PROJECT Kind

THE ULIMATE GLOW UP

NATASHIA TELFER

Copyright © Natashia Telfer
First published in Australia in 2022
by Women Changing the World Press
an imprint of KMD Books
Waikiki, WA 6169

All rights reserved. No part of this book may be used or reproduced by any means, graphic, electronic, or mechanical, including photocopying, recording, taping or by any information storage retrieval system without the written permission of the copyright owner except in the case of brief quotations embodied in critical articles and reviews.

Because of the dynamic nature of the Internet, any web addresses or links contained in this book may have changed since publication and may no longer be vaild. The views expressed in this work are solely those of the author and do not necessarily reflect the views of the publisher and the publisher hereby disclaims any responsibility for them.

Edited by Chelsea Wilcox
Typeset by Dylan Ingram

 A catalogue record for this work is available from the National Library of Australia

National Library of Australia Catalogue-in-Publication data:
Project Kind/Natashia Telfer

ISBN: 978-0-6455140-2-5
(Paperback)

ISBN: 978-0-6455140-3-2
(Ebook)

"

To my littlest loves, Cadence Myee & Nate Michael,

You are by far my proudest and greatest achievement I could have ever hoped, prayed and fought for. No matter where life may lead you, always remember our rule; be kind, be brave, be true.

Hanisiof, Mumma
And to my greatest love,
Forever, forever.
I finally believe you.

NT xx

CONTENTS

INTRODUCTION

THIS IS ME 5
Lesson 1: You are not a label. 7
Lesson 2: Your inner critic is a big jerk. 11
Lesson 3: Don't stand in your own way. 16
Lesson 4: Don't set unrealistic expectations. 22

PAST TRAUMA 29
Lesson 5: You are not responsible for another person's actions. 31
Lesson 6: Face the ghosts of your past. 36
Lesson 7: Recognise and embrace your differences. 41
Lesson 8: Home is a feeling, not a place. 48

THE FIGHT OF MY LIFE 57
Lesson 9: Tequila flu is not a real thing. 59
Lesson 10: Of course people care about you. 63
Lesson 11: It could always be worse. 69
Lesson 12: Sometimes you just gotta roll with the punches. 76

F*CK CANCER **85**
Lesson 13: Limit your self-pity parties. 87
Lesson 14: Sometimes life calls for the extreme. 95
Lesson 15: All actions have consequences. 100
Lesson 16: Bottling up feelings is never good for anyone. 110

SECOND CHANCES **115**
Lesson 17: You can find strength in unexpected places. 117
Lesson 18: Purpose can come from the most unexpected of places. .. 123
Lesson 19: Follow your real-life #influencers. 127
Lesson 20: Twenties are for making and learning from mistakes. 136

ADULTING IS F*CKING HARD **141**
Lesson 21: Don't do drugs. 143
Lesson 22: You deserve a happy ending. 147
Lesson 23: Miscarriages suck. 154
Lesson 24: Don't assume you are always the problem. 160

HAVING IT ALL **171**
Lesson 25: Sliding door moments are a real thing. 173
Lesson 26: Don't overthink things. 177
Lesson 27: Work-life balance is bullsh*t. 184
Lesson 28: Decline unsolicited advice. 188

WHATEVER IT TAKES **197**
Lesson 29: It's okay to be batsh*t crazy. 199
Lesson 30: Ditch the impostor syndrome. 209
Lesson 31: Level up. 212
Lesson 32: Kindness above all else. 220
Lesson 33: Be unapologetically authentic. 226

IT WAS ALWAYS WITHIN...233
Lesson 34: Shine bright..235
Lesson 35: Nothing grows in a comfort zone.............................243
Lesson 36: You already have everything you need. 247
Lesson 37: Break the rules if it feels right. 249

YOU DO YOU...259
Lesson 38: Pause, the world won't end. 261
Lesson 39: Recognise your own burnout....................................268
Lesson 40: Put your own oxygen mask on first. 271
Lesson 41: Work smarter, not harder. 276

BUILDING AN EMPIRE...283
Lesson 42: Build your dream team. 285
Lesson 43: Find. Appreciate. Worship your tribe. 292
Lesson 44: Setting boundaries is mandatory...............................298
Lesson 45: Haters gonna hate. 307

BEYOND MY WILDEST DREAMS 315
Lesson 46: The right time to start is now. 317
Lesson 47: Celebrate the good. 324
Lesson 48: Always keep perspective. 329
Lesson 49: Know when to walk away. 332
Lesson 50: Be a silver lining seeker. 337
The ultimate: Be you..340

INTRODUCTION

I have had my share of hardships. From child abuse, end-stage 4B cancer, toxic relationships, eight tumultuous years of IVF, multiple miscarriages and heartache, postnatal depression, starting up businesses, taking on government agencies, being a perpetual people-pleaser yet failing at maintaining friendships and so much more. All of this was an absolute walk in the park compared to overcoming the challenges of my own mindset and finding my voice, my worth and my place in the world simply by extending myself the same kindness I show others.

I have never been one to learn from the mistakes of others. I prefer to make all the messy mistakes myself and often learn and grow the hard way. However, I have always found comfort in the stories of others who bravely share their experiences. To know I am not the only human struggling in life some days is sadistically reassuring. To hear or read about someone who may have been through a similar situation as myself, and came out the other side wiser and stronger, gives me hope that I am not a lost cause and I do share commonalities with humans I may even look up to and admire. If I can help just one person in realising their potential and their worth simply by sharing my story, my experiences, my thoughts and lessons learnt ... then maybe all the late nights, continual rewrites and soul-bearing words will have been worth it.

So, who am I to be dishing out the advice? What would I know? What have I experienced? Well, in a nutshell, quite a lot. Nobody knows me and my story like I do, right?! My past brought much adversity, trauma and resilience. Today, I am a kick-arse businesswoman. My primary business, National Community Care, is a multimillion-dollar business, and I own FIVE businesses in total, all varying in size and success, and have been recognised as businesswoman of the year 2021 and a handful of other humbling accolades. I have been a keynote speaker for various events including International Women's Day and have run a handful of online workshops around empowering women stepping into their own light. In 2021, I was recognised by Nine Network's *Today* show for simply showing kindness to others amidst a pandemic. I employ over eighty amazing nurses and carers to provide a service that can literally change the lives of those most vulnerable within our community. I keep a small circle of fierce and loyal people I consider family – as I have always believed quality over quantity. I am head over heels in love with the most supportive husband in the history of ever and have two perfectly imperfect mischievous children I absolutely adore.

Most importantly, I can look in the mirror each morning and know, in my heart of hearts, I am happy with who I am at my core. I have zero regrets, and I am utterly grateful for my place in the world which makes me so excited for the future. I live a life I have designed for myself in a way I choose to do so. To have such freedom to do that and actually do it is beyond empowering.

This book unpacks my path and the endless lessons I learnt

along the way – and as always, I have learnt the hard way in both personal life and business. I show my scars because I want others to know they can get through whatever it is, survive, heal and come out even stronger. My path has never been simple, but regardless of the goal or the destination, through the good, the bad, the ugly and the insane, I survived it all and I'm so much better for it. I promise, it's all here. Authentic. Real. Raw and unfiltered … and all it took was a little self-kindness.

These stories are my perspective, my recollections, my experiences, my feelings and my truth of events throughout my life.

SELF-SABOTAGE

THIS IS ME

Self. [self]

noun
a person or thing referred to with respect to complete individuality.
a person's nature, character.
personal interest.

pronoun
myself, himself, herself, etc.

Sabotage. [sab-uh-tahzh]

noun
any underhand interference with production, work, as by enemy agents during wartime or by employees during a trade dispute.
any undermining of a cause.

verb
to intentionally prevent the success of a plan or action.

> *'Darling, the world's not really against you. The only thing that's against you is yourself.'*
> – Unknown

LESSON 1: YOU ARE NOT A LABEL.

If I were a book, I would be one of those fancy-looking books that everybody judges before even reading … Yes, I'm referring to the age-old saying 'don't judge a book by its cover'. I feel like this happens to me a lot. I also feel my 'resting bitch face' is on point and is quite possibly a contributing factor to this first impression I give off. Nevertheless, I do feel it's not a fair or correct assumption.

Today, I can confidently say I am a successful, grown-arse woman with an amazing support network of my choosing that I absolutely adore, live and breathe for, a multimillion-dollar business doing what I love and striving to create change and a difference in the world, as well as a handful of passionate side-hustles. Yes, I have a couple of nice handbags, an ever-changing wardrobe, an amazing, kick-arse hairdresser and my lashes are always on fleek (thank you, Emmalene at Eden Hair and Alex at Battle Lashes) … but let me make it very clear – as both Emma and Alex can concur – it never comes 'easy'.

Cue the labels.

I am not 'lucky'. I am not '#blessed', I am not 'fortunate' or 'destined' for what I have today. My life and what I have built within my life has come from hard work – and I am not talking about the nine-to-five kind.

It's come from seeing opportunities and grabbing them with both hands.

It's come from turning shitty situations into stepping stones, lessons and silver linings.

It's come from my heart and soul.

There is nothing more annoying and disheartening than being told you are lucky or something was handed to you. It diminishes the blood, sweat, tears, woman-hours and sacrifice I have put into said shiny thing you see in front of you. Don't do it. Don't downplay my hard work. Don't assume to know what it took from me to get where you see me today. I did not just wake up with this lucky life. I didn't inherit wealth or buy my success. I, like all humans, face opportunities and choices every single day. In fact, I have clawed my way through life to have what I have. It is how you react and what you do with those opportunities that can only ever belong to the individual. So please, do not judge me by my cover.

… But just quietly, how amazing is this book cover, if I do say so myself!

Labels and stereotypes bestowed upon me by others have always existed within my life – sadly so, it just seems to be the norm. When I was seventeen, I was in my final year of high school and the school formal was approaching. Like most school traditions, we had a series of questions to vote for the 'most likely' awards. Let's be honest, they were just stupid titles and labels such as 'Who is most likely to be a millionaire? Who is most likely to be named King and Queen?

Who is most likely to be a sports star?' and so on. I remember my friends had all stereotyped me to be most likely to get knocked-up. I don't even think it was one of the award categories, just an in-joke they had within our group. The assumption was because I had steady boyfriends through high school that I would settle down and be a Betty Crocker homemaker and have babies, I guess.

This infuriated me. The simple thought that my existence had been boxed up and titled by my so-called friends just did not sit well for me. After spending my life as an olive-skinned coconut RAAF brat, trying to assimilate myself into school and fit in with the crowd, this made me stop in my tracks. I realised I didn't want to think like that. So small-minded. That was the beginning of my discovery to finding a small bit of myself away from 'the pack' – but I wouldn't realise that until much later in life.

As the future unfolded, I was not the first to have babies – and my babies came after marriage, a successful multimillion-dollar career, IVF and after the age of thirty! It is safe to say, I am no longer in contact with those individuals who stereotyped me in such a small-minded way. This is exactly why I dislike labels. They are nothing more than a generalisation, with little to no actual evidence, often exaggerated or oversimplified, and most frequently, just downright offensive. With all that said, I know I cannot change the actions of others but rather the actions and responses of myself.

There is also merit in acknowledging that there are kind and positive labels to have bestowed upon you, but it seems to be human nature that we tend to absorb the negative over the positive. Turns out, this is a neurological response our bodies are hardwired for. Negative information causes a surge in activity in a critical information processing area of our brains, resulting in our behaviour and attitude to be shaped more powerfully by negative information. Research supports the idea of praise to criticism ratio of 5:1. Meaning, for every negative, you need to have five positives in order to have balance.[1] This research supports the concept that negative labels are five times more likely to impact you than a single positive label. No wonder we can recall every negative name we were ever called in school. To be honest, I can't recall any of the positives word for word.

When I was twenty-three, I was working at an acquired brain injury house. There I worked alongside a woman named Winnie. Winnie was so grounded and always seemed wise beyond her years to little old me, despite only being five years older. Winnie once told me she was trying to be more mindful about her own personal thinking, and for every negative thought she had about someone else, or about herself, she would stop herself and actively think of at least one positive trait about the person. I found this to be so thoughtful and is something I continue to practice a decade on. For example: my neighbour likes to mow his lawn at 7am every Saturday morning. It is really annoying, and then the kids are up. It is the only day we have a chance to possibly have a sleep in. The positive mind shift would be, *The neighbour is very thoughtful. When he mows his lawn at 7am, he is also kind in doing our council strip of grass as well.*

In addition to this, I have made a conscious effort to accept praise and actively attempt to spend just as much time analysing the positive as I know I do with the negative. It's taken me some time and is still something I must consciously make an effort to do. I know it sounds so pompous, but what it boils down to will surprise you. You either learn to see your positive qualities equally or, if you find that uncomfortable, you should at least be spending your time equally, resulting in less time spent dwelling on negative qualities. Life is all about balance after all, right?! So, ask yourself:

Are you really the bitch you were just labelled, or perhaps you are just too honest for those who prefer to live in the shade of denial?

Are you brutal, or perhaps authentic, so it scares some people?

Work-obsessed? Or confidently hold good work ethic?

Fence-sitter? Or just have perspective and can see either side of the fence?

Fake? Or perhaps you are just actually a decent and kind person with no hidden agenda?

Are you selfish? Or is it drive?

Overconfident? Or eternal optimist?

Pessimist? Or realist?

Scared? Or cautiously proceeding forward?

Failed your business? Or made some tough and smart business decisions to call it?

Overachiever? Or goal-orientated?

Struggling working mum? Or balancing life while having it all?

Too 'busy'? Or simply living to the fullest?

Troublemaker? Or game changer?

Round peg? Or square hole?

My point is, it is the language in which you view your labels that will ultimately impact your self-worth and your ability to grow. For me, identifying this was the first step to learning to be kinder to myself. It's by shifting this that the magic can really begin, because how you think and feel about yourself will literally impact every other facet of your life.

LESSON 2: YOUR INNER CRITIC IS A BIG JERK.

So, what has more impact than labels given to you by others?

The labels you give yourself!

I had a good sense of my self-sabotaging behaviour from an

early age. However, it took me thirty-five years of life to confidently do something about it. To change my language and acknowledge I'm not a selfish, shitty mum, mentally crazy workaholic who has had opportunities handed to me. I am an unapologetic kick-arse, fierce, kind, crazy, courageous, boss-girl Mumma. I'm living the life that I created with authenticity, determination, hard work, a lot of hustling, a side of sass and a whole lot of stubbornness and grit. Not a single soul can take that away from me because only I own my actions and my place in the world. Yes, opportunities will always present, but that does not mean things were handed to you. You still must put in the blood, sweat, soul and tears to mould it into whatever success you wish to cultivate and grow for yourself.

The craziest part about this realisation was it took me thirty-five years to action. Worse yet, I literally had so many checkpoints along the way that one would think I would have awoken to this revelation well before now. Ignorance is bliss, I guess. Don't get me wrong, there were lessons learnt along my journey, but strangely, it wasn't surviving multiple traumas, it wasn't facing death, it wasn't having others believe in me and starting my business, it wasn't the handful of side-hustles, it wasn't any other life adversity, achievement or milestone I've had that brought me to life. It was simply stopping and looking within myself, and realising and allowing myself to believe **I am enough.**

In such a fast-paced society, we all go for the quickest route to reaching our end goals. Whether that's that magic diet pill or the twenty-minute EMT workout over the conventional healthy eating and gym session. We seem to want instant results. But if history is anything to go by, nothing worth waiting for happens overnight, and self-development is one of the biggest inside jobs you will ever have to face. Realising this is an inside job is the first step. It's a continual development and learning process of yourself. Who else knows you better than you know yourself, right? You create the narrative. Loving yourself starts with liking yourself, which starts with holding some respect for yourself. This starts with thinking of yourself in positive ways. So, for me, it was overcoming my inner critic that always kept me in my box. That little voice in your head that tells you that you suck, that you'll fail. That you don't have what it takes and that you are undeserving.

Meet Nancy.

In my 2021 podcast, *Kindness & Courage*, 'Nancy's a B'[2] episode, I identify Nancy as a life-sucking, goal-crushing bitch! I'm talking all things inner critic. My podcast unpacks identifying her, calling her out and shutting her down to ensure she doesn't stop you from living your best life. Nancy is any thought that diminishes your ability to live your best life. Nancy tells you you're going to fail your exam, that guy won't call you back, you don't deserve the pay raise.

Nancy and I go way back. She has pretty much dictated most of my life. She has told me I couldn't have children, I didn't belong in business, no-one would marry me, my husband would leave me – heck, she even reared her ugly head again more recently and made me stop and think about whether I have what it takes to write this book.

So here are my top tips for dealing with your inner critic:

1. **Acknowledge your inner critic.**
    Acknowledge that there's more at play here than just you. Your inner critic is easier to conquer when you realise she will never leave you. She's stuck to you like your shadow. But it's imperative to acknowledge she is not you. By thinking of Nancy like

your shadow – she only exists because you exist, but unless you find Peter Pan's Neverland, she is never leaving you – we can performance-manage her arse to ensure she is not in charge of this circus that is life.

2. **Catch your critic.**
    Pay attention. Notice when you're being self-critical. A good rule of thumb is to remember that if it's not something you would say out loud in front of someone, then I bet the thought should not be entertained by you. When it comes to your inner critic, your thoughts are not reality, and I guarantee you they certainly do not depict how others actually see you. So logically, Nancy doesn't know shit. She's making uneducated calls on your behalf, and to date, you have been allowing her to do so. Don't allow her to.

3. **Name your critic.**
    As you guessed, my inner critic is Negative Nancy. Because I just love a good rhyming name. There's plenty to choose from. Hateful Hannah, Sour Sally, Whinging Wilma. I've heard others name theirs Frank, George, Karen. By naming them, they become less threatening and something outside of your body, which makes separating this behaviour easier to manage, effectively allowing you the clarity required to realise they have no merit.

4. **Change negative to neutral.**
    If you struggle to stop her, back it up a little and try changing the intensity of your language. Instead of 'I can't ...', it is 'I can't *YET*'. Instead of 'I hate', try 'I dislike'. This mutes a

lot of Nancy's negative-toned power. By doing this, it allows you a fighting chance to proceed forward in taking back your control.

5. **Question Nancy.**
What the hell does Nancy know? Cross-examine her. Challenge her. What qualifications does she have to make these uneducated comments? Is what she saying a fact or a feeling? I guarantee you if she were a real-life person, you would be stalking the shit out of her socials to figure out her credibility. Nancy is that social media user with absolutely no content or friends on her social platforms. It screams 'total scammer', right?!

6. **Perspective alignment.**
Is what Nancy telling going to impact you in five minutes, five hours, five days, five weeks, five years? Is your critic's message truly life-shattering in the grand scheme of things? Something that may seem so serious in the heat of the moment may be utterly insignificant in the bigger picture of life. Without the ability to align your perspective, you can unknowingly allow Nancy the power to eat you alive.

Prior to turning thirty-five, I would not have considered myself confident. Nancy ensured my only belief was that I was a pushover. A people-pleaser. A submissive passenger within my own life. A supporting actor in the movie of *my life*. I never gave myself credit and couldn't understand what anyone would see in me and my potential. If someone wanted to set a meeting with me, I would just about move heaven and earth, cancelling any personal plans and appointments I may have had to ensure I didn't disappoint the someone setting a meeting. My own needs and wants have always been second for longer than I can remember. I know this was a choice of mine – and a choice I do not regret – but looking back now, I do really see how passively I was living within my own life because I allowed Nancy to limit my thinking, and ultimately, stunt my success. This limitation affected me in every aspect of life – both personally and professionally. This theme will appear throughout most of the stories I will share and unpack in this book, providing you with a small sense of how submissive I was in my own life and how this ultimately impacted my ability to show myself any kindness.

LESSON 3: DON'T STAND IN YOUR OWN WAY.

Bad behaviour. Not to be confused with Negative Nancy. She creates the self-doubt and thought process in your mind. Bad behaviour is all YOU. These are your physical actions and inactions because of listening and believing that inner critic. It's like being an accessory to a crime. You might not have been the mastermind of the said crime, but you sure as hell committed it.

I call this phase two of self-destructive, self-sabotaging, self-doubting, self-loathing. Any of these skills sound familiar? We have all been there. Whether it's beating yourself up over not achieving something to the standard you hoped for, purposely ruining your diet for the week, missing a gym session, putting off starting something, waiting for the 'right' time, exceeding your weekly spending budget, missing a work deadline, telling yourself you are hopeless and basically placing all others above yourself … these are all skills I am AMAZING at. Pro-level! Seriously, if these skills were Olympic sports, I would be a gold medallist!

What is worse, I have always had a good level of self-awareness, meaning I have a clear understanding of my self-sabotage, yet I still do it. The term self-sabotage is used when this destructive behaviour is directed at yourself, and the negative habits consistently undermine your efforts. In 2019, I would learn from my psychologist that my self-sabotage can be considered a form of psychological self-harm. Now, I didn't want to be harming myself in any form. Yet, there I was, doing it. I wasn't allowing myself to succeed. But I had this self-talk creating a narrative telling me if I'm aware of the problem then it's not really a problem.

A key reason identified in those that self-sabotage is due to lack of self-esteem. Now, I never thought I was a low self-esteem kind of person. In social settings, when I want to be, I can be the life of the party, I love and own my share of eccentric and loud statement clothing, so surely this couldn't be true. But how often could I be the exception to the rule? It would turn out, my self-sabotage set me up to fail in several ways and had become so ingrained in who I thought I was. It was ultimately because I thought I was controlling my life by controlling my failures. Expecting the worst saves you from disappointment, right?

This mentality reinforced my negative behaviours that ate away at my potential for success. I constantly found myself falling short of my goals. For example, dieting. I would be on a health kick and doing great, but by Thursday I would eat a chocolate bar and then tell myself I failed my diet, so I might as well start again on Monday, and then ruin myself between now and Monday. So, I would take two steps forward, fall back one step, but instead of persisting, would jump back an additional three steps, ironically putting me further back than where I initially started. My biggest confession of bad behaviour and prime example of self-destruction was yet to come. I feel like we all have a little self-sabotage within us at one time or another. It's how you deal with these moments of sabotage that matters.

For me, my self-awareness game is strong. I would manage this by keeping a journal or habit tracker, or most commonly, a note on my iPhone. Doing this made me more aware and gave me something tangible to action. This allowed me to identify the facts from feelings and make small changes and minor adjustments in the right direction and permit myself to cut some slack. I don't need to be my own worst enemy. The world is full of enough shade-throwers, I didn't need to be one of them too. I needed to get on my own team!

I've come to learn personal development is not a destination but rather a continuous path you must stay on. I have learnt my weaknesses, but rather than just pointing them out, I've accepted that the only way those weaknesses change is if I actively do something about them. I know I suck at accepting praise, recognition, self-care, asking for help, waving the white flag. These are all skills I am actively working on. Some days are better than others. We all are so hopeful to win the $100 million lotto on Saturday – even if I never buy a ticket, I still find myself hoping to win! Surely you have, one time or another, thought about what you would do if you won. Pay off debts, buy a house, a holiday, quit work? However, the odds of winning the lotto are so ridiculous – and completely impossible if I haven't even got a ticket in the game – yet we feel like there is a higher possibility of winning the lotto than achieving any of the skills we are not so great at. It's utter madness. Why do you think that is? It is because we tell ourselves it is. The most powerful impact you can have on yourself are your self-thoughts.

Imagine our potential if we all believed in ourselves as much as we believe we will win the lotto! Humans love the idea of hope. Hope is amazing. Hope is an optimistic state of mind where we believe and hold an expectation of positive outcomes. Hope allows you to continue. Continuing allows space for change.

Self-sabotage is easy to do. Everyone can do it. But why not rise to the challenge and allow yourself to be your best self? Amongst the sabotaging, labelling, inner critic, self-worth, unrealistic expectations and bad behaviour there is always one common thread. Feelings. Feelings are not facts. Let me say that again ... *YOUR. FEELINGS. ARE. NOT. FACTS.* So, let's break this down. It's only when you understand the process and mechanics of things that you can cultivate the change you desire.

There are countless ways we sabotage ourselves including procrastination, self-medicating with drugs or alcohol, overeating from stress and interpersonal conflict. These actions can be especially dangerous because they're so subtle, you may not notice the extra cookie you're taking or the additional drink you have. At the time, they may even appear to calm you down and relax you. But as these actions increase, self-sabotage builds and can create a pit of self-defeat that's hard to climb out of.

For me personally, I am all too familiar with self-sabotaging diets and work deadlines! So why do we do this to ourselves? Here's my take on why and how to overcome it:

Fear.

Fear of failing.

Fear of succeeding.

Fear of the opinions of others.

Take your pick. It's human nature to develop traits in how we think and operate. Know your typical thinking patterns, your default settings. Our personality and experiences influence us to dominant modes of thinking, but obviously these can be biased in ways that are unhelpful in the majority of situations.

For example, people who are prone to anxiety tend to be hypervigilant to signs of threat and often may detect threats that aren't really there. This happens to be one of my personal patterns of self-defeating thinking. Cue Nancy! The way this manifests for me is that problems initially always seem bigger than they really are; whenever anyone asks me to do something that at first seems beyond my comfort zone, I (internally) overreact and perceive whatever is being asked as more onerous than it is. If I were two years of age, it would most likely be perceived as a toddler tantrum.

How do I deal with this? I find questioning my motives to be of benefit. *Why am I doing this to myself? What is the purpose? Does my behaviour support the life I am trying to create?* I must acknowledge my thinking bias, my inner critic and my behaviours – I factor it into my judgements. I discount my initial reaction, take a step back and review. Nine times out of ten it is one hundred per cent my brain overreacting as if it's a threat, when most likely it's an opportunity that has presented. You must remember, self-sabotage isn't an inherent part of your character, nor does it define who you are or erase your strengths and talents; therefore, it is possible to replace self-sabotage with self-advancement. I find it equally satisfying that there are a number of self-help books and resources specialising specifically in self-sabotage. That reassures me of two things. One: I am normal. Two: it can be changed.

An article in *Psychology Today*[3] sums it up perfectly with four steps.

1. **Identify and understand the pattern.**
   Why am I doing this to myself? What is the behaviour that I activate when I commence my sabotage? What cues do I have leading up to the behaviour that I could use to actively make

myself more aware in understanding my behavioural patterns? What is my inner dialogue?

2. **Consider the cost.**
   What is this behaviour taking away from me? What does it make me lose or fail at? What is the impact/the consequence of my actions? Identify these in black and white – exactly what it is you are ruining for yourself. Something tangible. It could be your health, your happiness, your wellbeing. This links in with good-old perspective.

3. **Clarify your values and goals.**
   Are your goals value driven? If you routinely struggle with committing to actions or fulfilling your goals, it might be helpful to clarify your values and ensure that your goals are aligned with them.

And lastly, my favourite:

4. **Do the opposite.**
   As simple as that right! *Ha*. No, but it doesn't have to be difficult. If you notice that you often sabotage yourself, list how. For example, do you forget to answer texts from friends and alienate them? Ignore assignments and then fail a subject for a degree you want? Terrible at managing your emails? Break the difficulty down in as much detail as possible and formulate a plan to act the opposite.
   Keep a habit tracker. (Check out my awesome trackers I created for you to download at www.projectkind.com.au A habit tracker can paint a snapshot of your behaviours and habits. Write all the

things you think you do each day and capture when it is that you are actually getting that task done. I think I'm going to wake up early and go for a walk. But my habit tracker will quickly tell me I'm lucky to commit to that one morning a week. Shift the task to the afternoons: suddenly my habit tracker is capturing four to five days a week. This is clearly a better time frame for me. My habit tracker also indicated that I was terrible at maintaining my multiple emails. As much as I try to maintain a work-like balance and not do emails outside of normal business hours, I found I had to do the opposite, and find a compromise to ensure I wasn't blurring my work and home life balance. So, I began filtering all emails and cleared out any junk first thing in the morning … literally before I'm even out of my pyjamas because there's no way I'm wasting the day when I get to the office to delete the spam. I have most recently allocated myself 'email hour' too. Now, I know that won't always work out as planned. We all know someone that loves to send their urgent email request to you COB on a Friday. If leaving things until the last moment is a problem with great cost to you, then it is helpful to get a diary or workplace calendar and start planning. I personally love a good Post-it Note reminder.

LESSON 4: DON'T SET UNREALISTIC EXPECTATIONS.

Unrealistic expectations. Come on, we have all been there. There's the small stuff like thinking your parents could just jet you off to Disneyland or wishing for snow on Christmas Day despite living in the Southern Hemisphere in Australia when December marks the beginning of our summer weather. There's assuming you will just breeze through school and study, figure out what you want to be and go off to university and become a somebody. Then there is getting yourself a Jennifer Aniston haircut with the assumption it would automatically enhance your appearance. Sounding familiar? They were just some of my smaller expectations in life that would lead me to great disappointment; I didn't get to Disneyland with my family, I learnt it would never snow in Australia for Christmas, I barely made it through high school, would go on to flunk out of going to university and that the only way the Jennifer haircut would make me look Anglo-Saxon is if I taped the picture to my face.

Then there is the big stuff. Life. It's a funny little thing. I've always wondered what the meaning of it is and what all our existence is for. Not a small topic to cover straight off the bat but a huge evolving focus within my life over my years of living. Life, to me, is an unknown time frame of sunrises and sunsets, full of many physical and mental challenges along the journey. It's a series of choices and risks from start to finish. Each life is unique, yet one's life is intertwined and influenced by the lives of others. The most basic primitive purpose: to continue the magical cycle that is life. Birth, grow, mate, procreate and die. I thought this is literally what the female human body is designed to do, right? Bear children. Now, don't get me wrong, these days there is a million and one things women can choose to be, but for me, in my ideas and narrative I had created for myself, I thought this was MY ultimate purpose. To be a mum ... along with being a princess, a ballerina and a schoolteacher, of course.

One consistent memory I have from throughout my childhood is that I always just wanted to be older than I was at that point in time. I wanted to be a grown-up. I wished so much to have the responsibilities and freedom that 'grown-ups' have. I literally spent my childhood wishing it away. Don't get me wrong, I had a happy and loving childhood. I just couldn't wait to start 'living'! I wanted it all. At six years of age, my idea of having it all included being married, with three kids, living in our own home by the age of twenty-six with one dog and one cat … Morbidly, I also thought I would die at the age of thirty-six because that was unimaginably 'so old'!

This became the first of many benchmarks I created for myself, and it became a measuring point I would continue to compare myself to and continually feel like a failure when I was not meeting the checkpoints and standards I had set upon myself at the age of six. TWENTY-SIX … I look back now and can't believe I thought I would have everything figured out by twenty-six, let alone put that kind of pressure on myself. I guess I thought that women did it in the old days, marrying young and having families at a young age, so it's not like I was asking the impossible of myself. But the reality is, these days, most women choose to and/or are required to return to work purely for financial income or personal sanity! So, this becomes another benchmark you set upon yourself, and this is all assuming you've even found that soulmate in your early twenties to settle down with and 'have it all' by twenty-six.

Turns out it would take me a few more years on earth to really understand MY purpose and path in life. However, I would discover this much earlier than most. I can confidently say I found and knew my realistic purpose by the age of nineteen. Today, that same purpose is still strong for me; however, with a few more laps around the sun, I've also learnt that one's purpose does not have to be just *one* purpose. I'm not sure how we, as a society, got to the conclusion that a person can only have one sole purpose. Even as children we want to be everything under the sun, and as we age, we are confined into believing we must choose one single path forward. It seems so ridiculous we would believe that something we want in our teens remains the same in our twenties, thirties, forties, fifties, sixties and beyond. We grow, we age, we evolve – so why wouldn't our dreams, desires and purpose do so too?

Hindsight always allows us to see how unrealistic our expectations may have been, but how does one harness that hindsight into a worthwhile tool to grow forward with setting future realistic expectations? Simple. By setting bite-size steps in the direction of where you want to ultimately be. Also known as a plan of attack and/or goal-setting.

Without goals, you can lack focus and direction. Setting personal goals puts you in control, giving you the power to alter your path in whatever direction you desire. However, in many circumstances, the initial goals we set out to complete are abandoned somewhere along the way. For example, for those wondering, I did give up on going to Disneyland as a child, but I did get to Disneyland at the ripe old age of twenty-two. A white Christmas in New York is on my bucket list, and as for university, it would turn out I was meant to be a self-made woman anyway.

To accomplish your goals, you need to know how to set them. This process begins with careful consideration and breaking down the goals into attainable and achievable steps. Write your goals down and schedule dates for their completion and evaluation. This can be the key to success, as writing down your goals will position you as the creator and highlights their importance. Having them somewhere that you see them every day will help to reiterate their significance and increase your chances of achieving them. When I set my goals, I have always favoured the SMARTER method because it's heck-easy to remember and it's foolproof. Seriously! If it works for me, you will be all over this.

Specific: Say/write/vision board exactly what you want to achieve.

For example, my current vision board is broken into sections that are important to me. Family, self-care, work, personal goals and rewards for when I achieve said goals, of course! In the work section, a big goal I have set myself reads: *Service coordination: my growth will only be as big or as small as I allow it to be. I need to employ someone to take this journey with me and lead the program within my company. I will know I have succeeded in this when I can advertise that support coordination is an additional service we can provide.*

Measurable: Decide on a metric that marks success.

This doesn't have to be dollar value or a number, as such. For example, my work goal for service coordination outlines my metric to be the ability to offer the new service as something my company can provide.

Achievable: Ensure your goal is realistic to your lifestyle.

My work goal example is in line with our company purpose, thus making it realistic to set. There's no point setting a goal that is so left-field I'd just be setting myself up to fail.

Relevant: Connect this goal to your overall vision.

The goal encompasses our company vision and allows us to stir further change within the system to improve our sector and services for our most vulnerable.

Time-bound: Set a deadline.

For me, I always struggle to commit to time frames. I know this is purely because I'm afraid I will fail, so I set myself a safety net, in a way. I know this is my weakness, so instead, I create vision boards each year. The board has no time frame, but I always find by the end of the year I have reached all of my goals and/or am on track.

Evaluate: Determine when you will check in on your progress.

I look at my board daily as it is strategically placed on the wall above my home office computer. When I look at my work section, I see I have achieved 75% of the work-related goals. In relation to the example of my support coordination goal, I can proudly say, in October of 2021, I employed not any old support coordinator, I employed THE best support coordinator in the state, whom I have always admired, respected and looked up to as a bit of a mentor. This man holds the same values and ethics as me and is without a doubt a disruptor and game-changer in our industry, continually advocating for systemic change to better the lives of our most vulnerable.

Readjust: Stay flexible if goals need to shift or change.

Life happens. Sometimes we choose other directions, these aren't necessarily failed goals, but rather readjusted or redirected to something that aligns to our current goals. For example, I have every intention on expanding into other states. However, that is not my primary priority right now – as such, the goal time frame is pushed back.

In line with my SMARTER goal-setting approach, I also like to set myself some safety measures to keep me goal orientated and on track to achieving said goals.

These include:

Accountability: When you are working towards a goal, things are bound to get tough. When facing adversity, you must hold yourself accountable. Telling your family and friends about your goals may give you the responsibility you need, helping you gather the support system to give you a push. If you remain accountable in your everyday life, you will also surround yourself with constant encouragement from those who are following your progress. For me, my business bestie knows the goal, and that right there holds us both accountable. Another example might be a gym buddy if your goal is to go to the gym five days a week!

Help: When entering a new venture, it is crucial to learn from those around you. Asking for help is nothing to be ashamed of, as freshening up your skills may be the thing that sets you apart. Seeking advice may come in a variety of different forms: asking a friend, a mentor – these will only get you one step closer to achieving your goals. Many people find that going back to study is one of the most beneficial steps when attempting to successfully achieve a goal. This is something I have continued to do to ensure I have knowledge about the happenings within my company. Knowledge is power, and professional and personal development is priceless.

RESILIENCE

PAST TRAUMA

Resilience. [ri-zil-yuhns, -zil-ee-uhns]

noun

the ability of a person to adjust to or recover readily from illness, adversity, major life changes.

the ability of a system or organisation to respond to or recover readily from a crisis, disruptive process.

the power or ability of a material to return to its original form, position, etc., after being bent, compressed or stretched.

'You have always had the power my dear, you just had to learn it for yourself.'
– Glinda the Good Witch

LESSON 5: YOU ARE NOT RESPONSIBLE FOR ANOTHER PERSON'S ACTIONS.

> ***Warning:*** *the following content contains reference to abusive experiences which may be triggering to some. Please be kind to yourself and please seek professional advice if you are struggling with your past experiences.*

Practicing introspection to better know yourself is no small feat. It is about looking into your insecurities and understanding why they are there in the first place. Looking into your past is usually the best way to dive in and untangle the endless possibilities that were the driving force for your current emotional state. Think about that. We do not come into this world with fear or insecurities. These feelings are learnt. As such, the only way to overcome our own inner demons may be to look within and break it down to break the cycle. I found this process really confronting, yet also a level of detachment from my past which I'm almost certain is self-preservation mode, but when I was honest with myself, I could see exactly why I am the way I am. Equal parts nature versus nurture. I was raised in a beautiful loving family home (nature) but was subject to some external factors (nurture) that would ultimately impact who I would become.

The earliest memories I have are fragments of being preschool age in South Australia. I fondly remember growing up in those early years with my cousins Luise, Sera and Amoe who lived at the end of our street. I remember the Australian Grand Prix being held in Adelaide. I remember the Christmas parades and my mum use to cut my carrots into flowers and that this boy in my preschool class stole my artwork despite my attempts to clearly write my name on it. These memories are vivid. Colourful, detailed, happy memories.

My only other memory of this age is of the family that lived next door to us. More specifically, their eldest son. I'm going to call him Mark as I honestly cannot remember his name. I'm sure that is probably some deep-rooted suppression right there. My memories of Mark are vague. They feel foggy, dark in colour and distant. Like a dream I'm trying to recall from a few nights prior. A polar opposite to the vivid and colourful memories of my positive experiences at this age.

I was four years of age at prep, and Mark would have to have been twelve years old at most, as South Australian schooling was prep to year seven. We were your average family in the average neighbourhood with kids playing in the street until the streetlights came on or playing at the neighbour's house.

But nothing is ever as it seems.

Mark would sexually assault me at every opportunity possible. He would make me go into his room and tell me to take off my clothes and lay down on the floor just behind the door so he could hear if grown-ups were coming.

He would sexually abuse me and pinch me.

I don't remember these details too intensely, but I do recall that the pinching on my legs and stomach hurt. Afterwards, he would always tell me that if I told anyone we wouldn't be allowed to play together anymore, and I would get in trouble from all the parents.

This would occur countless times until we moved interstate.

What the actual fuck, right? What's worse is, at the time, I did not know this was wrong. By the time I realised right from wrong and body awareness, we were living in Newcastle, and I somehow felt what had happened was my own fault. It was my fault for not knowing any better. I was compliant, after all. If I knew it was wrong maybe I would have spoken up. But maybe I wouldn't have because he told me I couldn't. It was my fault for not telling a grown-up. It was my fault for allowing myself to be in situations where this could repeatedly occur.

To this day, I have never really articulated that story from start to finish with anyone. I guess this is because I had this mentality that it was in the past and so I left it exactly there. I figured what was the point in bringing it up now … what good would it do? Little did I know how much the situation would impact and shape me forevermore.

I also think of Mark. Did he know what he was doing was wrong? Surely if he was aware it had to be kept a secret, he would have known? But how can a twelve-year-old be capable of such horrible acts? Was I just as naive when I was twelve? How did he even know what to do? Was he a victim of abuse himself? Was it something he told the other kids at school about? Was he mentally unwell? Did it stop with me? Was there another little girl moving into my old house? Did Mark grow up to be a horrible human? Did Mark wake up to himself and join the church to repent for his sins? What became of Mark?

I feel sorry for him.

I know that's probably weird, right? But seriously.

What a misguided boy to feel he had the right to take what he wanted from me whenever he pleased. I am sad for him. I do hope he had a brighter future ahead and turned into a respectable human. As I grew up, I came to realise I could not be responsible for his actions. For me, this shaped an idea in my head that boys just take what they want, and objectifying women was somehow just the way it must be.

This reshaped my future in one aspect, but it would also become my earliest memory of acknowledging that some humans are just awful, and I cannot be held accountable for their actions. This lesson would go on to serve me well when dealing with all types of demons in life, both personally and professionally. Every person is responsible for their own emotions, words, reactions and behaviours, just as I am the only person responsible for my own. We cannot expect to change how somebody else feels or change how or what they think. The only person who can do that is themselves.

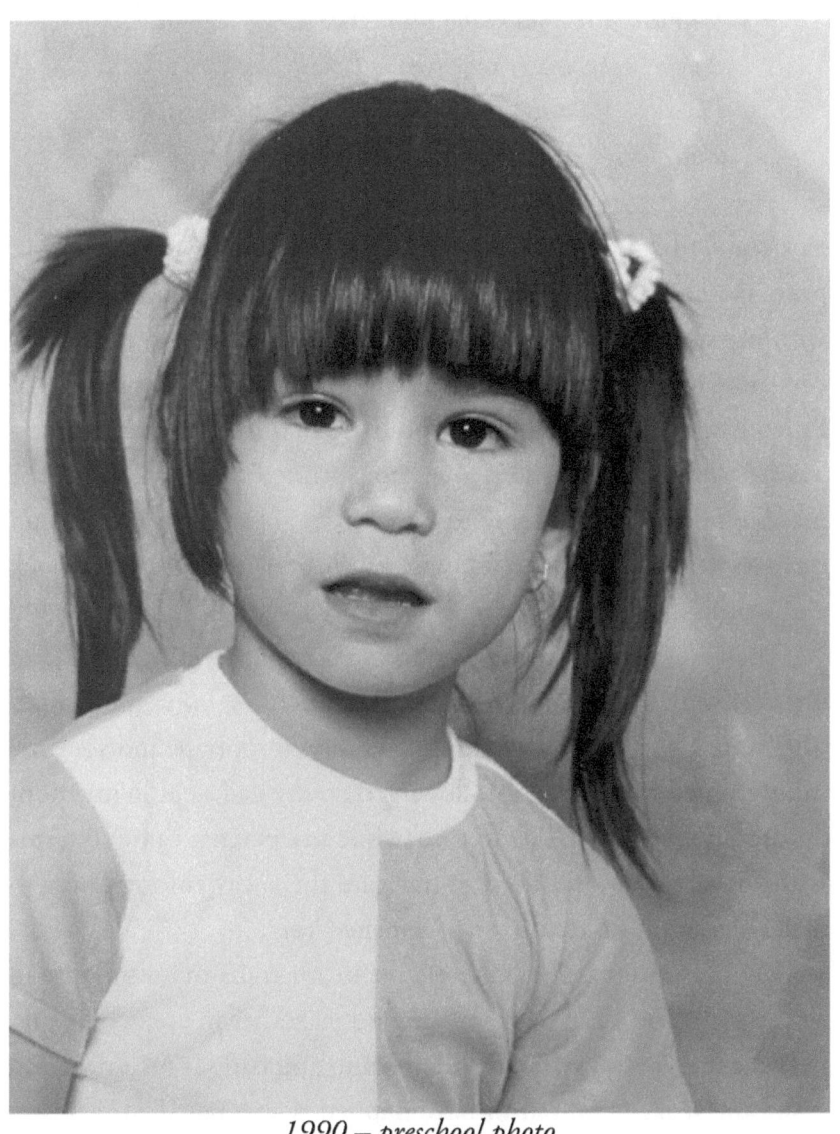
1990 – preschool photo

LESSON 6: FACE THE GHOSTS OF YOUR PAST.

> *Warning: the following content contains reference to abusive experiences which may be triggering to others. Please be kind to yourself and please seek professional advice if you are struggling with your past experiences.*

Fast-forward six years, at the age of ten, I was your average kid in primary school, I did little athletics on the weekends and fought with my sisters regularly. It was Christmas holidays and my mum's dad came to stay with us from Darwin. He began buying me lots of little gifts. I know that sounds about normal for any grandparent, however, my younger sisters were not recipients of these gifts. Just me. Grandad would ask me to come in his room to wake him up early so we could go bird watching, but I didn't own an alarm clock and would inevitably sleep in every time.

Then he began writing me strange, coded messages that, in essence, were inappropriate for a child, much less your grandchild. This time I was acutely aware this was inappropriate and told my mum immediately. For the following days my dad slept in my room on the floor with me 'just in case' while my parents came to terms with the situation and tried to navigate their way through how to manage a situation that hadn't happened yet.

My grandad was the only relative in Australia my mum was in touch with, and I can only imagine it placed her in an awful situation she didn't wish to be in either. Mum and dad sat me down and asked me what I wanted to have happen. I was petrified. I mean, nothing had happened. Was I meant to wait until it did? Then it would have been easier to act upon? I didn't want my mum to send her only relative she had contact with away, so we arranged for me to go and stay with my best friend Hayley and her family for the two weeks until my grandad was scheduled to fly home.

I was chuffed. I got to go have fun at my best friend's house over the school holidays for an entire two weeks! I returned home, grandad was gone and I never saw him again. I look back on this now and realise this was me conforming to the easiest path. The least-disruptive path. The path that ensured I did not burden anyone with my problems. Meaning I am the only one that suffers in silence so others can continue undisrupted. It was the path easiest travelled, and I was happy to take it. Turns out, I would continue to have this mentality for years to come.

When I returned home, I guess my parents had done some research or something because they asked me if I wanted to speak to someone about what had/hadn't happened, and my mum asked if I wanted to place all the items grandad had brought me into a plastic bag and smash them up by throwing them at a wall. I remember at the time thinking, *Why the hell would I wreck some trinkets because grandad was a weirdo?!* As the years passed by, I have had no further contact with my grandfather. He still lives in Darwin and sent me gifts for the major life milestones up until my twenty-first birthday. Last I heard he had become a bitter old man with no-one left in his life as a result of his actions. I am sad for him and what has become of his life, but it is not lost on me, his life today is merely a by-product of this own actions.

Trauma is an emotional response to a negative event. It could be an accident or tragic event, child abuse, relationship trauma and/or abuse, or possibly even something as simple as the company you keep. Being raised in a family with a high-achieving sibling with a big personality can breed insecurities. This is something my sisters love to tell me. The effects of trauma can be overwhelming and difficult to understand, process and move on from. Because trauma can be so hard to process, it's often difficult to understand the full impact it has on our lives and can often reach further than one would anticipate.

For me, when I look back at my past trauma, I know they were never closed traumas. Just because the physical abuse ended, it did not end the psychological impacts that would stay with me a lifetime. The cost of these instances was great. This was not something I would recognise within myself until speaking with a psychologist in my thirties. I wasn't talking to a psychologist to deal with past trauma specifically, but unbeknownst to me, the ghosts of my past still had a strong hold on my present. This became a hurdle I had to overcome before moving forward with today's problems. It would be highlighted to me that my approach to every intimate relationship I would hold was tainted by the everlasting impacts of my past traumas.

That's the ironic thing about trauma. It hides within you and unknowingly has the power to shape your views. These instances impacted my self-worth. How I see myself and how I assume others must view me. Most importantly, it impacted my personal views on my body and heightened my insecurities. These all point to the leading symptom of trauma being fear (followed by self-hatred). So, naturally, my defence mechanism to this would become my many plates of armour I would shield myself with over the years. I perfected my poker face and never allowed anyone to get close enough to see the real and vulnerable me. I essentially became a vault. Totally healthy, right?!

The only way through this, for me, was not revisiting every single detail of the traumas in my past. That had been packed down deep. In fact, writing this book is the first time I've articulated some of the details. To break any trauma down, you must have a good hard look at what it is that you are afraid of going forward. Recognise that the way you may think of the world isn't necessarily how it is. Identifying this is a vast step toward achieving your own inner wellbeing. For me to move past this, it was not about recalling the pain but rather the strength I gained. I have acknowledged that, yes, I went through a lot, but I've also grown a lot too. We need to credit ourselves for our resilience and step forward with grace.

Processing trauma works best when you engage what may be your distorted views with the clearer and more insightful views of a wise friend or professional. It is only then we can take a step back and see that perhaps we are not a failure, we are not alone, it wasn't our fault, and we are not inherently disgusting and perhaps my views are, again – only thoughts. Not facts. This is only the first step toward years of personal self-development when recovering from any kind of trauma. This is followed by acknowledging the actions of others are no fault of your own. It wasn't because I didn't know I was supposed to say no, it wasn't because I didn't know any better, it wasn't because of my clothing. I didn't invite these experiences to happen. These experiences I faced were the actions of others over which I had no control. They are not mine to own. This approach can be said for many more situations I would find myself in throughout life.

Things inside & outside of my control

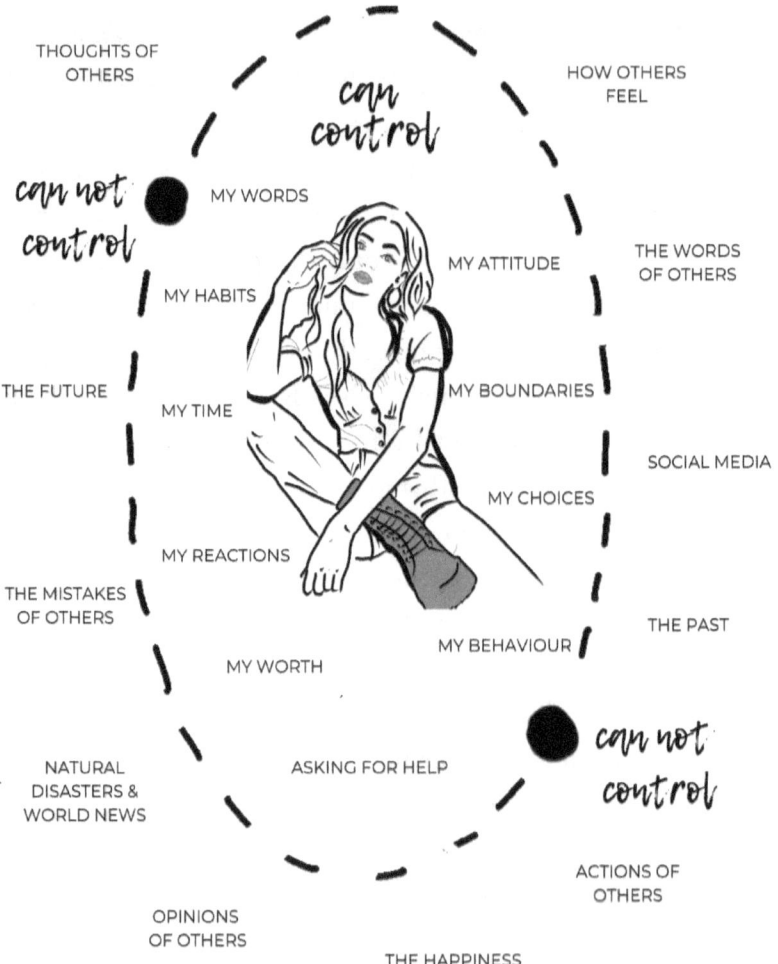

can control
- MY WORDS
- MY ATTITUDE
- MY HABITS
- MY TIME
- MY BOUNDARIES
- MY CHOICES
- MY REACTIONS
- MY BEHAVIOUR
- MY WORTH
- ASKING FOR HELP

can not control
- THOUGHTS OF OTHERS
- HOW OTHERS FEEL
- THE WORDS OF OTHERS
- THE FUTURE
- SOCIAL MEDIA
- THE MISTAKES OF OTHERS
- THE PAST
- NATURAL DISASTERS & WORLD NEWS
- ACTIONS OF OTHERS
- OPINIONS OF OTHERS
- THE HAPPINESS OF OTHERS

LESSON 7: RECOGNISE AND EMBRACE YOUR DIFFERENCES.

At the age of twelve, we were posted to Canberra. We moved into a small country town Queanbeyan, just on the other side of the ACT border. I was going into year eight, and all I wanted was to fit in. So much so, I stopped sprint running and changed my name! Natashia is my birth name, and my family and friends prior to Queanbeyan called me Tarsh. When I started school, I decided to drop the 'r' and become Tash. I reflect on this now and see that I basically just wanted to culturally assimilate to fit in. Anything to avoid the labels. I was told I wasn't dark enough to be an Islander yet nicknamed 'FOB' (fresh off the boat), I was told I looked 'abo', I looked Indian, gosh, at one point before I grew boobs, I was even told I looked like a 'hungry Ethiopian'. A kid at school told everybody I was adopted because my 'mum' was white. This kid went on to become a co-captain of a national sporting team.

The nicknames bestowed upon me by my classmates were all references to my appearance. They included Choc, Chicko, Boobs McGee, Pocahontas and Harry-barge-arse. There was such cruelty and racism weaved through my early years of primary and high school I even began to question if Darwin (my birthplace) was in Australia. Now, I'm first to admit I am, without a doubt, 'geographically challenged' and my family will attest to that fact, however, the racism I experienced made me question my nationality as if others knew me better than I knew myself. Maybe I wasn't Australian? So, I did what any normal kid would do before the times of mobile phones and Google … I asked my mum! Seriously. Because other children questioned me due to my skin colour, it led me to question my entire identity. I didn't understand why I had to be brown. What did I do to be punished with my olive skin?

Maybe as kids we just didn't know any better, but the fact of that matter is we all learnt that behaviour from somewhere. I'm so sad to say this undercurrent of racism was just the 'norm' during my time at school. It wasn't questioned. Kids can be cruel, yet I am totally ashamed I took the easy path. The quick route to fit in and be a 'normal white girl'. I didn't want to stand up and be different or even proud of who I was, just the way I was. I just wanted to fit in and be like everyone else. I wanted to assimilate myself in every sense of the word and beyond. Cue identity crisis? Your real self is the characteristics that do not change over time. Your core beliefs. It's the unchanging pattern of behaviours and interactions that make up the core of who you are. Then there is your 'environmental self' which is the part of you that changes and evolves since the day you were born. This includes your physical attributes, your mental and physical growth, and experiences in your immediate environment.

We all have a complex relationship with our identity. It's the one thing that defines us most, yet we are never sure what it is exactly. I know I struggled with my own sense of identity for a long time, and it took me years to find out who I really was. Who it was I wanted to be. The path to finding my identity wasn't linear, but I feel like any journey in life worth travelling never is. Although I have a stronger sense of myself than I did when I first started, I still do not attach my identity fully to anything because I believe there is no final destination when it comes to growth. I believe that we always have a chance to learn, change, grow and evolve, and I hope I can do this until the very end.

I can confidently say I would not be where I am today without my identity growing with me. I believe that knowing who I am at the core made me a stronger person and gave me the courage to take a stand when I feel there is an injustice. Finding your identity is ultimately about finding out what makes you, you. It is about understanding who you are and what makes you tick. I can assure you, you are not your parents, the place you were born, the colour of your skin or what you do for a living, even though we tend to identify with these things. Being an authentic person means having values, interests and passions that make you unique. There is also your environmental self that may influence your behaviour or physical attributes, but it's important to know they do not make up your core self.

I'm proud to say I woke up to myself in some respects, however, even in today's society, there is a lot of pressure to be someone you're not. We are constantly bombarded with messages telling us who we should be, how we should look and what we should have. With social media platforms available on every electronic device, we are conditioned daily to believe these messages. So how does one find your true identity? I feel like that should be the handbook given to kids in school! That shit right there is more important than algebra, surely! So, here is my top six to taking inventory of who you are:

1. **What is your CORE?**
    Your values are what you believe in. By identifying these, you discover who you are and what makes you tick. These are enduring qualities that will help you forge a strong sense of yourself. Your identity is the centre of your story. Who are you? What do you want? Why do you do what you do? They may be little things but it's usually what seems inconsequential that makes a difference in how you feel about yourself. Some examples could include:

- Loyalty
- Empathy
- Religion
- Honesty
- Integrity
- Optimism
- Equality
- Adventure
- Patriotism
- Authenticity
- Recognition
- Enjoyment
- Family
- Money

2. **What are your beliefs?**
   Your beliefs are your perceptions or what you accept as truth. Research shows that our beliefs are formed from our experiences which, in turn, are shaped by our environment. Your identity is made up of what you believe and how you act on those beliefs. This affects the way you live your life, how you react to your environment, the way you approach your relationships. It also affects your values, actions, goals and any plans you have for your life. Identifying your beliefs will also help you let go of any that are holding you back. Some examples of limiting beliefs could be: *I am too young/old/inexperienced/over-experienced.*

3. **Identify your strengths and weaknesses.**
   One way to find your identity is to make a list of your strengths and weaknesses. For me, the weakness list is always first and

easy to compile, but applying facts, not thoughts, will shorten your list. When listing your strengths, don't be shy or modest about it. What are you good at? When you identify your strong points, you'll be able to see how those strengths can be applied in different roles, projects and aspects of your life.

4. **Practice mindfulness and awareness.**
Mindfulness is about being aware of what is within and around you. It goes hand in hand with awareness and allows you to be in the present moment, which allows you to stop and assess situations as required. A big part of mindfulness can include meditation. Hold on. Hear me out. If you are like me, your first response is, *Forget it, I've tried all of these things before, and they don't work,* or, *But I don't have time to sit still and do nothing.* Just be opened to revisiting the possibility. The trick is just finding the right method for you.

For me, I love anything that is quick and easy and fits in with my already chaotic day. So, when I came across the physiological sigh (double inhale, long exhale breath) I learnt from the gorgeous Chelsea Pottenger of EQ Minds,[4] I was SOLD! It is simple, easy and can be done anywhere without screaming to the world you are meditating to avoid a meltdown moment. It calms the mind, reduces stress immediately, oxygenates the body and balances your nervous system, creating equilibrium between alertness and relation. A quick google of the physiological sigh will provide you with overwhelming information on the benefits and how to.

It can be done sitting or standing; begin by exhaling fully. Eyes open or gently closed, take two full inhales through the nose followed by an extended exhale through the mouth, breathing all the air out.

5. **Accept who you are.**
   Easier said than done, right?! Accepting yourself for who you are can help you find your identity because you're not judging yourself or measuring yourself with someone else. (We have all been there!) We often criticise ourselves because we don't look the way we're supposed to or we don't fit in. But you don't really gain anything by going with the crowd, and it will be hard to find out who you truly are if you can't accept yourself.

   If you feel overwhelmed, overly lost or confused about finding your identity, then getting help may be the smartest thing you can do. Discussing your life with someone else, like a confidant or professional, can be very beneficial. There is power in knowing that you are not alone and we all, at some point, question ourselves. Professional help might assist you to gain a clearer understanding of yourself, the world around you and your place within it. Getting support for what's important to you can take the stress out of making big decisions in your life and provide you with clarity and peace of mind.

6. **Change.**
   Create change in the areas of your life that you want to improve. But how does change happen? Some change is inevitable and happens to us – for example, puberty. Other times we create it ourselves. For example, changing up how I introduce myself to others. Sometimes change may require asking someone else to act. Such as asking the office team to all chip in with creating the stationery supplies order – this way, we are each responsible for ordering the items we individually need and nothing is forgotten. Sometimes change is created by working together in collaborative partnerships. For example, our community

company has partnered with ACT Health in a number of projects with our aligned goals to approach government agencies for larger-level change. It's never easy, but if it is required, it must start somewhere. Ironically, working on my personal growth and change is uncomfortable, yet I am always ready to advocate and fight for change for others!

My Rotuman roots have always run strong. While none of my siblings grew up in Fiji, so many of the cultural customs are surprisingly strong. One is order of birth. As the eldest, this has always meant the default was it was up to me to speak up on behalf of my sisters. Whether it was negotiating more sprinkles on our ice cream as kids or raising a serious concern like expressing the collective opinion on whether our parents should sell our childhood home. I know you're probably thinking this is often an age custom more so than a cultural one, however, one of the defining cultural aspects to this custom is that if the eldest (me) believes the topic at hand is not valid and chooses not to raise the topic, then it is dead, and the siblings essentially fall in line.

Growing up, I guess I never knew any different and this seemed to be a role I just happily assumed. Recently, I was watching a new Disney movie with my daughter called *Encanto*. This movie really conjures a lot of emotion around family and the roles and stereotypes we play. (Highly recommend it for all ages!) It's about the Madrigal family who live in the mountains of Colombia in a magic town called the Encanto. The magic of the Encanto has blessed every child in the family with a unique gift – every child except the main character, Mirabel. As the story unfolds, Mirabel feels like the outcast of the family but will come to learn that each of her sisters and cousins all have their own insecurities in life. Enter sister Luisa. I felt an instant connection with Luisa. I'm not sure if it was the fact she is the biggest sister of the three – like myself – or the fact she had great responsibility to uphold within the family.

Luisa's magic gift is strength. She is the strongest and most reliable member of the family. Having been gifted with super strength, both her family and the people of the town rely on her power. In turn, Luisa greatly appreciates that she can be of significant contribution to her community. Soon Mirabel learns her sister isn't all platinum-and-diamonds tough. In Luisa's words: *'Under the surface, I'm pretty sure I'm worthless if I can't be of service.'* Hello, soul song! This Disney song became a favourite in our household, and probably by Mum more than the kids. I love that sometimes a reminder of who you are and who you think you are can come from the most unexpected of places. Thank you, Disney.

As for my younger years of rejecting who I was, thankfully I discovered my core values and realised my olive skin was a blessing that most would purchase in a self-tanning can. As for my name change, thankfully, today, I see the silver lining in the fact only my nearest and dearest call me Tarsh. Those that know the real me. Tarsh is something my husband Guy calls me and as such, many of our closest friends have picked up on this and have now adjusted how they pronounce my name. Sometimes Tash world and Tarsh world collide, but it's the Tash world that is made to feel the uncomfortable minority now. As for 'Natashia', that's reserved for big trouble from Mum and formal business email signature blocks.

LESSON 8: HOME IS A FEELING, NOT A PLACE.

My resilience to my childhood traumas is, in part, a result of the amazing family network I have. We are very close, well at least that's what outsiders say. My family and I do not live in each other's pockets. We don't talk on the phone. We don't have to update when we arrive somewhere safe. Our motto has always been 'no news is good news'. If you call, you are most likely going to receive 'what's wrong?' as your initial response when the call is answered. However, we always have a standing Friday night dinner gathering at Mum and Dad's. We always have Good Friday together, birthday dinners, and most importantly, always stick together when shit gets tough – but in a non-mooshy kind of way.

My dad is a coconut (self-proclaimed title for 'Islander') and a giant teddy bear. He is the third of four and was the only sibling fortunate enough to have been born in Sydney, Australia, before his family returned to Fiji where he grew up. Dad is from a small island off Fiji called Rotuma with a population of 1,594, so if you are Rotuman, there's a 99.9% chance we are related! We have always felt a deep connection to our cultural roots in Fiji. My dad moved to Australia at the age of eighteen and joined the Royal Australian Air Force (RAAF).

This was my entire childhood, and we lived across four states in Australia. In total, I have lived in nine childhood family homes, which might seem like a lot, but since leaving home I have lived in an additional thirteen homes. I admire my dad. I know they say daughters are the apple of their father's eye, but I feel like my dad is the apple of mine! Today I look at my dad and see the glue to our family. He is our moral compass. Our true north. Our light at the end of the tunnel. Our safety net. Dad is a self-educated wonder brain, literally the only human in the Southern Hemisphere with the skills and expertise to do what he does for our Australian Defence Force. Dad is sixty-one and still playing hockey. He has the spirit of Peter Pan and runs on Fiji time … late.

My Mumma bear is of English descent with a somewhat gloomy childhood, from what I know of it. She was orphaned at the age of eleven when her mum passed away from leukaemia and her father fled back to Darwin. As a result, mum and her sister grew up in a children's orphanage in England until the age of fifteen when her father called for their return to Australia. Upon their return, my mum's father and partner at time decided it was all too much and he set off to North Queensland for job opportunities, orphaning my mum and her sister a second time. That same day, child services arrived to collect my mum and aunty and they were placed in another children's orphanage. A year later, my mum ran into her dad in town. It seemed he and his partner had moved back to Darwin, and he had 'forgotten' to mention it. He said he had a place, however, there was only enough room for one of the girls to move in. My mum told her sister to go, and Mum stayed in the orphanage until the age of sixteen when she was deemed old enough to fend for herself. So from sixteen, Mum was on her own.

Mum's body is here in Australia, but her heart is in the UK with her soul sister and cousin Jeannie. Mum was a stay-at-home mum doing the Betty Crocker mum gig. Literally, up until I finished year twelve, my sisters and I received a packed lunch box every single school day. She was the type of mum where I had to warn my school friends before they came over that she wasn't a regular mum. She was a *scary* mum. She liked to swear and tell it exactly how it was … and God help any soul who picked on us at school. Mum would be up at the school office faster than you could blink, demanding an explanation, an apology and an expulsion, she didn't care who they were or where they were from, no-one was bullying her kids.

When we were children, she truly embodied the term 'Mumma bear'. When I was two years of age, my sister Ebony was only weeks old, and Mum and Dad had taken us to a family club with some friends for dinner. Mum popped me on the floor, instructed my dad to watch me while she and her friend took Ebony to go and order dinner. Apparently, my dad was unaware of this request, and had not noticed I was on the floor playing. Furthermore, he and his friend did not notice my abduction. A complete stranger walked into the club, picked me up from the floor and ran off with me. Just as the man exited the building, my mum walked back into the room and saw me over his shoulder. My mum went into an absolute panic and rage both at the same time, screaming and throwing my baby sister at her friend. Mumma-bear mode kicked in and she ran after the man who had just abducted me. She chased him down into a nearby alleyway and was a raging screaming slapping Mumma bear, roaring at this man to give her back her baby ... Thankfully, it is safe to say, my mum won that battle.

***

Once I was out of the nest, Mum went back to the workforce after eighteen years and has continued to dedicate her life to children as a child care coordinator and runs an OOSH centre. We love to tease Mum, telling her she doesn't have any friends over the age of ten as every kid in their local shopping centre yells out, 'Hi, Gerry!' as they pass us by. Mum has that British hard exterior but she's a ball of moosh at heart. I suspect this is where my love for a good steaming-hot Yorkshire tea comes from and where my stellar resting bitch face was inherited from.

I also have two younger sisters. Ebony and Jayde. Across the three of us, we span six years, and we are told we look the same, however, we are each very different in personalities. I was your stereotype firstborn child. I followed the rules, was a leader, over-achiever, people-pleaser, reliable, protective, righteous and bossy.

Ebony was stereotypically the second and middle child. She is the fence-sitter, peacemaker, rebellious more so than I, independent, and according to her: 'left out of everything'. Jayde is the youngest … through and through, and still fits the stereotype well into her thirties now. Jayde's charming and outgoing, attention-seeking, spoilt and the biggest rule-breaker of all. Jayde has faced many adversities but, on the outside, looking in, seems like she has always just breezed through life carefree. This is probably a firstborn statement to make, but Jayde is the most spoilt and favoured child. #truth

We were raised the old-fashioned way. Always dressed the same in homemade sewed dresses, ridiculous home haircuts (why my mother allowed me to have the mullet haircut I requested at the age of six is beyond me!). We were raised to always respect our elders, always give up our seat on the bus to the elderly, disabled and/or pregnant, always use manners, wooden spoons were ridiculously threatening when whacked on the bench to put the fear of God into misbehaving children, we would never ever have even contemplated speaking disrespectfully to our parents and especially our grandparents. Then there was the good-old timeout in our bedrooms until the oven timer went off. Just quietly, I am convinced my mum would add additional time on the oven timer. We played outside after school and on school holidays with all the neighbourhood kids. We did little athletics, television was a luxury, sugary cereals were a never, and we didn't whine and complain, otherwise mum would threaten to 'give us something to complain about'. This extended to our health. This old conversation played out many times throughout our lives:

Me or sisters: Mum/Dad, I fell over and hurt my *INSERT INJURED BODY PART*

PROJECT KIND

Mum/Dad: Is it bleeding?
Me or sisters: No …
Mum/Dad: Is a bone poking out?
Me or sisters: No …
Mum/Dad: Are you dying?
Me or sisters: No …
Mum/Dad: Then off you go, you'll be right!

In the event it was bleeding, we were told to get some toilet paper and stop complaining. Yes, you read that right … toilet paper. This was our norm. We didn't have a first-aid kit, and Band-Aids in our family house were a commodity. If you go to my parents' house today, you'll find the same thing. No first-aid, a couple of old random Band-Aids and maybe some baby Panadol since grandkids have come along. But you know what, I feel like this raised us tough and resilient with a high pain tolerance. I would go on to break many bones in my early twenties playing sport – none of which I knew were broken at that moment. These included broken hands, wrists and even my eye orbital bone. It would only be in the days following that the niggling pain would have me going to get it checked out, only to find I had sustained fractures and breaks.

I love the memories of my childhood, even if there were some unsavoury moments. I look back on these moments, and while they were not all within my control, I would not wish my experiences on any person. I have accepted it is 100% my responsibility how I choose to allow these moments to impact me today and the power I allow these moments to hold over me. What I could control, I did. As a child having lived across nine houses as a RAAF family, and my tendency to move house as I've aged has not yet changed. Being a RAAF kid meant culling unnecessary belongings each time we moved. This led me to be not much of a sentimental keepsake keeper. In fact, we joke in my house now, that my husband is the oldest thing in the house. I've learnt from all the years of moving and adversities we faced, that the things we choose to live amongst are nothing but materialistic things that can, for the most part, be replaced. Any sentiment they might hold is a feeling I hold within me, not the object. So, naturally, I grew up with a strong belief that a home is a feeling, not a place.

Firstly, I acknowledge there are far too many people in the world who do not have a safe home, and the thought of that saddens me. Every person should have the right to feel what it is to have a safe and loving home. To me, home is a feeling of safety, warmth, love, acceptance and moral compass. A feeling that allows me to feel safe and the first space I could be unapologetically me. For me, this has meant I have felt 'at home' within many places, including our family home my parents reside at, the house my husband and I live in, the houses our siblings and their families live within, and even my great aunty who lived in Hornsby and my grandmother's house in Lautoka, Fiji. No matter where we are in life, it is being with those people that create my feeling of home. All homes that we know, we can enter without knocking, contain fridges we can open without asking and couches we can pass out on without judgement.

Guy, Cadence, Nate, Mum, Dad, Ebony, Adam, Jayde, Luke, Ma, Pa, Brooke, Scott, Uncle Henry, Aunty Miri, Luise, Sera, Amoe, Aunty Rita, Uncle George, Mapiga and Pa. These people are my heart. And my home.

2019: Christmas family photo. Dad, Mapiga, Mum, Guy, me, Nate, Adam, Mahlia, Ebony, Lani, Luke, Jayde, Cadence, Elijah, Iggy and Noah.

SURVIVAL
THE FIGHT OF MY LIFE

Survival. [ser-vahy-vuhl]

noun
the act or fact of surviving, especially under adverse or unusual circumstances.
a person or thing that survives or endures, especially an ancient custom, observance, belief or the like.

adjective
of, relating to, or for use in surviving, especially under adverse or unusual circumstances: survival techniques.

'At the end of the day, we can endure much more than we think we can.'
– Frida Kahlo

LESSON 9: TEQUILA FLU IS NOT A REAL THING.

I was your typical seventeen-year-old. Loving life, taking it for granted, acting like I was invincible and consuming far too much alcohol and underage nightclubbing Thursdays through to Sundays with my fake ID.

Moving across many states in my childhood also meant changing school systems. When I was in kindergarten, I completed terms one, two and three in South Australia, before moving to New South Wales and entering year one for term four. The following year I was straight into year two. This meant I was always one of the youngest people in my school year. In year twelve, when I was only sixteen, turning seventeen in May, most of my friends were already eighteen, if not far off from turning eighteen, so a fake ID addressed my massive case of FOMO (fear of missing out).

Never in my wildest of dreams could I have predicted I would be fighting for my life within the space of a year after graduating high school.

It was 22 March 2004, my usual Saturday night out, now with a legitimate ID and with my boyfriend at the time, Ryan, and a group of mates. Early in the night, one of the boys – Jack – got into a heated argument with another partygoer. I intervened and did what any good friend would do, and distracted Jack with tequila shots! A bellyful of tequila later, Jack had forgotten about the altercation, and I was violently throwing up by 10:30. For the record, I was not normally a spewer, so this was unusual.

The next morning, I woke up feeling very sick and sorry for myself. I had a cracking headache and sore throat – presumably from my excessive alcohol consumption and violent vomiting. I also was feverish all day long with all-over body aches and excessive sweating. I am talking drenched hair and wringing-wet PJs and bed linen. With the sweats overnight I had excessive thirst. I am not a great water-drinker at the best of times – and yes, I know all the benefits but the best I can do is consume my water intake in the form of a cup of tea or ten! However, these night sweats had me guzzling down two litres of water just overnight. When my symptoms persisted into the week, I was beginning to think I had influenza. During that time, I would get the shakes in the morning when I got up if I did not have breakfast immediately. In addition to all of that, I broke out in a red rash all over my stomach and arms. This tequila flu raged on for three long months.

Yes, I know what you are thinking, after a week of symptoms, any normal person would be booking a doctor's appointment. Today, I would totally have my arse at my GP surgery ... By my nineteenth birthday in May, I somehow lost 9.5kg within one week, and this caught the attention of my mother. Mum suggested I go to a doctor. So, naturally, I panicked because my parents would never suggest such a thing. According to Mum and Dad's usual theory, I wasn't bleeding, I didn't have a bone sticking out ... so they must think I'm dying, right? No not really, however, there was a family history of diabetes, and being of Polynesian decent, I was ticking all the boxes. I was now nineteen years of age and did not have a GP. I had never needed one in my entire existence to date. So, Mum and I found a GP in our hometown at a family practice. Given I'd never had one before, my only stipulation was a female doctor.

On 1 June 2004, I attended my first-ever GP appointment at the age of nineteen. Legally an adult, yes, but I still needed my mum to come with me! Doctor Joan. This incredible human was sending me hard wholesome loving mum vibes. She had a calming presence, is empathetic, and most importantly, listened! Now I know what you're thinking ... *Isn't that what doctors are meant to do?* Well, yes, however, throughout my journey ahead, I would meet plenty of doctors that lacked 'bedside manner', which I feel is a doctor's way of saying they have no people skills. I also feel like this is 'essentials 101' in any role within the health care sector, right?

Turns out I did not have tequila flu, and furthermore, tequila flu was not a real thing! I know right, I was shocked too!

My primary symptoms did indicate grounds for diabetes testing, however, we would rule out diabetes within that same week. For the next three weeks, I underwent every blood test and scan known to mankind. It seemed I had a few things bubbling at the same time, so we needed to identify each of them and rule out anything else. Early on in this process, I remember Joan calling our family house phone (remember those things!!). I thought it was odd because it was Friday, and she didn't work Fridays. She was calling for a few reasons. One, to ask me if I was experiencing any new or additional symptoms. No, I wasn't. Two, to give me her personal home phone number in the event anything did change when she was not in the GP surgery. And three, to ask my permission to take my medical file home with her so she could continue to research and investigate my case. What a champion! These days, if you want to raise two things with a GP it's a long consult and $150 later.

One morning, I was getting ready to head back down to Joan's surgery to do our usual thing. When we got there, the receptionist said Dr Joan was off sick today, however, Joan had asked I still come in and was rescheduled to see one of the head doctors there. Let's go with Doctor Smith. So, in I went with Mum to see Dr Smith. He was fascinated with my case, and while I was in his surgery room, he made a call to an immunology buddy of his to pick his brain about my medical conditions. I could only hear Dr Smith respond to the immunologist on the phone. It went something like this …

Dr Smith: No. No history of diabetes.

Silence listening to the immunologist

Dr Smith: No history of smoking.

Silence listening to the immunologist

Dr Smith: No history of drug taking.

Silence listening to the immunologist

Dr Smith then turned to me, reached forward with the phone tucked between his shoulder and ear. He used his two free hands to grab my arm and pull up my sleeves. He then did this to the other arm.

Dr Smith: Nope. No signs of track marks on her arms.

Silence listening to the immunologist

The rest of the conversation kind of blurred out for me. I was in a state of shock, I think. I had mixed emotions. *How dare he* … I had a sense of vulnerability from someone with authority physically checking me without my consent because he chose to disregard my normal GP's clinical notes and what I had already verbally told him. I felt so still. It took me back to eerie feelings when I was younger with males objectifying females. Mum, on the other hand, was raging inside! As soon as we got out of there, she was formulating a formal complaint. Mumma-bear mode was ON. I was grateful for this because I felt like I was happy to retreat and take the easy path again and not rock the boat.

LESSON 10: OF COURSE PEOPLE CARE ABOUT YOU.

Are you ever surprised and humbled with the love you receive on birthdays, milestones and achievements? Or the love you are surrounded with when you are in your darkest time of need? I'm sure it is Nancy at her best but I am always overwhelmed beyond comprehension that my little old existence can have such an impact to be worthy of others wanting to support me. My heart feels so heavy with love, it feels like it could burst in my chest, and I just turn into a ball of moosh.

***

Ryan was growing increasingly distant, but I was too consumed with being sick and undergoing countless tests. So, I did what I do best, activated self-sabotage mode and pushed him away. I can't get hurt if I push him away, right? I couldn't cope with having to worry about him worrying about me. I can manage my emotions; I can't manage his. So, I broke up with Ryan to 'protect' him from having to go through anything that was ahead for me. Many years later, my psychologist would tell me that the reason I pushed him away was more deep-seated than that. She believes it was due to my fear of Ryan thinking less of me and/or abandoning me in my time of need – as such, I would default to pushing people away. Now I see she is right; however, I still say I dodged a massive bullet. To this day, Ryan is the only human that was present in my life at that time, that treated me differently and couldn't deal with what I was going through, and as a result, disappeared.

By the end of June, I finally had multiple diagnoses. My rash was still somewhat of a mystery. Not linked to any other diagnosis but presented very similarly to a rash that is contracted in some African regions. No, I had not been to any African region, nor had anyone that I had been in regular contact with. I was diagnosed with a heart murmur, significant anaemia, a gnarly heart infection: mycoplasma infection with a side of myocarditis, and lastly, a query diagnosis of sarcoidosis – pending further testing. Sarcoidosis is basically when tissue clumps together on organs and in your lymph nodes. Sarcoidosis symptoms included many of those I was presenting with, including the rash. It was all equalling up. The only way to officially diagnose sarcoidosis was to have a biopsy.

As it was linked with the lymphatic system, cancer was also thrown on the table, however, every doctor and specialist suspected sarcoidosis. Dr Joan referred me to the specialist Mum and I would go on to name Professor 'Perve-A-Lot'. I had never needed to take my clothes off to have my chest listened to in the prior three months. What I find more disturbing is this specialist is highly respected within his field and within our health system. Professor Perve-A-Lot discussed sarcoidosis treatments which would be ongoing cortisone injections and referred me to a surgeon through Calvary John James Private Hospital.

On Tuesday 13 July, I was admitted to hospital at nine in the morning. Surgery was scheduled for twelve. I had my shower with the iodine soap bar and was gowned-up with my hairnet, TED stockings and tie-on underwear. A nurse entered my room to tell me the wardsman would be up in a minute to take me to theatre. The wardsman entered, and to my absolute embarrassment, it was a friend of Ryan's. We exchanged pleasantries and it was totally awkward, but he was sweet. Tainted with a tinge of pity in his voice, but I couldn't do anything to change my circumstances in that moment. Mum and our family friend, Tracey, walked down with me to the surgery doors where the nurse said, 'You have to say goodbye to your mum now. You'll see her in one hour.' I looked at Tracey and Mum ... for the first time all day, they both looked concerned and visibly upset. Meanwhile, I was sitting up waving and smiling like the Cheshire cat saying, 'See ya!' With my adrenalin starting to surge in fear and excitement of going in for surgery I defaulted to pretending everything was okay to ensure Mum and Tracey wouldn't worry about me.

Sitting in the surgery waiting bay, that adrenaline I was experiencing when I left Mum started to wear off. I was beginning to shiver, and the nerves were kicking in as I waited by myself. A few minutes later, they wheeled me into the theatre. I remember everything was stainless steel and cold. The bed was in the middle of the theatre room, and they transferred me across. It was during this moment one of the nurses must have noticed my nerves. Once I was across, the nurse came to my side and held my shaking hand and spoke to me softly, reassuring me that everything would be okay. As my eyes got heavy, the last thing I remember seeing was the clock. It read 12.08pm and I was thinking, *I hope Mum will be okay. It's only an hour. I'll be out at 1.08pm. I hope she will be okay.* Then I drifted off ...

The next thing I knew, I woke in the ICU and could sense two nurses hovering over me attaching cords and sticky tabs to my chest. One of the nurses was asking me to open my eyes. I drearily opened my eyes and the first object in my direct sight was a large white clock. It read 2.30pm. Panic. Sheer panic overwhelmed my body immediately. The nurse asked how I was feeling. I responded, 'I need my mum. Where is my mum?' as I ripped at the cords they had just attached to me in attempt to get up. I was so worried about Mum and Tracey because I knew they would be stressed out thinking something had gone wrong because I was gone for two and a half hours. Turned out my surgery was a little more complicated than anticipated and as a result my right lung collapsed.

That afternoon I had a flurry of visitors. I don't remember too much of their visit, but one thing I do and will always remember is the overwhelming appreciation I felt that people other than my immediate family cared about me enough to visit me in the intensive care unit. Seriously! I've always had this uncanny ability to underestimate my value to other people. I know this was because I obviously lacked self-esteem and confidence for a long period, but I can say that even today I get emotional when I feel like someone has gone out of their way for little old me. When kindness is directed towards me, I'm overwhelmed and so impostor syndrome kicks in. Receiving this much love and support also pointed out to me that my situation must not be good if the hospital were allowing me to have the half-a-dozen visitors I received within ICU, as the unit is usually only reserved for immediate family!

That night I was a mess. I wanted to go home. I was in pain because I now had a drainage cord hanging out of my rib cage and felt ill from the morphine. There was one nurse on that night that showed me such kindness. She brought me a spew bucket – and yes, I know that is her job ... but it wasn't her job to sit with me and just talk about mundane things in the middle of the night to distract me from my misery. It was so comforting. I think that night I was lucky to have slept an hour between two and three in the morning, even if I was sitting upright hugging the spew bucket. This nurse and the kindness she showed me would stay with me forevermore.

A couple days later I got transferred back onto the ward where I continued to have more visitors and flowers from work and family for the next three days. I was still attached to several metres of drainage tubing protruding from my lungs, and attached to the tubing was a clear plastic container for all the drained fluid, goop, blood and clots from my lungs. However, I could carry this around with me so long as I kept the plastic container lower than my lungs. This gross contraption became known as my plastic handbag. Basically, wherever I went, it was with me. I remember going for a walk with Mum to grab some lunch from the cafeteria because the hospital food was awful. I had my food tray on the slide-along bench rails and my handbag on my food tray as I was selecting all the foods I wanted. Onlookers weren't sure whether to be mortified, disgusted or concerned for me but nobody was going to say anything to the sick girl. A few days later I had a scan and got the all-clear that the tubes could be removed, and I could get rid of the plastic handbag. Finally, things were getting back to normal … however, denial was a place I had decided to take residency.

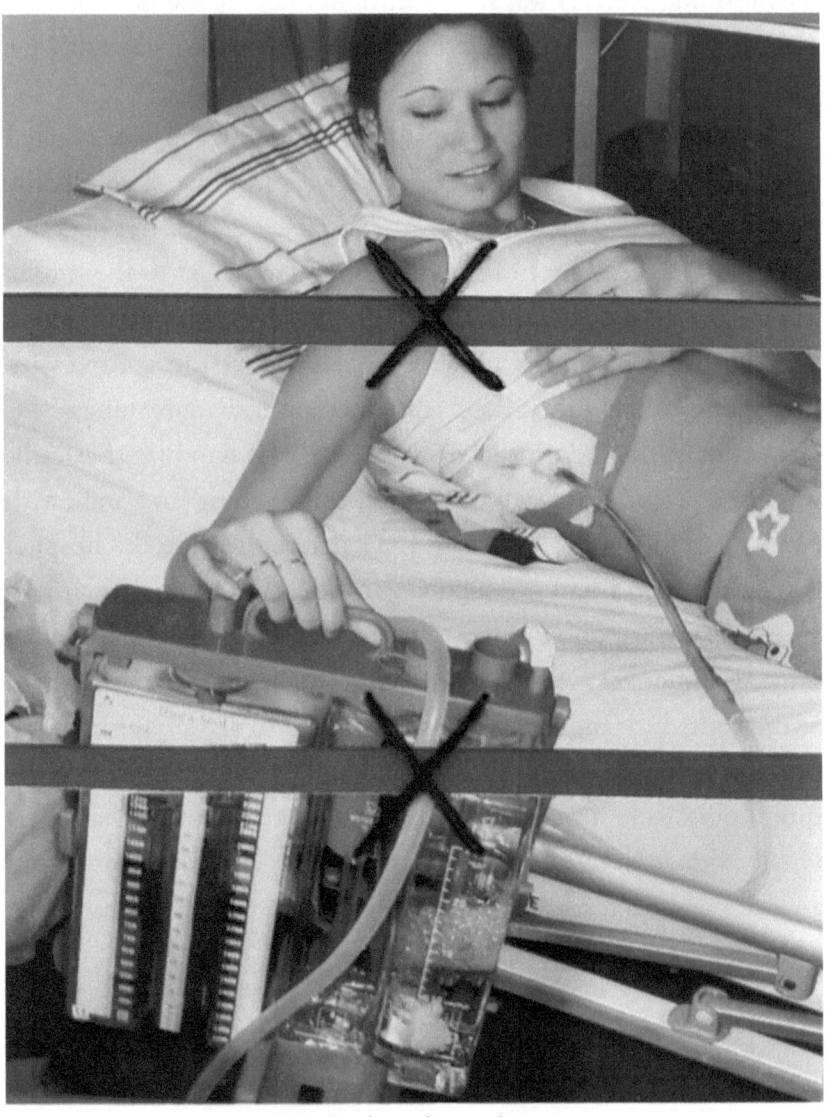

2004 – days after my biopsy

LESSON 11: IT COULD ALWAYS BE WORSE.

In this life, few things are undeniably right or wrong and this is because we all have different perspectives on any one thing. The key is having the 'right' approach to your perspective. So, what does that look like? It's not about being right or wrong. It is simply having an open mind and the ability to acknowledge that your view is not the *only* perspective, nor do you have the *alpha* perspective, and more importantly, other people's perspectives matter as well. One could choose to argue and hold onto their idea of what is right, or they could look at the bigger picture for a moment and acknowledge there is a different way to view said idea. *That* is perspective. This can be taken a step further, when applying that perspective view to the grand scheme of all things. Does this situation impact your life today? Tomorrow? Next year? Or is it something more like white noise which we shouldn't give any time and energy to?

Wouldn't our world be a better place if people understood and respected all perspective views? In this ideal world, a lot of conflict, wars, and ultimately, deaths could have been avoided if people saw things from another person's perspective. We would raise better, empathetic and more responsible adults if we just taught kids what perspective is, its importance, and why we may need to alter our views when faced with new information. Our world has a lot of white noise. Sometimes it takes a serious event to filter that white noise out. To truly see what really matters in the grand scheme of all things. Sometimes this stops us in our tracks before we can realise: it could always be worse.

***

Friday 16 July 2004. It was three o'clock on the dot when I heard the doctor on my ward headed toward my room. I was sitting upright with my hospital bed raised, rocking my *Sesame Street* Elmo pyjamas. Mum was sitting in the corner of my hospital room knitting and Nat was in the chair next to my bed. I was holding onto my trendy pink 2100 Nokia mobile phone. No words were being spoken but the love and support was abundant. My surgeon entered the room and exchanged pleasantries before jumping straight into it.

Surgeon: The biopsied tissue I extracted has returned a negative result for sarcoidosis.

Me: *Silent. Thinking to myself – Thank goodness.*

Surgeon: However, the tissue does appear to be cancerous and malignant.

Me: *Silent. Staring at my feet under the hospital bed blankets just nodding in acknowledgement.*

I don't recall the rest of the conversation.

It just became a fog.

An unknown world of nothingness.

I couldn't hear words anymore, just muffles. It was as if the world was suspended in time, and I was so calm. I just remember being so still and so calm.

It must have been the poker face of the century. I would later find out that Mum was questioning the surgeon for answers, but the essence of conversation was that he could not determine the type or treatment as I would require further testing with my referring specialist Professor Perve-A-Lot. The surgeon then left. Just like that ...

Within three minutes ... 180 seconds ... my life changed.

As the surgeon left, it's like the slow-motion suspended time suddenly stopped. It's like my subconscious had re-entered my body and the room was overwhelming with tension and my head was flooded with overwhelming thoughts but none of which I could isolate to actually articulate. My head was so noisy. Suddenly I felt so warm and short of breath.

I turned to look at Mum. She was sitting in the corner but as soon as she realised I was looking to her, she was up on her feet in a frantic tizzy, packing up her knitting, shoving it into her handbag. This redirected my mind to focus, and I asked if she was okay. Mum nodded her head so vigorously it was as if she were trying to convince herself of her response more than me.

She didn't speak or look at me.

I knew she wasn't okay, but I wasn't sure how to navigate my way through this one.

I wasn't sure if I was okay either.

She mumbled she was going outside for a smoke, and I asked her to come over and give me a hug because I knew she was tearing up. Mum burst into tears and hugged me so tight. I got a little upset myself because I always did whenever I saw my mum cry. Mum let go of me and quickly exited my room to go outside for a smoke. I turned to Nat who was just glaring at me. I asked Nat if she was okay. She just nodded, not saying a single word. I knew she felt helpless and at a loss for words. Which was extremely unusual for chatterbox Nat. However, I knew Nat's worry for me was also tainted by losing her mum unexpectedly just three years prior when we were in year ten. Death was something Nat was far too familiar with, and I imagine this was igniting a lot more emotion for her.

I contacted Tracey; she told me she would be up in fifteen minutes.

She arrived in ten.

Tracey came in with Mum. I would find out later that when Tracey arrived, my mum was at the front of the hospital sobbing her heart out. Tracey picked her up, calmed her down and helped her to deal with a day that would change our lives forever. When Tracey walked into my room, she took one look at me and wrapped me in a big Mumma-bear hug. That was my undoing. The hug I didn't know I needed because both Mum and I were so alike in trying to pretend we were each okay for the sake of the other but only resulting in utter despair.

I burst into tears for the briefest of moments. One of the two moments I would cry throughout this chapter of my life. Tracey brought me back to earth with a few of the undeniable facts I never really comprehended until that moment, on account of my utter denial. At the end of the day, I was always leaving hospital with a disease. But like the doctors, we were just so certain it was sarcoidosis. Regardless, I was never really prepared for any disease, no matter the diagnosis.

I am so grateful for having Tracey in my life. In hindsight, Tracey was the glue to my sanity that day. She is fierce but loving, strong but soft, real but empathetic. A true angel on this earth. She and her family took me in when I was a feral runaway kid in year twelve and loved me unconditionally. That day, Tracey was very realistic with her logical planning and coordinating. She started to rattle off things as if it were a cancer checklist.

Tracey told me I must 'concentrate on beating this awful disease'.

First steps would be to let family and friends know, and she warned me I might lose a few friends along the way that couldn't deal with my situation.

Tracey went on to say I 'need to pull my head in and settle down. No more partying or drinking'.

Wait.

What?

Suddenly my freefall was stopped by a concrete-slamming thud.

At that exact moment, reality hit and my stubborn streak was ignited.

Wait, let me get this straight, because I have cancer now, this places limitations on my existence? Who has a right to limit my life other than myself? I don't think so, absolutely not happening.

I nodded to appease everybody while I silently made a vow to myself. I was not going to stay home like a hermit. If I was going to die, I swore I would die having fun. Living life, not waiting idly for death while the rest of my world felt sorry for me. This mentality was not because I was brave on any account but rather because I was a stubborn nineteen-year-old girl who wasn't going to let cancer limit her or disrupt her social life.

Within the hour, word had spread quickly. Now, this was amazing. This was a couple of years before social media platforms were on Australian shores. So, word was spread the old-fashioned way by the good-old phone tree. Within that hour I received messages and calls from my workplace, family and friends. Even my other bestie Jes who was living in Wollongong. I was so overwhelmed with the number of people who gave a damn about little old me. These humans took time out of their day to contact me. I was so extremely grateful Mum, Nat and Tracey were with me that day. I honestly cannot have imagined having to pick up the phone and telling anyone 'I have cancer'. I felt like they were my damage control team. In a flurry, they were scheduling, contacting and coordinating everything and everyone. Meanwhile, I was still sitting motionless in my hospital bed gripping my phone as my world crumbled.

I feel like I was silent for most of the day. I remember my mind was still. There was nothingness. Everybody had gone for the afternoon and Mum was about to leave and would return at dinnertime with the family as she still had to get home to my sisters returning from school. Before she left, she was walking down to the cafeteria and asked if I wanted anything. Normally when Mum asks me if I want something to eat, I want everything on offer, but food was the furthest thing from my mind. Instead, I asked her to bring me back a notebook. This notebook would become by lifeline for the next six months. The only way I could survive each day as I went through something not a single soul around me at the time had experienced. It was lonely. That notebook became by little green chemo book. Unsurprisingly, I didn't sleep Friday night. I began writing …

Friday 16 July 2004 - The news. (Extract from my diary)

I have cancer. I don't think I will ever get used to saying that one. I thought only old people got cancer. How did I get cancer? Why did I get cancer? What type of cancer? Is there better or worse types of cancer? Why do I only associate cancer with old people and death? Am I going to die? I haven't even lived yet.

I can't sleep. The hospital lights annoy me, and well, I was told today I have cancer … Well at least I don't have to worry about telling everyone. I feel like word has spread already. Now my biggest worry is for those close to me getting upset and how they will act around me. On a selfish note, I'm mostly petrified of my hair falling out. I know that sounds vain. But it's an honest concern.

I feel like I am at a fork in the road. I could just quite easily fall into a downward spiral and feel sorry for myself, but I don't want my loved ones to get upset. I don't want to disappoint them. The last thing in the world I want to do is shut myself off from civilisation and wallow in self-pity, but I feel like that would be so easy to do. Okay … no sad faces. I'll focus on those around me. No sad faces. No sad faces.

PROJECT KIND

No sad faces. It could always be worse. No really, it could be! Losing my five senses or my limbs would be worse to me. Losing a loved one would be worse to me ... I just need to remember that.

It could always be worse.

Why can't I just go back to work and carry on like nothing has happened? That nothing is wrong with me. Oh shit ... what if this is God's way of weeding out the weak? If it's meant to be, it is meant to be! No, no, no, no. I know I'm in for a long haul, but I've just got to keep my head above it all. Stay focused and really stick it out. Everyone today kept telling me 'you've got to do this for yourself'. In all honesty, I'm shit at that. Every time I have ever attempted to do something for 'me' it always falls through. I never stick it out. I quit. I give up. I fail. Doing this for me won't get me through this. Doing this for me won't keep me alive.

No. I won't tell a soul, but I won't be doing this for myself. I can't. I'll do this for Mum. It kills me to see her so heartbroken and helpless. It would destroy her if I gave in. I can't let Mum down. This way I have some accountability. I'm going to win this. I don't know what I'm in for but I'm not going to give up. It's 4am now and I'm so scared. I'm shit-scared. I have no idea what is next. How do I do this? How do I beat cancer? Oh my gosh. Theme song ...

Matthew Wilder's song – 'Break My Stride'.

Okay, I need to put this notebook down. I feel like I am delirious and gibbering. I need to sleep. Maybe tomorrow will come and this will all have been a weird dream.

***

So how can anything be worse than this? Easy! Once my situation sat with me a few days I began to bargain with myself. In a way this was my grief process. I told myself it could always be worse. I could be losing my eyesight. As someone that loves art and being creative, this would be awful for me. I could have lost my limbs. That would take me a lifetime of adjustments lasting long past any cancer could. My biggest 'it could always be worse' moment was thinking it would be so much worse if it were happening to any person I know and love. Let me face this any day over my loved ones.

LESSON 12: SOMETIMES YOU JUST GOTTA ROLL WITH THE PUNCHES.

I woke the next morning and felt like I had been hit by a bus. Everything I hoped would not happen, happened. This was real. This was happening.

After being discharged, the punches kept on coming. There was literally nothing within my control. I felt like I was beginning to drown. Ryan came to visit. It was awkward and definitely cemented the fact that we were finished. I know I have a disease but fuck. He acted like I had a contagious flesh-eating airborne disease that he might catch from me. Throughout this entire journey, no-one would make me feel more alone, ashamed and disgusting as he did that day. What was worse, my parents liked him so were disappointed in me for ruining things. I didn't have the heart or the energy to tell them otherwise.

Jes drove down from Wollongong to see me. She spent the day with me just keeping me busy from my own thoughts, I guess. With Jes here, we went out Saturday night. My first night out of hospital and I went out, stitches and all. I had life flying at me in all different directions and none of it was in my control. So naturally, becoming intoxicated and losing any little control I did have over myself sounded like a great idea at the time.

PROJECT KIND

Three days later, Mum and I went to Dr Joan to get my stitches removed and to thank her. Joan put countless personal hours into my case and didn't stop until she got to the bottom of it. She was amazing. Joan is now my ongoing GP, despite now living thirty minutes away – I'd travel interstate to see her.

Dr Joan saved my life.

I returned to Professor Perve-A-Lot for my official biopsy results. My official diagnosis was nodular sclerosing Hodgkin lymphoma. Yes, that is a mouthful. It is also the exact cancer Australia's beloved Delta Goodrem had and beat, and many people would go on to tell me so, as if to say Delta beat it so you will be okay! My new diagnosis meant I no longer had to remain under the care of Professor Perve-A-Lot and was referred on to haematologist and oncologist Dr Matthews. My appointment with Dr Matthews was scheduled for Thursday 24 July 2004. I was excited to go because finally I would have a road map on what needed to be done and how. Some action. The last week felt like my family and I were stationary, waiting in limbo to hear our fate. How our lives were to play out.

Dr Matthews was a small-statured man. However, his mind and heart were the biggest I'd ever had the pleasure of knowing. He is a humble human and one of the best in his field. Mum came with me, and he spoke to me with compassion and in plain English, giving me all the facts. It appeared from all previous investigations the cancer was in my lungs. Dr Matthews went on to explain statistics like one in one thousand people will get leukaemia, but now being a cancer statistic, my chances increase to five in one thousand. This was a scary statistic for me and my family – noting my mum's mother had died when she was eleven from leukaemia. I am also more at risk of getting a secondary cancer. Of all the cancers, I did have the 'better' one to have. On the presumption I survived, my chances of the cancer never returning were 85%. That's pretty good odds so long as I was going to get to that side of the fence.

Next topic was fertility. At the age of nineteen, the idea of fertility was so embarrassing ... the furthest thing from the minds of any other nineteen-year-old I knew, but here I was. Dr Matthews went on to explain that normally there would be three options.

Option one would be to have my eggs harvested and frozen, however there was no guarantee of success as the science wasn't as amazing as it is today.

Option two was also down the IVF path. It would be freezing embryos. This option would involve nineteen-year-old me undergoing IVF and finding a baby daddy to fill me up a cup!

Ummmm ... That was a hard pass.

Option three would be to opt for a 'safer' chemotherapy treatment which would reduce the chances of infertility, however, it equally reduced the chances of getting rid of the cancer. This option would only be possible dependent on what stage my cancer was at, which would be determined in the next few days with additional testing.

Until my cancer could be graded, I had to go away and think about my fertility options, and we would discuss this at our next appointment once we had a clearer picture of my situation.

I was booked in at the hospital for a bone marrow biopsy the following day. That wasn't very fun. It was just a day procedure on the chemo ward. They gave me a twilight sedation and said it would relax me and most likely put me to sleep. It didn't. I didn't feel the initial incision, but Mum said I was moaning in pain. I remember the nurse telling me to close my eyes and I would drift off. The procedure was uncomfortable but thankfully it was quick. A needle is inserted through the cut and a liquid sample is withdrawn for testing. Having the marrow sucked out was painful. I remember Dr Matthews holding my hip securely as he used the surgical tool to remove the core of tissue (trephine) which is the size of a matchstick. This felt like a corkscrew was being twisted into my pelvis to remove bone.

Gallium scan was next. This required radioactive nuclear medicine. So naturally, I was thinking of *The Simpsons* episode 'The Springfield Files' with the glowing alien Mr Burns. Two days prior to the scan, Dad took me to get a gallium citrate injection. It is so radioactive; the injection comes in its own metal chamber and is injected by an automated system rather than by a person. So that was kind of concerning ... Apparently, the gallium then travels all over your body. It builds up in any cells that are actively dividing, such as the cancer cells in my body. Two days later, I went in for the scan. It's basically lying flat on your back for over an hour with a rotating scanner constantly moving around you while the imagery picks up all your glowing radioactive cancerous cells.

Friday 6 August 2004, I had my second appointment with the haematologist to discuss results and treatment plan. Finally, everything was tested and now it was time for action. The gallium scan revealed the cancer was metastasising across my body a lot more than we had initially anticipated. The scan revealed cancer lumps varying from 1-2cm in diameter. The many marble-sized tumours I had were cancerous cells that would continue to grow uncontrollably and spread across my body, invading my blood stream and lymphatic system.

So basically, I had cancer everywhere.

It was in my left side of the neck.

Both lungs.

Left shoulder joint.

Both underarms.
All through my abdomen.
My diaphragm.
My hip joints.
Lower part of my spine.
And the cherry on the cake ...
My bone marrow.

The biopsy came back revealing it, too, was riddled with cancer and may require a marrow transplant. All this cancer riddled throughout my body put me at stage 4B. Now, I wasn't too sure what that meant. How many stages are there?

One hundred? Fifty? Twenty?

Ten? If so, stage 4B looks pretty good right!?

... Nope

There are only four stages of cancer.

FOUR ... Stage one, two, three and four. I don't know what I did in my past life to deserve this, but there I was ... with cancer, and the severest form of cancer, at that. It has the highest risk of mortality and my doctor just told me I was stage four plus a B.

... The stage before death.

Well F*CK.

I think I preferred the tequila flu. I think I could do with a tequila now ...

'Any questions, Natashia?' Dr Matthews asked me. I shook my head no, but internally I was thinking, *Can't you just cut the cancer out then it is gone? Just an in-and-out procedure? I mean, you just biopsied a lump and cut it out ... why not the rest?* Unfortunately, the reality was I had so much cancer throughout my body I would have to be butchered top to toe to successful cut out all the cancer. There would be nothing left of me.

Dr Matthews went on to explain my treatment. I would require chemotherapy for six cycles over the course of six months. The chemotherapy was the more aggressive treatment ABVD which stands for all the drugs I would be required to have. Adriamycin (*ey-dree-uh-mahy-sin*), bleomycin (*blee-oh-MYE-sin*), vinblastine (*vin-BLAS-teen*) and dacarbazine (*da-CAR-ba-zeen*). Chemotherapy is basically the use of drugs to destroy cancer cells. It usually works by keeping the cancer cells from growing, dividing and effectively spreading. Because cancer cells usually grow and divide faster than normal cells, chemotherapy has more of an effect on cancer cells. However, the drugs are powerful, and will still cause damage to healthy cells too. Thus, making me immunocompromised.

Dr Matthews went on to explain that with this diagnosis, my fertility options were no longer a safe possibility as time was no longer on my side. He then asked me if I had any questions.

I only had one.

'What if I choose to refuse chemo?'

I didn't really think about Mum before I asked. I just blurted it out. Immediately, I felt Mum turn her head sharply and the warmth of her hot glare, but I refused to engage eye contact with her. Dr Matthews went on to explain I would basically be looking at end-of-life planning within three months. I could feel my Mum's glare burning into the side of my face now. Mum dismissed this and redirected us, asking, 'How soon can she start?' Clearly my mother was not pleased with me, nor was she going to entertain the idea of my refusing treatment.

Dr Matthews requested I start immediately. As it was Friday, I would have the weekend, then Monday morning would require pre-screening chemo bloods in order to calculate the dosages I would require, and Tuesday would be chemotherapy treatment: day one.

It was kind of crazy. It took so long to discover what was wrong with me, then I literally find out on a Friday and am booked in for chemotherapy on the next possible day. I seriously couldn't possibly take another punch. Leaving the hospital, I could see Mum was upset, but I left her be. She had a victory, I agreed to treatment, and I didn't want to make her cry again because, to be honest, I just needed a hot second myself. I felt like I was drowning. Like when a wave hits you in the ocean, disorientating you for a few moments and you don't know which way is up. You just hope the way you are heading is towards the surface as you gasp for air.

In theory, all the books and Doctor Google will tell you how to navigate situations like the one I found myself in. In theory, I should have leaned on my loved ones and expressed my emotions. I wasn't even able to label some of the emotions I was experiencing. In theory, I should not have avoided my thoughts. In theory, I should have prioritised looking after myself. These are the theories I encourage you to implement when dealing with distressing and traumatic experiences. However, here I was, not making anything easy for myself.

I went home and activated another default setting and went into 'helping others mode'. Don't worry about me, I'm too busy worrying about everyone else. I typed up a letter to all my friends. Don't forget, it was 2004, socials were not a thing yet, so I was going with the good-old snail mail. The letter would go on to explain to everyone what was going on with me. What I had ahead of me and that I was okay and to ask if anyone wanted to know anything. I felt I had no other viable choice. I couldn't sit and wallow. I couldn't bear the thought of pity eyes from my friends. So, I had to empower each of them with knowledge. I wanted to provide them with guidance on how to behave with me. I wanted them to know I was still me! I look back at this now and see there was a lot of fear there. I was fearful I would be outcasted by my friends and pitied by my family.

COPING
F*CK CANCER

Coping. [kohp-ing]

verb

coped, cop·ing.

to struggle or deal, especially on fairly even terms or with some degree of success.

to face and deal with responsibilities, problems, or difficulties, especially successfully or in a calm or adequate manner.

'I'm somewhere between giving up and seeing how much more I can take.'
– Anonymous

LESSON 13: LIMIT YOUR SELF-PITY PARTIES.

Coping is a funny thing. You think you can't cope then suddenly you look up and you did it simply because there was no other option. Whether you are coping through exams, job applications, health issues, bad relationships and more, the human mind and body is an amazing thing. Give yourself the chance and you might just surprise yourself.

Grief is a natural response to loss. It's the emotional suffering you feel when something or someone you love is taken away. In my case, my life as I knew it. The possibilities of the unknown were terrifying. I experienced all kinds of difficult and unexpected emotions, many of which I refused to acknowledge. Like all things in life, there is no real rule book on how to grieve. There's no right or wrong way, but it does take time. Time I felt I didn't have. Because of this thought, I know I didn't allow myself the appropriate space to explore these feelings, thus limiting my pity parties, convincing myself it was for the best. In hindsight, what I should have done is:

- Acknowledge my pain and the loss I felt.
- Accept that grief can trigger many different and unexpected emotions.
- Understand that my grieving process will be unique to me.
- Self-care including seeking out face-to-face support.
- Recognise the difference between grief and depression.

Instead of doing all the things I should have been doing, I chose to stay in denial. I allowed the whirlwind to sweep me up and was too busy trying to live to actually stop and feel.

On Saturday, Jes made another trip down from Wollongong for me, so Nat, Jes and I could have one last girls' weekend out before chemo began, or in case I didn't live to see another one. As morbid as it sounded, that was the reality I was facing. I remember we were at Tracey's house, and she asked to take a photo of us three girls together. That photo sat on their mantel piece for many years to come. Tracey would later tell me she thought that may have been the last photo she'd ever get of me. Nobody expected me to survive the year.

So, Saturday night we went out and I got absolutely smashed. It was amazing. Not a single care in the world. Probably due to the fact I couldn't thread a sentence – nor a thought – together that night. All my friends were out with me living our best nineteen-year-old lives. My friends were extremely overprotective of me that night and every night out that followed.

Monday morning rolled around. I went for my pre-screening chemo bloods, wrote myself a list in my green chemo book of things I needed to remember on the way to pathology. Mostly because it kept me task orientated otherwise I knew I would fall down the rabbit hole and allow myself to spiral. Only, my list wasn't very helpful.

PROJECT KIND

Monday 9 August 2004: (Extract from my diary)

1. *Double flush the toilet; urine will be red and toxic to others.*
2. *Use separate toothpaste as I am toxic to others.*
3. *Keep toothbrush separate from sisters because I am toxic to others.*
4. *No swimming as I am toxic to others.*
5. *No working on chemo days as I am MOST toxic.*
6. *Fresh towels every day to avoid infection and death.*
7. *Avoid sick people otherwise I will die.*
8. *Do not share food or drinks otherwise I could die.*
9. *No fresh flowers or plants ... they harbour bacteria that could kill me.*
10. *No temps over 37.4 otherwise I could die.*
11. *Don't upset others with my sad story.*
12. *No sad faces. No tears.*
13. *Don't die.*

Tuesday 10 August 2004: (Extract from my diary)

Cycle One - Day One. I had such a restless sleep last night. I was up coughing all night and had that nervous but excited feeling like you do as a kid for the first day back at school after summer break. I got up at nine this morning, had a shower and went to work. Dad picked Mum and me up from work at 10:30. We arrived at the hospital, and I'm not actually scared. I'm a bit excited to get this started. When we arrived, the receptionist directed me into the chemo room. It was a large room with eight leather chairs lined up side by side on either side of the room. I picked the second chair from the window on the right side. Prime real estate I have. Window view, but the right side also gives me a view back out into the nurses' station and reception area. The nurses are just setting things up now. Here I go. Hope I survive.

***

I met my chemo nurses Melissa, Kate and Fiona. Kate got my mobile number before we started and told me she was going to put me in contact with a girl close to my age named Crystal. She was three cycles from finishing her treatment, and Kate thought it would be good to talk to someone who truly understands the journey. I felt like a huge lifeline had just been thrown to me at sea. Someone that would know how I felt.

Fiona brought a wash bowl over and placed it in my lap to soak my hands in the warm water. Apparently, this was going to help find a decent vein in my hand to administer the cannula for chemotherapy. Apparently, I have very fine veins. The ones on the backs of my hands are no wider than the metal of a paper clip. Once cannulated, they hooked me up to a bag of saline and anti-nausea serum. Two of the drugs were push drugs administered by the nurses. One of them is referred to ironically as 'red devil'. It is red in colour and highly potent in its toxicity. It is also the wonderful drug that is responsible for making your hair fall out and your pee bright red for the following days. The other two drugs were IV bags. The nurses had it running at a slower rate for me because my veins were so small. I was grateful for this because it felt like someone was shoving a pen down my veins. Like a square peg in a round hole. My arm ached and pain radiated all up my forearm. It was like I could feel the drug moving up my blood stream and it was disgusting. It felt like someone was jumping on my arm over and over and over. The nurses gave me a heat pack for the pain, but it was useless. I just had to endure this as waves of nausea washed over me like waves in the ocean.

Toward the last thirty minutes I was done. I had had enough.

Five whole hours. I could feel I was getting emotionally overwhelmed and didn't want to do it. I couldn't allow myself to feel like this. Not now. I was only one session in. I had a mammoth trek ahead. Thankfully, it was over soon enough. I was unplugged and free to go home. I felt on top of the world because it was over. I survived my first day of chemo. That feeling was fleeting. On the journey home, I began to feel ill again. I was experiencing sharp pains behind my eyes and the thought of any food made me want to spew. By 6:30pm I already spiked a temp of 38.8 which meant I would have to go to emergency, but I had had enough of hospital for one day, so I told my mum the temp was fine and didn't show her. Safe to say chemo sucks and I don't really like it much. I now dislike Tuesdays. I honestly did not know how I was going to survive another chemo day.

I contacted Crystal that very afternoon. Looking to her for a path forward on how I was going to survive this. I feel like that was a lot of pressure. Not that I verbalised that to Crystal. After speaking with Crystal and hearing her struggle so close to the finish line made my finish line look like it was on the other side of Mount Everest. Crystal would describe to me how she was feeling, and there I was, after one session, feeling that way already. I didn't know if I could do this … Bury me on Mount Everest with the rest of the lost souls.

The following days were a mix between hating life and wishing for death. There was not much else between, but I was too stubborn to give up. I knew I would have to grieve eventually for the life I felt I was losing, but I couldn't. I felt that path was a slippery slope to self-pity party central and I couldn't go there. Not yet. I needed to put my energy into being present. I was scared that if I went there, it would all be over. I had to push through. One foot in front of the other, but it felt like time slowed down. I felt every painful minute of every day while I was enduring my treatment. As far as I was concerned this was a far easier option than seeing my friends and family mourn my pending death with their pity eyes. It became about accepting the idea that positive people also have negative thoughts and terrible days. The difference between a positive and negative person is that the positive people don't allow those thoughts to grow and destroy them. Some days, this was easier said than done.

Nat was amazing. She didn't know this at the time, but she kept me accountable for the daily mundane tasks that helped save me from myself and my spiral of self-pity. She would come over and we would go for walks every second day. I felt awful at first but loved being able to get up and out of the house for some fresh air and sunshine. We talked about everything other than cancer. Generally feeling squeamish seemed to be the new norm, even on a good day.

Thursday, I stayed at Jack's. Remember Jack? The boy who got me tequila flu, only it was actually cancer … well he and I had been hanging out. Jack was sweet. It was nice not to be treated like a fragile contagious freak, but we were just friends, so I didn't need to worry about going to my default setting and pushing him away. It was so easy. We would watch movies until I fell asleep. It was nice to be doing something other than being sick. There was no expectation to be anything.

I eventually agreed to be 'official', but it seemed everybody but me knew that was already the case. I feel like because my brain said, *No, we are just friends*, I was able to let my guard down. To this day, I truly believe Jack was a driving force of positivity in my journey. My memories of my relationship with Jack are sweet. He had a huge impact on me and my recovery. I wholeheartedly believe our paths were meant to cross. For those that believe in soulmates, I believe there are various types of soul connections and I believe Jack was a 'soul crossing' for me. It's like that saying 'ships that pass in the night' ... it's used to describe someone who comes into your life, but the timing and circumstances are not right, so effectively are not conducive to a long-term relationship, but Jack and I were thrown together and shared amazing experiences and awakenings that I will always remember and be eternally grateful for.

***

Turns out, in 1969, psychiatrist Elisabeth Kübler-Ross introduced what became known as the 'five stages of grief'.[5] These stages of grief were based on her studies of the feelings of patients facing terminal illness. So here I was, slowly moving through the textbook stages of Elisabeth's studies and I didn't even realise it.

Stage 1: Denial. 'This can't be happening to me.'

Stage 2: Anger. '*Why* is this happening? How did tequila give me cancer?'

Stage 3: Bargaining. 'Make this cancer go away and I swear I'll give up my ability to bear children if this is what the universe intends for me.'

Stage 4: Depression. Now, to be honest, it took me quite a few years to realise I was still grieving this chapter of my life.

Stage 5: Acceptance. I don't believe I was truly accepting of my circumstances for another fifteen years after my diagnosis. This would go on to have many adverse effects in other areas of my life.

Stage three started four weeks into treatment and became one of my core beliefs for a long period of time; stages four and five took a good fifteen years before I could honestly say my grieving process had ended and I was in acceptance. Obviously, I was none the wiser to it at the time.

2004: What we thought would be my last-ever photo ... Myself, Jes and Nat

LESSON 14: SOMETIMES LIFE CALLS FOR THE EXTREME.

My dad's family have strong Christian beliefs. So naturally, when I got cancer, everybody was doing a whole lot of praying. I remember, after being diagnosed, it was my great-uncle's eightieth birthday celebrations in Hornsby. Our family travelled to the Sydney celebration. We all thought it would be best if we kept my 'situation' under wraps to ensure everyone else would have an enjoyable gathering celebrating this amazing milestone. I remember sitting there with the family, all just kind of sticking to ourselves. While nobody questioned anything at the time, afterwards, the extended family called to check in as they sensed something was going on and clearly noticed my gaunt, deathly appearance. Once all the extended family knew, they came from Sydney to bless and pray for me. Literally.

At this stage, I wasn't sure what I believed in. I just knew there was something bigger than me. To be honest, I was up for trying anything. Chinese acupuncture, chemotherapy, prayers, raw foods … you name it, I did it. However, somehow through all of this, I created this negative self-talk. A narrative in my head that would hold me prisoner for the following twelve years, limiting my existence because I wouldn't open my mind up to accepting any other narrative. Enter stage three: bargaining.

My negative self-talk became the default dialogue I would regularly have with myself that ultimately limited my capacity to believe in my abilities and myself. Later in life, my psychologist would tell me that negative self-talk is within every person. When I did it to myself, I was diminishing my ability to make positive changes within my life and confidence. It was creating unnecessary stress and essentially stunting my success in life.

So, what was my negative self-talk narrative? Well …

I had this crazy idea, but in my mind, it seemed very logical and possible. I thought that cancer was one of God's ways of weeding out the weak. But if I used man-made medicine (aka chemotherapy) to go against God's will, I would be defying God and my fate …

Still with me? Hang in there, it gets weirder!

When I was on the brink of giving up and thought I was literally going to die, as I was slowly moving through the process of grief, I took residency up in stage three: bargaining. I made a pact with God, the universe, Buddha, Allah, Mother Nature, the devil … anyone who was mightier than me and listening. I promised if the higher powers that be allowed to me live, I would acknowledge and accept and vow to be the dead end I was destined to be. As such, I would give up my fertility in exchange for my life to continue. This would mean I would still be the required 'dead end' as per the universe's plans, thus, keeping the natural order of life and death in balance. I was just merely asking to extend my life sentence.

I know what you are thinking!

What the actual fuck was wrong with me?

That is some twisted and deep shit, but with my beliefs, and looking at that logically, it made perfect sense. Let me just remind you that I had cancer. I was dying. I was desperate. Ironically, I obviously subconsciously knew it was crazy self-talk because it was a belief I did not openly share with other people. Partly because I know politics, money and religion are just taboo topics in society that nobody ever agrees on. I was never one for confrontation and believe everybody is entitled to their beliefs and opinions, and so long as they don't impact others negatively, what's the harm … but I also know not everybody thinks like I do. As such, my ideas around this may have been considered extreme as they were an extension of my own personal beliefs, so I didn't expect others would understand. I already had so much on my plate, I didn't want to have to cope with their judgement or feel I had to justify myself.

The other part to me choosing not to share my thoughts on this was the mere fact that I was just nineteen years of age. I felt like cancer aged my mind and outlook significantly and rapidly. No-one my age that I knew was having and/or sharing their profound discoveries to the meaning of life, let alone having deep and meaningful soul-baring conversations like this. The nineteen-year-olds I knew were cramming for university exams on weekdays and out partying on the weekends or partying their way through a gap year trying to drink more than the night before. Sleeping with regrets. Dating mistakes. Doing the walk of shame and backing it up the next night. Being reckless and exploring our new-found freedom into adulthood. Making all the mistakes. Well, at least that is what the crazy nineteen-year-olds I knew were doing.

It was in this moment of negative Nancy self-talk, I realised – really realised – just how much I wanted to live. Have you ever actually stopped to think about that? No, seriously! We all 'exist', but are you actually 'living'? Would you be content to leave everything behind tomorrow? Have you done everything you hoped to do or are you at least on your way to doing it all? Did you fulfil your idea of a fulfilling life? Are you proud of your legacy? Would you be leaving with regrets? Are you comfortable with death? I personally had never given this topic a thought until now. Granted, I don't think this is something any nineteen-year-old gives any real thought to, but there I was, with a death sentence, and all I was certain of was that I did not want to die.

I wasn't ready to leave this world. I didn't feel like I had even begun living yet. What had I been doing with my life up until then? I was wasting it away. Until that point, I merely lived carefree like the rest of those nineteen-year-olds I mentioned. I was literally floating around the earth with little to no purpose … *yet*. I hadn't achieved anything; I had no nice legacy to leave behind. In fact, if I died tomorrow, I've got a lot of shady shit written in my journals from my pre-cancer days that would make my grandmother blush. I really need to destroy those!

As crazy as it is, this woke me up. It made me want to be present. Be alive. Give back. Destroy my embarrassing journals of the past. Do something meaningful. Make a difference. Be kinder. Create a legacy. I just wanted the chance to be able to do that and not die tomorrow regretting the sad excuse of an existence my life was up until that very point. I certainly wouldn't have put my hand up to step forward on the cancer line, but here I was, thrust upon it, trying to figure out how to get myself out of the damn cancer line the best way I knew how. All I had to do was survive and get through treatment as quick as possible, then I swore I would do something positive with my life.

If an early death doesn't give one the drive to live, I honestly don't know what would. I had no idea what that would be or what that would look like, and even more so, how my trade-off meant my future would not include biological kids. What was my purpose without bearing children of my own? Am I even a woman? Doesn't every woman that chooses to have children, dream of having children that look like them? Their eyes, their skin tone, their personality, a walking, talking mini-me?! I was just grateful that Jack was aware of this from the beginning, so it wasn't an awkward 'talk' we had to have later down the track.

I knew I wanted to live. I just wasn't sure what life without kids would look like as it was not a life I had ever envisioned but something I now needed to plan for. At the time, I didn't have anyone in my life who actively chose not to have children. I know we were in an era where women could have the opportunities afforded to them to 'do it all', and statistics showed women having children later in life or choosing successful careers over children. I am totally for all of that and why the hell not! I guess the gripe I struggled to come to terms with was that I was not afforded that choice. My right to my choice was removed from me. I felt powerless … and dare I say, I even felt worthless. Then throw in some guilt of feeling greedy for making such a deal with the devil, so to speak, I basically gave up my ability to have children before I even knew what that really meant for me. Are we greedy humans? We live in such a fast-paced world, wanting for everything, but at what cost?

Eventually, once I got through this deal and faced my negative Nancy self-talk, I vowed fully, knowing this time that I would never go forth in life with tunnel vision ever again. I would proceed through life with my wide lens on. I do truly believe this lens has become one of my strengths and has significantly contributed to my success today. What is my wide lens? Like used in photography, my wide lens allows me to fit more into the frame, aka my view, my thoughts. Simply put, it allows me to see the bigger picture within my own life and existence. This lens has allowed me to understand my actions and reactions, and the repercussions these have on others, and essentially make informed decisions on how I react.

For example, midway through treatment, I hit a mental wall. I was faced with the self-talk 'do I continue' OR 'do I call it quits and face death'? For me, I chose to continue because the wide lens of this was obvious. My death would alter and affect those around me within my 'bigger picture'. Continuing to fight would have less impact and disruption to those within my bigger picture. A bit of a drastic example, I know; however, everyone's wide lens can be applied to every situation in everyday living, and this allowed me at the time to cope the only way I knew how. It is making a conscious effort to ask yourself if your words and/or actions have the possibility of negatively affecting someone around you and weighing up the risk vs. reward. Thinking beyond just yourself.

LESSON 15: ALL ACTIONS HAVE CONSEQUENCES.

All actions and inactions have consequences. This is something we are told from a young age. If you touch the oven when it's on, it's going to be hot and burn you. In my day, it also meant I was probably going to get a smacked hand. Going out on an all-night bender knowing you have an exam in the morning is a consequence that will impact future you. Going on that bender and deciding to drink-drive home has potential lifelong consequences that can impact you and the community. For me, I felt I was losing grip on my freedom. So naturally, as a nineteen-year-old, I did everything in my power to do everything I was told not to do.

***

From my very first session of chemo, I became violently ill within hours.

Within twenty-four hours my hair began shedding.

Within two weeks all the side effects were in full effect.

Riddled with constant headaches, flu-like symptoms, nausea and vomiting all seemed to be as common as breathing. So, so, so, so, much vomiting. Red urine the following day or two after treatment was my new normal. My energy was depleting, so I felt like I only ever had a quarter battery life from the moment I woke up in the mornings, and not a single thing I did could ever recharge my battery above that level. The simplest of tasks exhausted me – including even turning the pages of my trashy magazines I would cart along to chemo. It physically exhausted me to turn a page! My veins were absolutely wrecked with lumpy scar tissue. Dr Matthews suggested I had a port put in my chest.

The port would be placed under the skin, usually in the right side of the chest. It is attached to a thin silicon tube that is guided into a large vein above the right side of the heart called the superior vena cava. The main advantage of this vein-access device is that chemotherapy medications can be delivered directly into the port rather than a vein, eliminating the need for needle sticks, and it can stay in place for many weeks, months or years. So basically, I would have a two-way tap. It would also allow the hospital to drain my blood for tests.

As a thirty-six-year-old woman with much experience in the health sector, I would totally opt for this option today. But not nineteen-year-old me. No thank you! I refused. I already had no body hair, shit eyebrows and thin ratty hair on my head. I looked pale and sickly skinny. I was not about to have a tap attached to my chest too. The consequence of my choice meant damaged veins. To this day, they are still visibly damaged. No regrets here, though. Not having the port allowed me to feel somewhat normal when I wasn't violently ill. To nineteen-year-old me, having the port would have been the final cherry on the top telling the world loud and clear, 'Sick girl over here!'

Additional side effects were loss of appetite, which was compounded by the fact I had also lost my sense of smell and taste. Everything was plain. During chemo, the catering lady would always come around with hospital sandwiches and the plastic cups of apple juice. They always wanted you to eat before you left the chemo ward. To this day, I cannot stand pre-made mixed sandwiches or hospital apple juice in a cup. It's like a smell-triggered memory. Takes me right back to that chemo sick feeling. Also, the nurses used medical tape to stick my IV line to my skin to make it more secure as my veins were so fine, they would often burst and/or become dislodged. The smell of the medical tape to this day makes me feel instantly ill.

I also lost my sense of touch. My fingertips couldn't differentiate the difference between hot and cold, smooth and rough. I had mouth sores, bleeding gums and ridiculously sensitive teeth. On top of that, I was also losing my fingernails and toenails. I was extremely susceptible to everything. I wasn't allowed near anyone who had returned from overseas travel, I wasn't allowed near anyone unwell and/or recently immunised with live vaccinations. I wasn't allowed to have flowers or plants. Everything had to be sterile. Clinical. Clean. And cold.

My hair was a huge vain point for me. It was the basis of me wanting to not do chemo in the first place. It was also the one thing that would signify to the world I was the token sick cancer girl. Thankfully I have always had thick hair, so I refused to shave my head and look like a chemo patient any more than I already did. My hair came out in clumps day in and day out. I'd do another round of chemo and it would start shedding all over again. My hair ties went from the thick hair bands to the dental elastics you would put on kids' braces! I think back now and can't believe how consumed I was about salvaging my hair. I devoted so much worry and time into my inevitable hair loss. I feel like if I got a do-over I would totally just shave it off and rock some crazy out-there wigs. But I also accept this was an age thing. I like to think I'm wiser these days and less likely to give a shit about what others think of me, but it is also not lost on me this is totally in hindsight, of course.

In my bid to maintain a regular life and ignore the consequences of the chemotherapy, I attended my social gymnastics class with Nat and one of the boys, Alex. We were all standing in a circle with our class and the coach instructed us to work on our bridges. I laid on the ground and bent my knees up and placed my arms back on the floor beside my ears, assuming the position to push up into a bridge. Alex was spotting me. I pushed up and all I heard was gasps and Alex put his hands over his mouth in shock. I broke my bridge and turned around to see what everyone was carrying on about. I looked down on the gym floor mat and there was an epic chunk of my hair.

Alex was standing on my hair when he was spotting me, however, due to my hair loss, I didn't feel it ripping from my head as I pushed up into my bridge. Alex was extremely apologetic. I just wanted everything to be okay. So, I brushed it off and played it down, 'It's okay, I didn't feel a thing!' and I really didn't feel it. I only felt shame once it occurred. I hated the idea everyone felt sorry for me. Oh ... there goes the chemo girl again!

Prior to tequila flu and cancer, my friends and I had all signed up for a cruise around the South Pacific in October of 2004. This now meant the cruise fell smack-bang in the middle of my chemotherapy cycles. Mum and Dad were 1,000% against me going on the cruise. But I was determined that I was continuing to live, and that meant doing as I would normally do. I notified the travel agent when I was diagnosed with cancer to adjust my booking health insurance. Turns out the insurance company didn't want to take a chance on me and would not cover me in any capacity. This did not help my case with selling it to Mum and Dad. But I was a grown-arse nineteen-year-old now. I was going! With my haematologist's approval and a letter outlining what would be required in the event I did become unwell, I was set to go.

I had chemo on Tuesday, and we were sailing out on Wednesday for eleven glorious chemo-free days! I was so excited to go to chemo because it meant I was closer to going on the cruise. I was a lot more alert throughout the five hours of treatment; I noticed a lot more within the chemo room. Details like I was the only person in that room under the age of fifty on treatment. Every cancer patient that entered the room came in fresh and positive, but a round of chemo left each one of us looking and feeling like zombies. It is literally as if chemotherapy sucks the life force out of you.

As soon as I was finished, I bounded home to pack and repack for the one-hundred-millionth time. My friends picked me up the next morning and we caught a bus to Sydney Harbour. Just as seasickness was overwhelming my friends onboard, I was sick from chemotherapy. I slept for forty-eight hours straight, only waking three brief times drenched in sweat with temps of thirty-nine-plus. My friends urged me to go to the onboard medical centre to seek medical attention. But with no health insurance approved, I knew I couldn't afford the care so decided to stay put and 'sweat it out'. If I was ever close to death throughout that journey, those few days were it! In hindsight, I see how ridiculously reckless of me this was, and how I didn't die, I will truly never know.

I eventually, by some miracle, got better and was able to join everybody else. The cruise was amazing. We made lots of new friends – none of which looked at me like the sick girl, which was refreshing. We drank and partied every single night, rolled out of bed by midday the next day to disembark onto whatever glorious South Pacific island we had docked at for the day. I felt like this was the time of my life. I even had photos during the cruise. Something I wasn't too fond of during this whole process, but I thankfully had time on my side as this was before mobile phone cameras and socials.

After eleven glorious days sailing the South Pacific, it was time to dock in and face reality.

Reality was worse than I remembered.

I had pushed my treatment back a week so I raced back to Canberra to have my pre-chemo blood work done ready to jump straight into the chemo chair the next day.

Having the additional time between cycles was amazing, but boy, did I pay for it. The next day, Sally connected me up to my chemo and put through the anti-nausea IV meds. No more than five minutes in, I began vomiting. I continued to vomit for the entire six hours of chemo. This day took six hours because I just couldn't tolerate it. Physically or mentally. I thought the cruise sweats were bad … this was misery. I spent the entire time in the chemo chair today wishing for it to just be over … and I wasn't talking about chemo. I was talking about life. Then it hit me. This was getting hard. I just wanted to stop. I had just come off such a high on the cruise to this poor excuse of an existence. Why was I doing this?

I started thinking of all the positives my death would bring. It would be a lot cheaper for my parents who were paying for their nineteen-year-old daughter's medical bills and private health insurance. I felt like the biggest burden to them. Dad was having to take so much time off work to get me to and from appointments (my mum doesn't have a car licence). I was constantly sick and the entire family household revolved around my health. My poor sisters were struggling in school and Ebony was in a dark place. Surely my life was not worth that much stress. In that split second, I realised I was done, and a single tear fell down my cheek. I quickly wiped it away before Mum saw. Knowing Mum was there, and I had to keep it together for her, was probably a good pressure to put on myself in that moment. She was about the only thing keeping me together even if she had no idea at the time. Mum asked if I was okay, so I just casually sighed and said, 'I've had enough,' passing it off as if I had simply had enough of being stuck in the chair for that day. Not as in I had had enough of living and was ready to welcome death any time then …

Dad picked Mum and me up and dropped us home. I got inside and Mum asked me if I wanted a drink. I responded just mumbling, 'Okay. I'm just going to the toilet.' I went upstairs to my 'designated' bathroom, shut the door and sobbed. Then vomited and sobbed some more. Like, really sobbed. I'm talking Kim Kardashian ugly-cry sobbed! (Cry number two of my cancer experience.) I had nothing left. I was done. I couldn't do this anymore. I didn't want to do this anymore. Everything ached. I was physically and emotionally exhausted beyond comprehension.

I wanted to die.

Next thing I knew, Mum was tapping at the bathroom door. 'You okay in there, Tarsh?' I pulled myself together to respond, 'Yes, Mum, just sick. I'm going to have a shower; I feel gross.' Mum acknowledged me and told me to come downstairs when I was finished as there was some mail for me. I got in the shower and continued to spew the second the water touched by back. I continued to cry in the shower. I don't know if that's normal, but I love a good shower cry! While I was in there, I was trying to muster up some courage to find the right words to tell Mum I couldn't do this anymore. Mum was going to be the hardest person to tell that

I wanted to give up. I wanted to quit. If that meant death, I was ready. The pain was just unbearable.

I got out, got dressed and took myself downstairs with no idea how this was going to unfold. There, sitting on the kitchen bench, was a pink envelope addressed to me. I opened it and read it.

I stood there blankly and read it again.

And again.

Mum asked me, 'Who's it from?'

I read it again …

'Delta Goodrem,' I responded.

I was so perplexed. How? Why?

It turned out, Tracey contacted Delta Goodrem's people about my story and she handwrote me a letter. I must admit, I knew of Delta, and knew she had the same cancer (stage one in her neck) a few years prior but beyond that, I wasn't a diehard fan, by any means. But I felt seen and as if someone that actually knew what it was like was validating me. A perfect stranger took time out of her busy schedule to write a little old nobody a simple note telling me to hang in there and keep fighting. The timing was uncanny. It was exactly what I needed to hear to get myself in check and reactivate my coping mechanisms.

Yes, I needed a good cry. I needed to acknowledge it was fucking hard fighting cancer and well beyond just sitting in a chemo chair for a few hours. But I guess life is worth fighting for. I feel like this part of my story is so lame. It was ridiculously good timing. Having someone my age that knew what it was like, and was still able to tell me to keep fighting was corny as hell but eye opening. Thanks, Delta!

Suddenly, I felt reinvigorated. I had to put my big-girl pants on and move forward.

I wasn't a quitter.

In fact, I'm the most stubborn person I know.

I wasn't giving into cancer.

Cancer was not going to take another damn thing from me.

I wasn't going to die and let my one regret be that I didn't keep trying. So, I picked myself back up and soldiered on for the remaining chemo. I continued my walks with Nat, the fresh air was a lifesaver for my mental health, and I continued to journal in my little green chemo book. It wasn't easy. In fact, it was shit. I progressively got sicker and sicker each visit and the symptoms would last longer each time but it's like I had a second wind in me, and I was not stopping … other than to vomit.

2004: Nat and me on the South Pacific cruise

LESSON 16: BOTTLING UP FEELINGS IS NEVER GOOD FOR ANYONE.

I rolled into Dr Matthews' suite for my review check-up on a high and feeling positive and strong, like I could take on the world now I had my self in check. Then Dr Matthews told me I was possibly looking at an additional three months of treatment and radiation on my lungs due to the severity of my cancer and the decline in the responsiveness my cancer cells were now showing in my weekly blood work.

No. No no no no no. No way. Not happening.

This rocked me. I was not prepared to face more time in the chemo chair. So naturally, I went home and did what I do best. Bottled up my true feelings and masked it with some good-old self-sabotaging behaviour. It came back to my relationship with Jack and those conducive circumstances I mentioned earlier. I eventually ended things with Jack. I really struggled to come to terms with this fork in the road that was my relationship. I felt I owed it to Jack to stay with him. He had, after all, spent nearly every night with me, rubbing my back, emptying my spew bucket, collecting my shedding hair and accepting me exactly how I was … dying. But was that a reason to stay?

I ended things with Jack because I couldn't drag him through more of that. He didn't sign up for that. At least, that's what I decided, so I pushed him away. I was good at that. The break-up was awful, however, Jack and I would always have this amazing connection and bond no other would ever understand. This would go on to cause much friction in our following serious relationships, despite being completely platonic moving forward from our break-up. To be honest, my next boyfriend had some big shoes to fill.

I had two more sessions in the chemo chair before I was hopefully done with the initial six-month plan of chemo. Then further testing to determine if the additional treatment would be required. But I wasn't focusing on that because I was not accepting it at all. Wasn't happening. My friends were all driving up to the Gold Coast for new year's. I was not going to miss out! So, off I went with my array of chemo pain drugs. It took over twelve hours for us to reach Surfers Paradise. Three days before New Year's Eve and we had not booked any accommodation, living life like free-range chickens. We managed to fumble our way into a backpacker's lodge for two nights, and it seemed like all of Canberra was in Surfers Paradise for new year's. We ran into various circles of friends and managed to hotel-hop with friends the entire week.

We were staying with some friends that went to our rival high school in our same year. We were walking down to the nightclubs. I was walking with Jay, chatting away, when one of the other boys behind us – Mike – made a smart-arse remark about how 'shit and thin' my hair was. Mike was an arrogant person with an 'I'm better than you' attitude. So, I wasn't fond of him to begin with. He continued commenting his hair made a better ponytail than my poor excuse of a rat's tail. I saw red. Mike opened Pandora's box. I spun around and bit back.

'That's because I'm having chemotherapy, you insensitive dickhead.' He didn't believe me. So, I literally marched toward him and said, 'Feel this,' and grabbed his hand and made him feel my scarred veins along my bruised skinny arms.

'Would my hair do this?' I gestured as I effortlessly pulled a clump of hair by the roots from the side of my head and threw it at him.

'Look at this,' as I reefed my top up to show him the fresh scars from my biopsy.

Mike was stunned. He looked at Jay to verify. Jay was his best mate. Jay told Mike to pull his head in. Mike knew immediately it was serious. Jay's mum had died of cancer only a few years prior. So, Mike knew this was not something Jay would joke about. I really struggled to forgive Mike for a long time. However, when I really unpack it, the way I reacted and treated him wasn't fair either. It's like Mike wore all the anger and resentment I had within me for being sick. Everything I had pent up inside throughout my entire chemotherapy journey came spewing out. Mike simply presented me with the perfect opportunity to blame him for a moment. It was beyond a comment about my hair. Let's face it, my hair was disgusting. What Mike said wasn't untrue! It wasn't Mike I needed to forgive. It was about me accepting the thing I had lost. My hair. My teen years. My dignity. My health. My confidence. My social life. My sanity. My purpose. My future family. Here I was, diagnosed, at nineteen years of age, and thrust straight into adulthood with absolutely no room for error because it was literally life or death.

This encounter really highlighted to me that I probably needed to speak up more for myself. I shouldn't have expected everybody to know what was going on in my head, let alone comprehend the overwhelming roller-coaster of emotions I was riding going through cancer and everything that was involved with that. But I also knew it was more than just sharing my thoughts and feelings out loud. There was so much more there to unpack to overcome this default setting of mine, but I knew that sometimes you must hold back speaking your truth because the situation requires you to do so. This was that time. The only way I could keep my head above water right then was to just keep pushing on to survive.

I would eventually learn to master speaking up; however, I know my people-pleasing setting is often primary to my speaking-up setting. As such, this is still something I know I must actively work on. Today I always remind myself of these things if I ever falter …

- Only a question not asked is a guaranteed no.
- Feelings, like perspective, can vary. Don't assume everyone feels the same.
- Being in touch with your feelings will make you a better person.
- Being true to your emotions leads to feeling better about yourself. This truth is ultimately you being able to be authentic.

When we are not honest with ourselves or in sharing our feelings, we act differently. We may not make ourselves available to others and may withdraw and/or, in my case, push people away. This is exactly what I actively chose to do throughout much of my treatment, thus leading me to react inappropriately when Mike made a simple observation. Because my unchecked emotions were pulling me in a different direction from where I really needed to go. I would learn that when you express how you really feel (in an appropriate manner), problems get solved, relationship issues get resolved – assistance is not failure, and life is easier.

STRENGTH
SECOND CHANCES

Strength. [strengkth, strength, strenth]

noun

the quality or state of being strong; bodily or muscular power.
mental power, force or vigour.
moral power, firmness or courage.
power by reason of influence, authority, resources, numbers, etc.
number, as of personnel or ships in a force or body.
effective force, potency, or cogency, as of inducements or arguments.
power of resisting force, strain, wear, etc.
vigour of action, language, feeling, etc.
the effective or essential properties characteristic of a beverage, chemical or the like.
a positive or valuable attribute or quality.
something or someone that gives one strength or is a source of power or encouragement; sustenance.
power to rise or remain firm in prices.

'Sometimes the strength within you is not a big fiery flame for all to see, it is just a tiny spark that whispers ever so softy, "You got this, keep going.".'
– Unknown

LESSON 17: YOU CAN FIND STRENGTH IN UNEXPECTED PLACES.

Today, as an adult woman, I know my family are a core strength of mine without question, and that is NOT an unexpected place. However, at the age of nineteen, my family, in my mind, were totally embarrassing. My sisters were annoying, and no way did I want to go do the grocery shopping with my parents and risk being seen my someone I knew doing uncool mundane things. I saw my family more as an embarrassing reminder of where I came from.

Thankfully, cancer did wonders to my priorities and my relationships with my two sisters. Don't get me wrong, I'm sure we would have also been just fine without the cancer too … eventually! However, the journey provided lessons for all of us. Most importantly, that tomorrow is never promised. This allowed us to become much closer than we thought possible because suddenly the small stuff was insignificant. For me, personally, the love and selflessness both my sisters demonstrated when shit got real was overwhelming with the fuzzy-feel-goods.

Growing up, we used to refer to Ebony as Oscar the Grouch (from *Sesame Street*) because, you guessed it, she was often serious and grumbly. Guarded with her emotions and never showed signs of affection. Then there was Jayde. She was … Jayde. Spoilt, bratty and is generally, still to this day, a bit of an oversharer. Ebony and I convinced Jayde she was adopted after we found her at the dump. Jayde would go on to believe this for many years of our childhood. We had a normal upbringing, I think. Best of friends one minute, tormenting each other the next. At first it was Ebony and me always telling Jayde she was too little to play with us, then one day things shifted, and Ebony and Jayde told me I was too old to play with them.

I was nineteen, Ebony was sixteen and Jayde was twelve when I got sick. Cancer changed all our lives. I wasn't sure how they were told about my diagnosis. I'm unsure if this awkward conversation was had by Mum or Dad to break the news to them. I don't know if they cried or didn't quite understand. All I knew was cancer did shift our relationships into a more appreciative and caring mode from that day forward. Eb never said much. At sixteen she was more of a mumbler and grunter so to receive any actual words of a kind or positive nature was exceptionally rare and even strange.

Over eighteen years later, Jayde would recount her experience with me, still remembering it like it was yesterday, telling me that Mum had returned home from the hospital after finding out the news. 'I was walking home from school through the local shops with my friend Amanda. Mum called me, crying, saying I had to get home right now. I told Amanda I had to go and ran home as fast as I could. I walked in and Mum was sitting on the kitchen floor crying. Dad was sitting at the kitchen bench silent. Mum blurted out, "Tarsha has cancer, and she is not okay." I didn't know where you were, so I sat with Mum on the floor and just cried.'

Ebony, the more sensitive and anxious child of the three of us, had an entirely different experience. Ebony recounts her experience to be much calmer. She was in the car with Mum and Dad. 'Mum mentioned you were still having tests and it looked like you would undergo treatment for cancer. I feel like the way it was delivered to me wired my brain to cope. I thought to myself – *Well, she has cancer, but she will go to the hospital and the doctors will fix it ... right.* I remember the honesty in their words. Dad said it was in the worst stage but you will have treatment, so it was the "but you will have treatment" part that I held onto.' The gravity of the situation would slowly unfold for Ebony when she would return to school and have teachers asking about my situation and essentially checking in on Ebony's welfare throughout this period. This raised the idea to Ebony that maybe things were worse than she thought.

I recall talking about my fertility and explaining it to Ebony and Jayde standing in the kitchen of our family home. Ebony turned to me in that moment and said the sweetest thing I had ever and probably will ever hear her say to me. In her moody teen ways, she mumbled, 'I don't want you to die. You can have my eggs. I don't even want 'em anyway so you can have 'em.'

Ummm, thanks ... I think? She said it with such tepidness, if I didn't know Ebony any better, one may have considered it was almost apathetic in her delivery. But I know it was as good as I was going to get out of Eb. It was Ebony's way of declaring her unwavering love and support for me. Ebony is her own worst critic, and her negative Nancy is loud, proud and always present, but her heart is bigger. Ebony went on to bless me with my beautiful, brave and fierce nieces Mahlia and Lani and became a nurse with a very different awareness on the gravity of the situation we once faced.

Then there was Jayde. At only twelve years of age, she had a heart bigger than any other human I knew. Jayde declared I could have her eggs too. She also went on to write her school principal a letter of absence stating she would not be attending school on Tuesdays for the foreseeable future as she would be caring for me. She went on to articulate that in the event the school had any concerns about the matter they would be able to find her sitting on the floor of the chemo ward by my feet. Pretty incredible, right?! That is exactly where Jayde spent her Tuesdays. Five hours with me, by my side. Jayde would rub my hands and turn the pages of my trashy magazine because I was literally too exhausted and fatigued to do it myself. She even held my spew bucket as I violently vomited.

As we got older, any serious boyfriend Jayde had would have to pass her prerequisite of acknowledging and accepting that one day she would be donating her eggs to me or possibly even being a surrogate. I'm sure that must have been confronting for a few of them, but it was a commitment Jayde never wavered from. Jayde would go on to be the first of us to have children. She gave me three nephews in total – Elijah, Izaiah and Noah. They are rough, sweet, sensitive, honest and kind. Jayde was first to make me an aunty, a role I am so proud to hold. Her eldest was my best friend. He told me so every day. He always told Jayde he wanted to live with me. I would visit nearly every day when he was younger to play with him. With no prospects of children in my life at this stage, my entire life inheritance, should I ever have any, was going to Elijah and I would be the crazy old aunty that left him everything. To my nieces and nephews, I am known affectionately as 'Gmpfy'. A name bestowed upon me by Elijah when he began to talk. I used to sing to him, and our favourite song was 'The Little Green Frog'. 'We all know frogs go la-di-da-di-da ... They don't go gmpf gmpf gmpf ...' So, naturally, he thought my name was Gmpfy. Ten years, and five nieces and nephews, later, I am still affectionately known as Gmpfy.

Collectively, as a family, we showed such strength. My family, at times, were my only strength when I had none of my own. This is something I never really articulated to them in words, so I hope, if they didn't know that before, then they certainly do now. Mum, dad, Eb, Jayde ... thank you.

Then and now: Me, Ebony and Jayde

LESSON 18: PURPOSE CAN COME FROM THE MOST UNEXPECTED OF PLACES.

Imagine if you got a do-over. What would you change? What lessons did you take away from your experience?

After beating death, my greatest fear became finding myself in my seventies laying on the couch or in my bed, staring at the ceiling wondering where the hell my life went. The years slipped by and I did nothing meaningful and made no true connections. To me, that is the saddest existence I could possibly envision for myself. Thankfully, the silver lining to my near-death experience was the do-over it provided me. A new life. A new beginning. No more missed opportunities, no more shoulda coulda wouldas. I was going to be a doer. My desire to make a difference was burning within and I just wanted to contribute to our community and do something, anything, extraordinary. I had to make my life count for something now, otherwise what was the point of enduring all of that?!

I had a second chance. It came on 19 January 2005, to be exact.

My last scheduled chemo cycle. I honestly did not think I would live to see 2005. I was so excited, I couldn't sleep the night before. Last chemotherapy session, and of course, all my veins were shot. This last session, the only place they could connect my IV line was in the side of my forearm. It hurt like hell, but my excitement for this last session meant it was worth it! Mum came with me and then she was set to fly out to England to see the family for a well-deserved holiday. This trip would be Mum's first trip home since leaving there. I was so proud of Mum for doing this for herself. She needed and deserved a break. To see her child sick and not be able to make her better tore her apart, but she soldiered on to always keep a brave face for me. I would later go on to find out just how bad my mum struggled with my illness and that she required medication and counselling. Of course she did. For the first time in nineteen years, she couldn't fix me with a simple Band-Aid. I'm not sure if I ever verbalised to my mum how much she means to me, but it's safe to say, I bloody love her.

I wouldn't know if I would need to extend my treatment until my next specialist appointment on 18 February. Between now and then, I had scheduled in gallium scans, another bone marrow biopsy and CT scan. I went in for my gallium scan two days after my radioactive injection. After the scan was finished, they usually ask you to wait until they can see the images to know if it captured what they were after before letting you leave. I stared at the clock for fourteen minutes and twenty-seven seconds with nothing else on my mind other than praying the scan was clear.

The nuclear medicine specialist came out. *FUCK.* I literally held my breath. He told me there was some activity in the images, however, it wasn't clear enough to determine so they couldn't make any definitive judgements based on it and would require me to return tomorrow to do it again! Safe to say, I stressed over it for the following twenty-four hours. The scan went smoothly, and I was told results would be with Dr Matthews for my next appointment.

I went on to have my second bone marrow biopsy. Mum was still away so Tracey came with me. It sucked just as much as the first one did, and I swore, if it was in my bone marrow, then I was done. No way was I taking a bone marrow transplant from someone if it hurt that much just to extract a tiny amount.

Friday 18 February 2005. *(Extract from my diary)*

PROJECT KIND

I cannot believe it. I did it. It's gone. I BEAT CANCER. I fucking beat cancer. I cheated death. I AM a survivor. I don't have to extend treatment. I don't need radiation on my lungs! I'm not the sick girl anymore! It's over.

***

Mum was over the moon. Dad and I had a bond like no other. Everything felt great. It didn't get any better than this. This experience was hard and shitty, but the lessons learnt were beyond anything any life experience could possibly give me. I was seeing the bigger picture in another light … and now I was ready for life and ready for living. Within days of receiving my amazing news I was not wasting any time. I knew what I was meant to do now. I enrolled myself in a traineeship in independent living and aged care. I realised I wanted to give back. I wanted to help people. This was my new-found purpose. It married up with my desire to be a perpetual people-pleaser and the realisation that I wanted to provide others with the quality care they deserve.

By September, Jes moved back to Queanbeyan, and I moved out of home (again) and lived with Jes in our very own little apartment. It had green seventies carpet in the kitchen and a frosted yellow shower screen around the toilet in the laundry, but it was our little slice of independence and freedom. We got up to a lot of mischief living together. However, what happened in our Carwoola home, stayed at the Carwoola home. We adopted two cats. My cat Cobra was fated to death by snake bite a couple years later and Jes' cat Holly is remarkably still kicking at the age of sixteen, now living with Jes in South Australia.

The year 2005 was full of monthly medical appointments scheduled around my traineeship and studying, but I made it work.

Every scan I had would show something, but was never definitive, so I would have to wait for a repeat scan the next month hoping it was clear or that it had grown enough to diagnose and treat accordingly. I feel like 2005 was the year of the yo-yo, back and forth with appointments, emotions and bated breath, but having found my purpose provided me with a sense of intent moving forward and a meaningful life beyond cancer.

For me, this new-found purpose was the silver lining to my cancer. However, it also takes a lot of inward soul-searching. This search can be applied to all of us. It's about taking stock of your life and asking yourself the real questions. In doing so, you may not have the glaringly obvious answer presenting itself, but you just might find a recurring theme.

What do you want to be when you grow up?

What are you passionate about?

If money was no object, what is your dream job?

If you could change anything in the world, what would it be?

What issues do you hold close to your heart?

Do you have a cause that is important to you?

What do you believe in? What are your core values?

What kind of legacy do you want to leave behind?

Do those closest to you know what you are truly passionate about?

Is your current place in the world on the path to where you want to be? Or is it necessity?

What do you need to do to get yourself on track to the path you wish for yourself?

What holds you back? Finances? Partner? Or fear of failure?

Who is responsible for making your purpose become a reality?

When are you going to start?

LESSON 19: FOLLOW YOUR REAL-LIFE #INFLUENCERS.

Before the world of online influencers and hashtag trends, one was influenced by an action, environmental or physical factor, and/or a person. Today's essence of the word boggles my mind; someone who lives on the other side of the world that has no bearing to your actual existence, and you most likely have never met and/or will never meet. Yet, you make a conscious decision to be 'influenced' by this individual, thus buying whatever they are selling or believing whatever it is they are telling you with little to no scientific facts or evidence provided to back their claims. The only evidence that supports the said influencer is the silly notation that 'everyone is doing it', so it must be legit, right? Or that it looked super cute on her Instagram Reels?

Maybe I'm just showing my age here, but I find my influencers of importance in those that directly impact my existence. Yes, there are influencers I have never met; however, their purpose was passion driven rather than fame and/or dollar driven … For example, former South African president and civil rights advocate Nelson Mandela. He dedicated his life to fighting for equality. Pretty sure it doesn't get any humbler than that! Don't get me wrong, if Elle McPherson tells me on socials that product cream X is her secret to flawless skin, I'll take the bait … but not just on face value. I'll check out the company creating the cream. Are they ethical, is there scientific evidence to prove what Elle is telling me? What are the reviews like? If so – then 100%, I'm down! I'll order ten, but when it comes to the deep-level stuff that really matters, for me, these are individuals within your life that impact and influence you. The real influencers, rather than the PR marketing kind.

Your upbringing, your parents and family network. Your friends and colleagues; those fighting the same fight as you to try and make your world a better place. For me, I was also fortunate enough to find influence from individuals I cared for while working in a dementia-specific nursing home and some of the amazing people I worked alongside. Here, I created some of my best work memories and stories. Throughout my career across aged care and acquired brain injury, I met and had the privilege of caring for some amazing humans with so many amazing stories to share. I believe some of these stories and experiences will stay with me forever. Some of my favourite characters I have shared below (with obvious changes to their identity). These amazing humans each taught me something in one way or another that I hope will stay with me forever.

Mae

This interesting lady led a humble life, and according to her family, was very modest and led a private and introverted life. However, dementia led Mae down a path to where she had become unrecognisable to her family. Mae had become an exhibitionist. Her favourite thing to do within the nursing home was strip off her clothing and walk around the facility free as a bird. We were constantly chasing after her with the hospital-style gowns to cover her up. Mae also loved to wander. I will never forget the morning she was wandering in the dining room with her Vegemite toast. We prompted Mae to sit down rather than wandering around with food. Mae stripped her clothes off and shoved her Vegemite toast up her vagina so she could continue wandering. I guess she had no pockets, so she made do with what she had? I had to respect her resourcefulness. While this was not the Mae her friends and family knew, and they were understandably upset with her behaviours she was exhibiting, Mae was content. She was safe, and in her mind, she was living her best life. I loved that Mae gave zero fucks.

PROJECT KIND

Maggie

Maggie was the wife of a true Aussie farmer, and before moving into the nursing home, lived with her husband out of town on their property. Dementia had resulted in limited and repetitive speech. Maggie's days were like groundhog day. Her husband George would come to visit her every single day and assist her with lunch. This went on for years. George was hitting the ripe old age of seventy-five and was worried about undertaking annual examinations by his own doctor to determine whether he would be fit and able to continue driving. George failed his examination, and as a result, was unable to keep his driver's licence. While we were busy providing care to his beautiful wife, there was nothing in place for George. This news left him without means of transport and without purpose. George unexpectedly and ever so sadly went on to end his life on his property, widowing Maggie.

Maggie went on to pass a year or so later; however, both Maggie and George have stayed with me. Highlighting a gap in the system where George was unsupported. I know this was beyond any of my professional duties at the time, but today, it is something we are acutely aware of within my business and understand and support primary carers of clients in which we care for.

Bill

Bill was a wild one. Tall, active and mischievous. He was strong. One evening, I was with my work partner in another client's room assisting her to bed when we could hear the screeching of a table being dragged down the corridor. I popped my head out to see what was going on. Bill was in the corridor pushing a side table he had taken from another resident's bedroom. The side table had a TV on it with the cords dangling behind. Now, this was in the early-mid-2000s, so TVs in nursing homes were still your old-school box TVs where the depth was as wide as the screen. I proceeded to stop Bill and grab the table from the other end. Bill wasn't having that, so he tugged it toward himself. After a couple tugs between us, I knew there was no way I would physically be able to get the table and TV from him safely. So, I picked up the TV from the table, turned away from Bill and made a beeline for the nurse's station, waddling down the corridor trying to carry a box TV wider than my arms' reach.

Bill started yelling out, 'Police, police, help! There's a thief. Stop her!' He proceeded to chase after me trying to kick me up the arse. I knew, in Bill's mind, there would be no reasoning and he wasn't going to let up. My only option was to come up with something tactical before I fell over, smashing the TV and myself. I stopped, and thinking quickly, I pulled out a piece of paper towel I had in my pocket with my notes for the day scribbled all over it in my little shorthand codes. I told Bill, 'No, no, no, Bill, I just bought this TV, here look, it's the receipt,' as I handed him my bit of paper towel. He took it and looked at it and then smiled at me and told me to 'move along then' and let me go, gesturing me to keep moving.

Bill taught me not everything in life will make sense. Not everything is logical. When you are dealing with situations or people that are irrational, you cannot expect to rationalise the situation. You need to take a step back and look at the wider picture and see their perspective just for a hot second. It still might not make any sense, but that in itself should definitely change the approach you take in responding. Quite frankly, sometimes it is adapt or die.

Betty

Betty was my all-time favourite. Now, I know you are not meant to have favourites, but we are human. It's normal to feel connected to some more than others. She was born in the early twenties, widowed by war and went on to be a savvy businesswoman. She was a bit of a disruptor for her time, and I loved that. Yes, she had dementia, but by gosh, she was as sharp as a tack. Not much got past old Betty. She would always offer me direct employment if I just took her out of the nursing home and cared for her down the south coast in one of her beach-front properties, and Betty was very resourceful. One might say she was a lady of the finer things and high maintenance. She loved to look her best and have her finest Dior and Lancôme make-up done each morning. Betty knew just after lunch was when we would be busiest on a morning shift. As such, of course, this is the time she would request assistance with just about anything to capture your undivided attention. Betty would walk back down to her room with her wheelie frame after lunch then promptly buzz for a carer to attend for whatever reason she had mustered up each day.

One shift, she buzzed right on cue; I popped my head to Betty's room and she asked me, 'When am I going to get some attention?' I responded to her and explained after lunch as we were just assisting those who needed help getting to the toilet and needing bed rest. Betty quickly responded, 'So, I've got to shit my pants to have some of your time?' I promised Betty I would come and have my lunch break with her in her room once I was done. Clearly, that wasn't a quick enough time frame for beautiful Betty. She buzzed again twenty minutes later. I started walking down the corridor toward her room when I saw her door open. She started to back out of her door bum-first when I noticed her pants were around her ankles. Betty proceeded to squat and pee on the floor just outside her door before shuffling back into her bedroom, slamming the door and buzzing again.

What the fuck did I just witness?!

I went to Betty's door, knocked and opened it while avoiding the puddle of urine now on the floor. She was sitting in her armchair looking rather pleased with herself. I looked at Betty and didn't need to say a word. Betty smiled at me and said, 'Well, now I need your assistance here.'

I loved Betty for her no-bullshit approach to life. She was a go-getter and made things happen. She was a resourceful and successful businesswoman and raised her children as a widow in a time when it would have been expected of her to be a homemaker. She was upper class; she was fierce and as real as it got. She never sugar-coated shit, she ran her own race and she went places. I hope to have as much spunk as she did when I'm in my nineties.

Mapiga Ravai

This woman was brave beyond words. I don't think I have held as much respect for a single person like I have my mapiga. Rotuman language for 'my grandmother'. She was born in 1937 and lived until the age of eighty-four. She was the youngest of four sisters, and like my dad, always seemed like Peter Pan. Forever youthful at heart and in appearance. She grew up in a time and culture of arranged marriages, and this was how she came to meet and marry my grandfather. A time where my pa was head of the house, and that's just the way it was. Mapiga was the homemaker, a baker and crafter. During this time, she wanted me to marry a Rotuman boy, because in her words, 'Then I can boss him around.' I believe this is where my love for cake-making and craft originated from. When my Pa passed in 2009, one would have easily assumed my mapiga's life would surely end soon too, having no idea how to function without him – the man that managed their finances, paid their bills, took my grandmother to do the grocery shopping and to church. In the days after my grandfather passed, my dad and I were the only two with valid passports so he and I flew to Fiji to be there for the funeral, cultural burial and celebrations with my aunty and uncles.

I remember expecting to see my grandmother shattered into a million pieces. That was how my heart felt, so I couldn't begin to imagine how she felt. I remember walking into her house with Dad and hugging her so tight. As expected, she was heartbroken and lost. I wondered what my grandmother's life would look like moving forward. With three out of four of her adult children living in Australia, no immediate family were close by. After that first day we arrived, my grandmother showed nothing but strength and admiration for my grandfather.

In the wake of my grandfather's passing, my mapiga did the opposite to what I expected. She pivoted her life. She grew. She levelled herself up, spread her wings and flew! She found her courage to speak up in a culture and place where that isn't necessarily encouraged. She was so strong and chose to stay in her home, surrounding herself with the love of all her worldly possessions she and my grandfather had collected over a lifetime together. She surrounded herself with the love of her sisters and community. She became open-minded about the world we lived in and even accepted and approved of my then-boyfriend, now-husband, despite him being far too many shades of white for her normal liking. She saw our love, and approved the first white person into the family for one of her grandchildren! Seriously, my mum even had to work harder than Guy to gain that status! She would live on to meet all her great-grandchildren from myself and my sisters. This was an honour she was most proud of.

It was only in our adult lives I really came to appreciate my grandmother for all the hardships she endured and her ability to always remain true to her core beliefs and never waiver. I truly believe, in watching her, I learnt resilience and strength. In 2021, when she became suddenly ill, consumed by cancer, and with a pandemic grounding all international travel, we could not fly to be with her. It broke my heart into a thousand pieces when she passed because we could not be there. I felt like we failed her. We spoke with her on FaceTime every day until the day she passed. I was so angry at the world for not being able to be there. This is something I would have to come to terms with because it was beyond any person's control. This is something I am still working on.

When my mapiga was alive, she taught me kindness, she taught me how to ice a cake and the secret ingredient to her famous pineapple tarts.

When she was widowed, she taught me adaptability, that you are truly never too old to pivot, grow and learn.

In her death, she taught me resilience and strength.

With my perspective, I was able to find profound peace in knowing she had lived a truly wonderfully full life, with compassion, kindness and authenticity like no other. I am at peace knowing she truly lived. She was always true to her core and her moral compass was unwavering. Something she instilled in my dad. While we couldn't physically be with her in her final days, she was surrounded by an abundance of love, and I know her love continues to surround all of us. Her life was to be celebrated, not mourned, because to me, in the end, she was the epitome of authentic kindness.

Winnie

Remember Winnie, the down-to-earth work colleague that taught me to actively seek the good in others? Well, Winnie taught me so much more. While I was working at the acquired brain injury houses, I had also enrolled myself into an online university course in criminology and criminal justice. (I know right, how left field!) I was struggling to admit defeat in accepting the fact I was not enjoying criminology, and in fact, was more certain now than ever, that health care was definitely my jam. Criminals do not want my help. I found health care much more compassionate and rewarding.

However, before I would accept this goal readjustment (SMARTER, right!), I was talking with Winnie about my feelings of being a failure in having not figured out what I wanted to be when I grew up. (Yes, I was twenty-three already, but I still felt that maybe I hadn't found my forever job, and it would only be when I did find it, that I would see myself as 'grown up'.) Winnie so wisely corrected me with her words. 'Why do you have to find a forever job? Just find a today job that you like today!' Winnie would go on to tell me I could have twelve different careers by retirement age. As soon as the words left her mouth, I knew she was right. There I was, stressing I had to make a life-altering decision that I would need to honour until the end of time. Taking me back to year twelve senior year when we all so strongly believed the HSC was the be all to end all, and if we failed in that, we failed in life. All that algebra, textiles and ancient history was essential to our daily skills in adulthood, right!? NOT! (Well, at least not in my case.)

That afternoon I went home and dropped out of the only university class I would ever enrol myself in.

Yep. Totally owning it …

I am a university dropout.

According to a 2019 YouthSense Report,[5] I am proudly one of the 20% of first-year university students that dropped out.

Criminology and criminal justice was not for me. Winnie's advice would stay with me forevermore and be good sound advice that I, too, would go on to impart to others along my journey.

I am so grateful to have been able to cross paths with so many amazing humans. To be but a small fleeting chapter in a lifetime of memories for those I cared for. To have such an impact is all anyone can hope – to leave the world having done that is exactly what Mae, Maggie, Bill and Betty did. Meanwhile, Winnie has plenty of years ahead of her to impart much more wisdom and advice to the world around her. As for my mapiga, I know she will always remain with me until my final day on earth.

LESSON 20: TWENTIES ARE FOR MAKING AND LEARNING FROM MISTAKES.

And might I say, I made plenty of them. I was twenty years of age and beginning the restart of the rest of my life. I had beaten cancer. I had found my career calling and had amazing supportive friends. I had just moved jobs and was now working at an acquired brain injury unit in Canberra and studying again. Despite my new awakening to the notion that life is a gift not to be taken for granted, I was still a young adult doomed to make mistakes. Then I met an obnoxious, overly confident Richard … Why did I call this character in my life Richard? Because in the end, Richard was a 'dick' to me.

It all started when some friends and I were in Braddon wearing our 'For Sale' tour T-shirts we all had made for our New Year's Eve trip in Surfers. The next thing I hear is this person say, 'How much for those bad boys?' gesturing to my chest. It sounds vulgar in my head, out loud and even on paper as I write this … but twenty-year-old me thought he was trouble, and I liked trouble. (Yes, this is one of those moments I wish future me could go back in time and slap myself for thinking like that!) Richard was a bit of a wild one. Stereotype 'one of the boys' mentalities, but he did have a softness about him. We started dating. Turned out, Richard was in the USA Minor League Baseball for one of the more well-known teams at the time. This meant he was due to return to America for their spring training baseball season. What I thought would be just a fleeting summer whirlwind romance would become my life for the next five years.

Six months living in each other's pockets, and six months long-distance Skype calls and emails. It was tough, but at the time, it seemed worth it. Six months apart would pass and we would pick up together where we left off. Richard was crazy jealous of my friendship with Jack. Rightfully so. As I said before, they were huge shoes to fill. Jack and I had that soul connection, but we weren't soul*mates*. In hindsight, Richard wasn't my soul *anything*, but at the time, we were madly in love with one another. In five years, we built a life together. Travelled together and talked about the idea of marriage and our future. However, Richard was still a big kid himself, and it really was just all talk.

Fast-forward to 2010. We were twenty-five and in our fifth year together. Australia was launching their national baseball league and Richard was throwing the first-ever opening pitch. It was exciting. I was going to drive down with his mum and aunty and cousins to watch the series. I was all packed ready to go when I got a Facebook message from a girl named Aubrey. Turned out, Richard was a dick. He had an American girlfriend. She proceeded to send me all their photos and details of their relationship. I called him to say I wasn't coming and why. I then sent his beautiful mum a message saying, *Just got a text from Richard's American girlfriend. I'm not coming to*

Sydney. Travel Safe. XX Richard was sitting on the team bus on his way to Sydney when it all came out. His entire baseball team knew what was going on. The team were amazingly supportive toward me at that time and his family rallied around me.

In hindsight, I was ridiculously overdramatic about the situation. When Richard returned home late that night after the opening game, I had replaced every single one of our photos that hung on the walls of our house with an identical photo of Richard and Aubrey together. Richard and me at Disneyland. Swapped for Richard and Aubrey at Disneyland. Richard and me laying on the sand at the beach. Swapped for Richard and Aubrey laying on the sand in America etc. I kicked Richard out and should have listened to my gut then and there and called it. How were we going to come back from this, knowing he would be off to America again in less than six months to do it all again?! But I loved him. He said he loved me. So, we … no … I … it was just me attempting to make it work. The next couple of months were miserable, to say the least.

That saying 'beating a dead horse' had never been more true or applicable to my life than during this period. My relationship was the dead horse. I realised I wasn't a priority in Richard's life. He was overly confident and ultimately very selfish. I was so angry Richard had ruined us. Angry I was the one left with debt we both collected, angry that he had wasted the best part of my twenties. Six-year-old me thought I'd be married with a house and white picket fence and three kids by now. I only had twelve months left to achieve this expectation. I did not beat cancer for this shit.

My heart ached for the loss of his family, mostly. Ironically, I am still close with most of his family, they truly are beautiful souls. Would you believe since Richard and I ended things, I have never unintentionally crossed paths with him ever again! It was literally like that saying: 'a time and a place for everything'. Richard was no longer a requirement in my life, and as such, literally was no longer present within my world. Thank you, universe. The best parting gift Richard gave me was deleting me from socials. A clean cut, completely severing any relationship directly between him and me. For that I am grateful. Silver lining! Another cherished silver lining was having some amazing ex-in-laws and gaining some beautiful friends through Richard's family. For that I am grateful.

Today, Richard is no longer playing baseball, is happily married to a very kind soul with a couple of kids, and upon reflecting on our time together, as shit as I thought it was in the end, I can honestly acknowledge now it was simply a process I had to go through. We had fun, we were young and were living our best lives for that moment, I guess. I learnt from the experience, and it allowed me to make way for a better and brighter chapter to follow. I am ever so grateful to have the life I have now. Ironically, a life that could not have happened without crossing paths with Richard and Baseball Canberra, thus #silverlining.

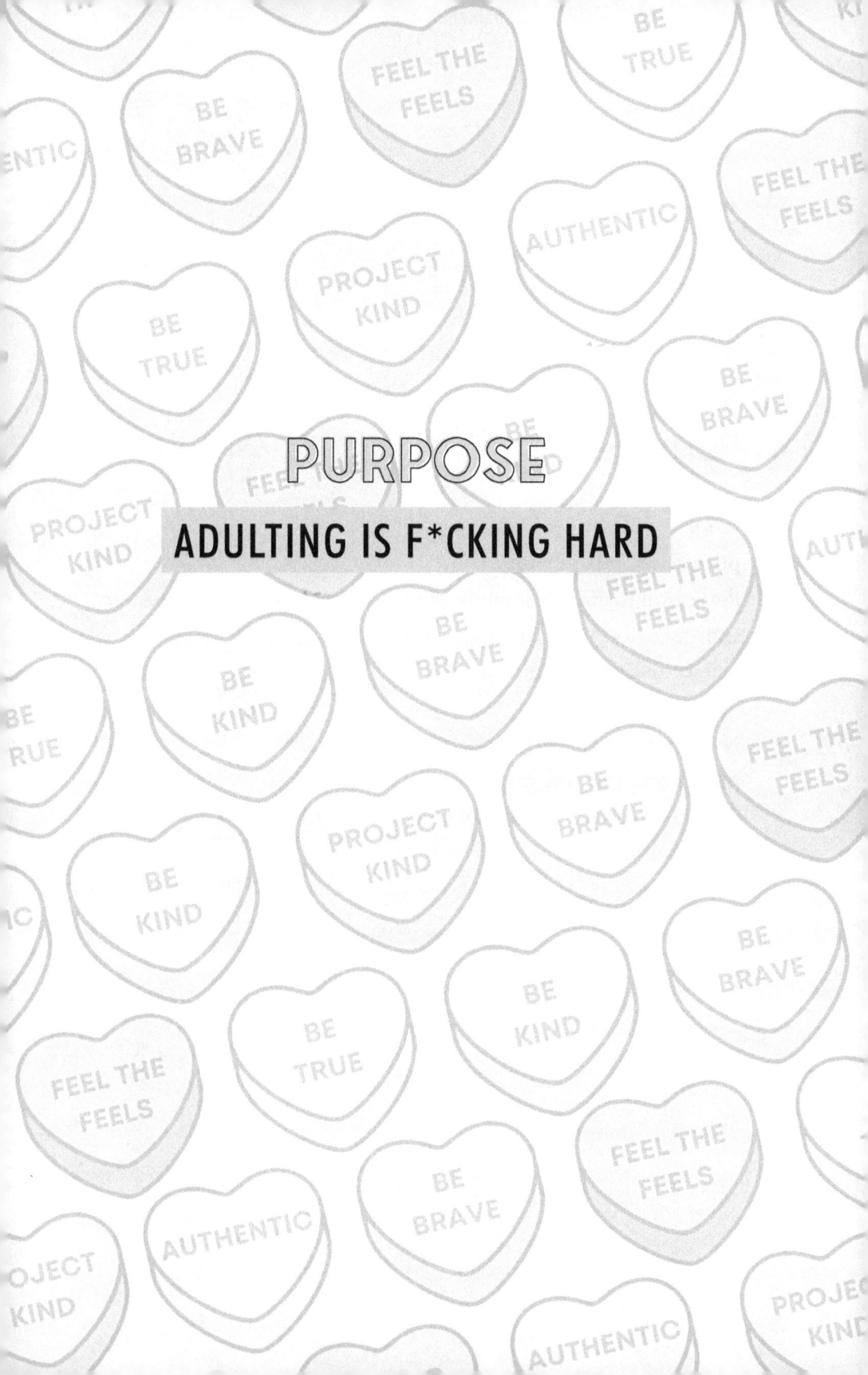

PURPOSE
ADULTING IS F*CKING HARD

Purpose. [pur-puhs]

noun

pur·posed, pur·pos·ing.

the reason for which something exists or is done, made, used, etc.
an intended or desired result; end; aim; goal.
determination; resoluteness.

verb

pur·posed, pur·pos·ing.

to set as an aim, intention or goal for oneself.
to intend; design.

'Purpose: how you use your experiences, talents and passions to better the lives of those around you.'
— L Perterson

LESSON 21: DON'T DO DRUGS.

We all have pasts. We all made choices that maybe were not the best ones. None of us are completely innocent or immune to poor choices. But we get a fresh start every day to be better and do better than yesterday. For me, it is safe to say this last chapter was very easy to improve upon.

***

Up until our twenties, I think it's safe to say, it is human nature to want to fit in. All a part of human development as we grow and find our identity. As kids, most of us want to do what all the cool kids are doing, almost as if we are chameleons wanting to adapt to our environment. I think one of my biggest examples of this when I was growing up was me changing my name to ensure I was not different! I also remember it being 'cool' if you smoked in high school. If teen smoking does not scream herd mentality, I do not know what does. You can't tell me a single 'cool' person I knew in school could honestly say they enjoyed and liked the taste of cigarettes the first time they tried it. It was the persistence and desire to fit in and be 'cool' that made it tolerable long enough to become an actual addiction. I'll admit, I tried to be 'cool', but I did not enjoy smoking at all, so was a 'social' smoker, aka only cool when it counts, right?! Thankfully it was nothing a dose of cancer and maturity didn't set straight. For a little while, at least …

In my early twenties, while making all those mistakes twenty-something-year-olds do, I was living a purposeful life because I had found meaning in my career. However, I did stray off the path, despite my life-pivoting experiences. Because my career was coming together, I thought I had it *all* together … turns out there were plenty of other facets within my life that needed much improvement. I'm ashamed to admit I started taking drugs in order to become 'cool'. Before you say it, I know, I know, I know! What the fuck was I thinking? I had just been given the biggest second chance at life. I had beaten cancer, and here I was, tempting fate again like I had a death wish of some kind dabbling with recreational drugs on the weekends. It became my mind-numbing escape because it was the cool thing to do. With Jes having moved away and Nat overseas, I spent my free time with Jack and some of the boys I went to school with. It started out with the odd music festival scene and grew to weekend benders, thinking I was living my best life.

By no means was I reliant on drugs, and I was never addicted; however, I acknowledge this was just disgusting and I take full responsibility for my actions; it was 100% my choice to participate, and I enjoyed it while it was short-lived. I enjoyed that, in that moment, I didn't have a single care in the world. I enjoyed that it relieved the pressure I (or Nancy) put on myself to ensure I did something worthwhile with my golden second chance in life. I know it is no excuse, but having been given a second chance at life, I felt immense pressure like I couldn't fuck it up. So, naturally, I fell straight into self-sabotage mode.

The boys were always super overprotective of me, but I just loved that it was easy with the boys. I didn't have to be anyone, and they accepted me as I was. Ironically, at the same time, there I was, doing drugs, because they were. I guess a part of me felt I was making up for the lost time I spent having cancer treatment being expected to be responsible all the time, then on top of that, because I was 'blessed', I was automatically meant to accept that I couldn't fuck it up in anyway … gee thanks, Nancy. No pressure, right. It was like I felt I missed out on a rite of passage to choose the scenic route of growing up or something.

Today, I look back on this and see I was just making stupid decisions.

Full stop.

It wasn't cool.

It wasn't safe.

And I went on to care for too many patients with drug-induced long-term brain injuries to know and appreciate how lucky I am by complete chance that I didn't end up like them.

I was reckless.

Plain and simple.

I feel like I'm hard on myself about my poor choices during this small chapter in my life as my dads' voice rings through my head, *You've been given a second chance, my girl, stay on the path.* Literally! For my twenty-first birthday, my dad made me a birthday DVD filled with home movie snippets, video messages from my friends and photos of my past. Cancer was a large chapter in the DVD, and in the DVD, my dad literally tells me to 'stay on the path'.

These experiences would go on to become steps along my path to identifying what I did, and more importantly, what I did not want to be, and I certainly still upheld the goal to do something meaningful with my life after cancer. By the time I figured out who I was and reached the age of twenty-five with a fully developed brain, I knew well and truly drugs and party life was not me.

I don't share this chapter of my life too often. Not because I regret it, but rather because it's not a topic that I want to be highlighted and associated with anything I condone. I know I was stupid, but if any message is taken away from this time in my life, I hope it is that I thought I had made informed choices at the time, but in all honesty, I had no grasp on how serious the consequences could have been, and in hindsight, I know they were ridiculously senseless decisions, but here we are …

What did come out of this chapter, for me, was gaining a clearer sense of self that was separate from the expectations of my parents and medical specialists. Along the off-road path I had taken, I realised I had lost touch with certain aspects of my true self. Thankfully, I was able to acknowledge it was an experience I gained, climb out of the gigantic hole I was burying myself in, take away another life lesson learnt and it was a path I no longer needed to explore. I felt I had just been given a third chance to get it right.

***

I would like to take this opportunity to point out some staggering facts to anyone who may think drugs are 'cool' … According to Australian Bureau of Statistics[6], in 2020 it was reported there were 1,842 drug-induced deaths and over two-thirds (67%) of these deaths were considered accidental. Let me say that again … 67% of drug-induced deaths were accidental. This is 1,233 people. One thousand, two hundred and thirty-three.

To put that into perspective, there were 898 deaths recorded the same year in Australia due to COVID-19 and a further fifty-five deaths due to influenza.

1,233 people using drugs, and as a result, accidently died! They thought they were in for a good night and never returned. It is that simple. So, the lesson here: **Don't do drugs.**

LESSON 22: YOU DESERVE A HAPPY ENDING.

Do you ever feel you are perpetually late to life in general?

If you google human brain development, you will be overwhelmed with studies and information that will essentially tell you the human brain isn't fully developed until the age of twenty-five. This scientifically backs up my own theory that my 'real life' started from twenty-five. Now, my theory is not a theory I've always had, I'd say it's more of a label for my own personal instances where my life did not go to plan.

Breaking up with Richard was not in my plans, and I truly and stupidly thought my life was over. I had just wasted what I thought was the best part of my twenties on what turned out to be a dud! What a huge pile of steaming shit I thought my life was at that point. Going back to my hindsight, theory of life starting at twenty-five, there is research around adult and teen brains working differently. Adults think rationally with the prefrontal cortex, resulting in good judgement and an awareness of long-term consequences. But pre-twenty-five me was processing information emotionally with the amygdala. My brain connections between the emotional part and the decision-making centre were clearly not fully operational for business, and as a result, explains my emotionally fuelled poor life decisions up until that point. The poor boyfriend choices, the lack of self-confidence, self-worth and self-preservation … So, when I came across this research, it sounded logical to me and explained most of my early twenties, so I'm sticking with it.

At twenty-five, and with a fully developed and fully functioning brain, I met a guy called Guy. Yes, that is his real name! I was such a pessimist regarding the idea of 'love at first sight', and I am certainly not claiming this now, but there was this weird connection upon our first meeting. Let me just remind you, it was 2010 and The Twilight Saga and all things vampire romance were all the rage. Girls all wished for their very own Edward or Jacob. That basic desire to connect with somebody so deeply. I think half the fantasy was because you knew the person would just about have to sparkle in the sun or howl at the moon to actually be true, but this interaction with Guy was like we imprinted on one another. Or like in James Cameron's *Avatar*, we saw each other. *'I see you.'* We connected instantly on a deep and raw level. I know, I know! It is so ridiculously lame and sappy. But it's the closest example I have ever been able to conjure up to describe it.

My inception with Guy was unexpected. Everything just started making sense and this 'guy' is the first human in the history of ever that sees me clearly and understands me. All of me. It was as if he had X-ray glasses and saw through all my plates of armour I had spent a lifetime keeping in place. We knew of each other because he played baseball with Richard. #akwardAF However, we had never actually spoken a word to each other until one night at a local sports club trivia night. We even had a photo together capturing our first meet – cute. Now, these trivia nights weren't your average trivia nights. They usually involved large amounts of alcohol, dress-up themes, karaoke and a lot of silly behaviour. In fact, several years before, at this fine establishment, I was so intoxicated I ran behind the bar into the back office to vomit, then also proceeded to clean it up. The owner and fellow baseballer offered me a job that night and I worked there part-time for the following couple of years while I was studying.

This amazing Guy is six years older than me, and I love to remind him of that. He was living in Canberra for work, his family are based in Newcastle, and he is actually one of the 'good guys'. Clearly my pre-twenty-five-year-old brain was making some inadequate boyfriend choices, always going for the troubled and naughty kind, so I figured a 'good guy' was worth a shot. From our first meeting, we were both a little perplexed at the connection we felt and initially backed away, trying to figure out what the hell had just happened. What had we just experienced? It felt vulnerable to be so seen. How was this possible? A few months later, we gave up avoiding each other and have literally never spent a day apart since – except for a couple of nights for a work trip!

Guy is literally too good to be true. He is fiercely loyal. Chooses to keep a small circle of friends who he would lay down and die for. He is selfless, calm, grounded, kind and has the ability to see through the day-to-day bullshit and see the bigger picture with a whole lot of perspective. (Meanwhile, it took me a good dose of cancer and chemo to give me such perspective!) He has a huge wide lens when looking at the world. He is respectful, loves cats AND dogs, calls his family at least once a week, has amazing intellectual conversations with my family, cooks and does washing, but best of all, he loves me! With all my flaws, all my crazy ... 100% just the way I am. I never believed it could be true and I always waited for that 'I told you so' moment where I'd ultimately get screwed over or feel I must default to my self-preservation mode and push him away. But this was something I could, for this first time, openly talk about with Guy. His response has always been, 'One day, I will prove you wrong. You will see.' He is seriously the sweetest human I have ever met. The universe broke the mould after making Guy. Of that I am certain. He literally makes me want to be a better human.

Within one week, we were living together.

Within the year, we were engaged and commencing the IVF process.

Eighteen months after that we were married.

It's true, when you know, you know! I had finally met someone with the same mindset as me. Our morals and core values were aligned. I wanted to spend the rest of my life with this extraordinary human, and for the first time, since the age of nineteen, I thought about seriously wanting children and if my deal with the devil could be renegotiated somehow. As Daniel Defoe, a 1762 English author, once said: ''Tis no sin the cheat the devil,'[7] right?

For years, Guy and I underwent IVF. Various clinics. Canberra and Sydney. Multiple miscarriages. Ovulation tracking. Ovulation induction. Intrauterine insemination (IUI). In-vitro fertilisation (IVF). Intracytoplasmic sperm injection (ICSI). I can really see and understand how some couples live and breathe fertility planning. It is rather life-consuming. (Side note: never tell an IVF couple, 'Just don't think about it, it will happen when it happens.' IVF planning is nothing but calculated planning and precision, requiring it to be at the forefront of any thought!)

Guy and I seemed to have a cautiously realistic approach to this journey from the beginning. I think this was because of my cancer history, and for me, knowing my pact with the devil. I was ultimately asking for something I never thought I could have since the age of nineteen, so I already knew we were asking for the impossible.

Initially, we openly shared our IVF story as it unfolded. It was an enormous part of our life and took up a lot of our time. I felt I had to be honest about it. We weren't – and aren't – ashamed of that, so while others posted on socials about their smashed avo brunches or bender weekends, I posted about our IVF journey. Today, this is nothing to flinch at. Every second person has their IVF story on socials, and it's considered the norm – as it should be – but ten years ago, when we started, it wasn't met with all good feedback. I wasn't aware how offensive my uterus could be to others simply by sharing my journey. So, I must say, I did begin to filter what I posted. Then as the cycles resulted in miscarriage and heartbreak, I found it quite confronting and disturbing that people … friends … thought it was their right to know all the details and/or provide me with their advice on a matter they had absolutely no experience in. I guess I get that if it's social, it's social, but heartbreak is still heartbreak. Just because it is on socials does not make it hurt any less, and I feel somehow that is lost in translation to the keyboard warriors at times.

Guy and I always communicated with one another, ensuring we were on the same page. We set a road map of sorts on how we would navigate the IVF world, but most importantly, we set ourselves limits. Each round, we would set our variable soft limits and hard limits. For example, we knew by the time I was thirty, for our own personal circumstances, we would stop the endeavour for children of our own. We knew we had everything else in life we could possibly want and hope for. As such, I did not want to waste what I felt would be the prime part of our lives worrying every day about the one facet we did not have in our lives. I didn't want life to blow me by.

Mid-2015, we had just done another round of IVF, I had fallen pregnant and miscarried again at our standard nine-week mark. After each miscarriage, I would initially want to jump straight into the next round. The IVF clinic would always suggest waiting a cycle for my hormones to adjust. It was in this period, I would realise I mentally needed more time to grieve and prepare to face another round again. It took me a good six months before I was ready this time. I was nearing my hard limit of consecutive losses.

2010: The first night we 'met and spoke'.

NATASHIA TELFER

LESSON 23: MISCARRIAGES SUCK.

*(**Warning:** this may be triggering for those who have ever experienced such loss. To you, I am truly sorry for your loss.)*

Seriously, can I just say they suck! They are also significantly minimised and often dismissed within our society, making it a very lonely process to go through. I must admit, I've done it myself. Prior to experiencing one, if someone told me they had one, the next natural question would be along the lines of, 'I'm so sorry, how far along were you? Why does that matter? Oh, before twelve weeks, that doesn't count. Wasn't full term, it's not a baby.' I once had one of my friends tell me I was the only person doing IVF she knew that wasn't falling pregnant first go! When I corrected her and said, 'No, I fall pregnant every go, I just always miscarry!' her response felt cold, 'Oh, that doesn't count.' The words of someone who has never experienced the heartache of such a loss. The mentality of it can be rather disturbing. I am ashamed I was a part of that mentality, and it took me having multiple miscarriages to realise the damage such dismissive attitudes cause you in that grieving process. You add IVF miscarriage to it, it's a whole other element of heartbreak and financial strain! The whole process is mental torture, and to face it alone and feeling shame or guilt on top of that is probably one of the hardest things a person can face.

My first miscarriage was awful and shaped my approach to every pregnancy thereafter with such fear and precaution. I was twenty-eight years old, and it was in the lead-up to our wedding. It was my first pregnancy, and we were that panicky couple, unsure of this whole new world we were entering. We went to go for our seven-week scan and the sonographer informed us we may be a little early as the scan showed a yolk sac (the structure surrounding the embryo or foetus) but it looked a week off from heartbeat stage. She wasn't panicked, she just told us to pop back to our GP for blood follow-up.

My usual amazing GP was not working that day, so we asked to see the next available doctor. Enter Doctor Insensitive. Guy and I went in and explained what happened and told her we were informed to see her for follow-up bloods and repeat scan next week. Dr Insensitive told me I am most likely miscarrying and that I must be spotting or bleeding by now. I wasn't … but what would I know? We asked for the repeat scan and comparative blood work, and she begrudgingly gave us the pathology form but told me to expect bleeding in the next twenty-four hours and not to go to hospital. I'm not past twelve weeks so I will just clog up the hospital system, she said. Just bleed it out at home. She then went on to tell me to go home, drink alcohol and take Panadeine Forte if I had any! Next thing we knew, she was shuffling us out of her office. We went to pay for the consultation and Guy asked me to verify something she had said but I was in a spin and didn't know. He turned to go back to ask her to clarify to which she rudely responded, 'I've given you all the information and explained it, if you need further clarification you will need to book another appointment.' I felt so let down. How did she know? She wasn't my normal doctor. She had no comparative blood work to see my HCG levels (pregnancy hormones) decreasing to suggest miscarriage, I wasn't bleeding …

Days passed and I was petrified but felt like I couldn't do anything and had nowhere to turn to. I went back into my GP a week later after having the bloods. Joan knew I was a mess. Guy told her about Dr Insensitive and Joan insisted we put forward a formal complaint. But it didn't matter. The damage was done. Joan would go on to tell me I was having a 'missed miscarriage'. A missed miscarriage is when the pregnancy has stopped growing but the tissue has not passed and there is still a sac in the uterus. So, basically, my body not only couldn't do its job in growing a baby, but it also couldn't even miscarry properly. Feeling like an EPIC failure of a human at this point, my beautiful GP called the Centenary Hospital for Women and Children antenatal ward. Strangely, the obstetrician happened to be at the nurse's station and answered the phone call.

Doctor Toby was so kind and was so heartfelt talking to Joan about my situation. Joan was calling to ask how I would need to proceed. Dr Toby went on to explain that normally I would be sent to emergency, however, given I am not bleeding, I would be sitting there for hours on end. Instead, he scheduled me in to come to the ward as an outpatient to book me in for a dilation and curettage (D&C). This is a surgical procedure to remove tissue from inside your uterus.

I arrived at the day surgical ward to prep for surgery. I got changed into hospital gear and sat out in the waiting room with all other patients awaiting their various day surgery procedures. The nurse came and got me and took me into the nurses' consult room to take my measurements and sign consent papers. She then gave me a medication called misoprostol (Cytotec) which she explained would promote the dilation and softening of my cervix over several hours to assist the doctor with the procedure. I was then sent back out to the waiting lounge with Guy. Within five minutes of taking the tablet, I began shivering. The nurse noticed I looked off and got me a bed and a private cordoned-off area. She told me I may experience bleeding and to call her if I did. Within twenty minutes I was moaning in agony, shaking, shivering and going into shock.

Guy grabbed the nurse who came over. She looked at me and asked to do an internal examination. I could barely speak but with my shivering stutter I agreed. She informed me I was dilating rapidly and would call the doctor to see if he was ready for my surgery as I probably couldn't wait the full two hours I had left. The nurse asked me if I wanted any pain relief. I declined and she asked me why. I answered honestly and said, 'Well it's been twenty minutes, if I can't handle this, how will I ever handle childbirth?' To which she replied, 'Honey, don't be silly. Childbirth hurts like hell; the difference is, at the end of childbirth, you have a beautiful baby that you get to hold, and that love makes you forget all about the pain. You won't forget this pain. Don't do it to yourself, take the pain relief!' I knew she was right, but again, I had this expectation upon myself that I should be able to suck it up.

Given my quick onset, my surgery was bumped forward, and I was going in. I remember just thinking, *I want this to be over. Just take this baby out of me and let me move on.* I felt like this missed miscarriage limbo was the worst torture. Being sedated was a welcome relief for a few moments.

I woke in agonising pain. I couldn't open my eyes yet, but I remember thrashing around and feeling a flurry of nurses around me trying to keep me still and calm me down. Pain. I remember feeling excruciating pain. The nurses kept giving me a variety of pain relief and asking if that was helping. Nothing was working. I just wanted to roll up in a ball. Fentanyl was the last option and they had given me a lot of it. Still nothing. Someone paged Dr Toby. He came in and was not happy with the team. I remember a nurse asking if the utensil count was verified, suggesting a surgical tool was left inside of me. Dr Toby asked if anyone had performed an ultrasound on my bladder. Next thing, nurses were ultrasounding my bladder. BINGO. Turns out I really needed to pee and the pressure of my full bladder on my newly curetted uterus was causing excruciating pain! The nurses catheterised me and ahhhhhh ... instant relief. My catheter would stay with me for a week after being discharged. Apparently, I was another unlucky statistic suffering from urinary retention which was contributing to the immense pain I was experiencing.

I thought once the procedure was done, I could move on. It was such a torment waiting for the D&C. Little did I know, after all the physical recovery of miscarriage, it was the unseen trauma that was unbearable and isolating. Experiencing so many feelings, suddenly bursting into tears without any obvious trigger, confused why this happened, especially given there were no signs anything was wrong. Some days I just felt numb, empty and lost. Angry at that awful GP. I felt a small sting at every pregnancy announcement and baby shower post. Lonely because no one person understood me in that exact moment; I had no control because I couldn't fix anything. I couldn't change my circumstances, and worst of all … guilt. Guilt that I was being greedy to want a child after making a deal with the devil. Guilt that, as a woman, I couldn't fulfil what I thought at the time was my purpose. Guilt as a wife that my husband got a dud.

The circumstances around this miscarriage made it the hardest, however, it would only be the first of many more miscarriages to come. I know there are some amazing resources out there and support groups, but in that moment, when it was happening for me, I couldn't. I couldn't leave the house or form my feelings into words. I also feel it was my way of punishing myself by allowing myself to suffer in silence because I felt like it was my fault. Circling back to that self-sabotage. I was the failure, and this was my consequence. I know now that is not the case, but hindsight and hormones are a wonderful thing. This was also the turning point for me with social media. I stopped sharing our IVF journey, as I couldn't face sharing all the losses as they unfolded. People wanted updates immediately because social media is instant. My grief was not.

If you know of anyone going through a miscarriage, here's the don'ts and dos:

Don'ts	Dos
'It wasn't meant to be.'	Know there are NO right words or actions, and everyone processes the loss differently.
'Maybe next time.'	
'Oh, you can have MY kids.'	Be supportive.
'At least you weren't further along.'	Offer an ear (not an opinion).
'It wasn't a real baby.'	'I'm sorry for your loss.'
'You can have another.'	'I'm thinking of you.'
'Now you have an angel.'	'Can I do anything for you?'
'It's for the best.'	'I don't know what it is you are going through, but I am here if you need anything.'
'You dodged a bullet.'	
'There must have been something wrong.'	Drop cooked meals on the doorstep.
'Why did you miscarry?'	Offer to pick up a load of washing.
'At least you know you can get pregnant now.'	Have a grazing box delivered.
'What about IVF or adoption?'	Send a care package with chocolate and some movies.

If you have ever experienced a miscarriage, I am sorry. I am sorry if you felt any of the above emotions I felt. Time is the only healer; however, the pain of a loss never truly leaves you. It simply becomes bearable.

LESSON 24: DON'T ASSUME YOU ARE ALWAYS THE PROBLEM.

Have you ever noticed how often women still are the first to assume they are the problem? Whether it's the great gender gap debate within the workforce, or why a woman must be the one that juggles mum life and a career or the couples' fertility. The assumption is always the female.

When it comes to fertility, it's always the female who has a barrel of tests to complete while the male partner has one job …

***

By 2016, after multiple miscarriages, Guy and I agreed, this next round was it. I was thirty, and this was our cut-off we had discussed. No more after this. I just had nothing left to give. We decided not to tell our family this time around. It was just getting too sad to constantly update them with such sad news and disappointment. I commenced injections as usual and was on track for my egg retrieval procedure. Then the clinic called me to say they had double booked and couldn't fit my egg collection in, but I could go to the new sister clinic located in Wollongong and the nurse would take my file there as she worked across both sites.

I agreed as I did not just go through all those injections for nothing! I had a meltdown the night before but arrived in Wollongong the next day ready to do it. At this clinic, for egg retrieval they give you two valium and two Panadeine Forte for the procedure. Then, while in surgery, you have the happy gas. I remember the procedure had just finished. Five eggs were collected and the surgeon was walking me to recovery when he said to me, 'I read your file and it says you had a successful pregnancy last year. What happened?' I responded, 'I miscarried.' The doctor looked at me and said, 'Oh,

I like miscarriages,' to which I said, 'Oh great; I don't.' We reached the recovery room where he sat me in the chair and went to get Guy.

When Guy came in, the doctor brought my medical records in. He proceeded to tell me that his niche is infertility and reoccurring miscarriage. He believed that the clinic continuing to implement the same process again and expecting a different outcome was the definition of madness. As such, he asked us if we would be willing to freeze my eggs collected and undergo full fertility screening again. Given this was our last round, we figured we would give it our all, so we agreed.

After the egg collection, Guy and I went into Wollongong to grab some lunch and have a slow wander around the shopping centre before driving back to Canberra. We were in David Jones, and I was wanting to buy a Marc Jacobs watch. As usual, on a weekday, not a single salesperson in sight in the area you need them. A lovely lady from the Jurlique cosmetics section came over to serve us. Guy was wandering around and the lady exchanged the usual pleasantries as she served me. She then saw my hospital band on my wrist and asked if everything was okay … I was taken aback for a moment because nobody knew we were in Wollongong, let alone doing IVF. I didn't know what to say so I just blurted out the truth.

The lady went on to ask further questions but in a non-invasive way. I found myself talking to a stranger about my fertility journey. Then, from nowhere, I was openly telling her about my deal with the devil! I hadn't even shared that with my closest friends and family because it does sound batshit crazy, but here I was … The lady looked at me kindly when I told her. She responded, 'Don't you see? For somebody to be willing to give that up and make such a sacrifice, makes you the most deserving of all. You will see.'

And just like that, this perfectly kind stranger was able to lift the block I had held on my own so firmly for the past twelve years! This conversation stirred something in me. Maybe I was the reason I had not fallen pregnant and stayed pregnant all this time. Not because I couldn't have children, but because I convinced myself and truly believed that I could not? Is that even possible? This amazing human broadened my horizons and opened my mind to the possibility. She gave me hope. Suddenly I could allow myself to be cautiously optimistic for my future.

Guy and I had to go through all the usual tests again, including egg count, semen analysis, genetic testing, prenatal testing, etc. The doctor also wanted to do a semen DNA defragmentation index (DFI) and a procedure to test my uterus tissue. Both of which were not general fertility screening tools as they were not covered under Medicare or private health. We travelled to Wollongong for me to undertake the uterus tissue procedure. This would be the last test on the doctor's list. Prior to the procedure, the doctor asked us to step into his office to go through our results to date.

We walked into the consultation room and sat. The doctor walked in with two files. One was thick with papers poking out and looked rather dishevelled, while the other looked brand new and only had a couple of pages in it. The doctor placed the files on his desk as he sat. The newer file was on top. He opened the file, telling us we would look at Guy's results first. He started to circle numbers on the page as he went. 'Sperm count looks good. Swimming well. Good number of swimmers.' He paused for a moment ...

Then with a cocky smile, he suddenly circled a number as he said, 'Ah, this is it. This DFI is your problem.'

'Pardon?' I spoke. I glared at the doctor. Looked at Guy whose mouth was covered by his hand, looking perplexed and concerned at the same time. It was awkwardly silent, and I began to smirk and get the giggles. I couldn't even complete a sentence … 'You mean … he … I'm not … It's not me?' The doctor responded, 'Fertility is not a blame game.' I quickly replied, 'No, no. All this time, for over a decade, I thought it was me, but it's not me? You're telling me I'm not the problem? Guy is?! Just give me this moment for a minute …' I looked at Guy, and he looked worried. I had just been given the best news in my life and Guy had been given the worst. Way to be supportive, Natashia!

Guy finally mustered up his voice and asked the doctor if there was anything he could do, or were we out of the baby race? My head snapped around so quickly to hear the doctor's response. He told us that if we had undergone the DFI testing six years ago when we commenced IVF, it would have been identified as the contributing factor of our infertility. We would have been told to consider sperm donors or end our quest for biological children altogether. But there was a higher power in play here. There had to be. There were too many coincidences to ignore. At the same time, six years ago, our doctor was only just discovering the cause and treatment for this very fertility issue.

He conducted a study and presented his findings across America and Europe. The doctor went on to explain sperm DNA basically needs to be below 15% DFI for excellent quality sperm, 15-24% DFI for good, 25-29% DFI for fair and more than 29% DFI for poor quality. Well, here we were, with a whopping big fat 69%. This was the highest level our doctor had ever recorded and still stands today! He went on to explain if each sperm were a taxi, the DNA within each sperm is the taxi driver. The index was effectively the toxicity of the taxi driver ... how drunk the sperm was, and obviously the drunker the driver, the less effective the drive. This was the reason I was continually miscarrying.

The irony in all of this was, of all the practices we had gone through, it took being double booked and redirected to a sister clinic that landed us in the laps of the actual doctor who discovered the treatment for our 69% DFI. All we had to do was go home and have sex every day for a week and repeat the DFI. Clear to say, Guy thought this was the best medicine in the world. The theory was that, by the male flushing out his semen, it wasn't left sitting in the 'taxi bay' becoming intoxicated, aka not keeping the nutrients it required to be a viable sample.

A week later, we were at 26%. We now had average sperm. But average was better than toxic drunk sperm. This result meant we could effectively fall pregnant naturally. However, due to chemotherapy, my cycle was much like a panda, and I only seemed to ovulate every fifty years. So, the doctor suggested we proceed with a fresh cycle of IVF from scratch and for Guy to do seven to nine days of flushing out his system and we should have a winning combination. As we left the clinic with all our IVF drugs in tow, I turned to Guy and said, 'We will do twelve to fourteen days just to be sure,' to which he grinned enthusiastically. I quickly burst this bubble, 'Oh, no way. I'm shoving hormone needles in myself for the next fourteen days; you can sort yourself out buddy. You're on your own!' and that he was!

My extension on the doctor's theory paid off! Guy's DFI dropped to a tiny 3.4%. Another record in the largest reduction the doctor had ever recorded. This meant we would be going into IVF with the best variables. To reduce and control these variables further, we went with ICSI where the 3.4% swimmers would be injected directly into my eggs to remove a few more steps from the process to provide us with the best chances of a viable pregnancy. I proceeded with such confidence knowing it was not me, and that there was a treatment to give us our best chance. I opened myself up to the possibility of this happening. I still was cautious – but optimistically cautious.

Guy's statistics were the most significant improvement our specialist had ever recorded. So much so he asked Guy to write his story that would eventually be included in the fertility textbook he went on to publish that supports the idea that men are equally responsible for fertility issues within couples.

By day one of fertilisation, four of the eggs had accepted the sperm. Now they were put into a chamber until day five which would be implant day to provide the eggs their best chance at continued fertilisation. On day five, we only had three viable embryos. When we arrived for implantation of the egg into my uterus lining, the doctor informed us, of the three, only one was of good enough quality to proceed. ONE! Only one. One singular blastocyst for transfer. I began my negative Nancy thinking again, telling myself this was doomed.

The two weeks wait post-transfer is always the longest two weeks of your life. If you've been around the IVF traps for a while, you know a few old wives' tales and cheater tricks like wearing socks, eating pineapple cores, etc. Trust me, I have done it all. The best trick I learnt was the early testing. Particular pregnancy home kit tests are more sensitive than others. So, this meant, provided you purchased a few of the sensitive brands, if you were pregnant, you could get a positive reading. The earliest I got a positive reading was six days. In IVF terms, that was 6DP5DT, meaning my embryo was eleven days old. I liked knowing before the blood test and having the clinic tell you the results, but you still never really believed it. I would continue to pee on sticks every day to ensure my lines were getting darker. I felt like this allowed me to control my response when I got the 'official' results from the clinic after the two-week wait.

Two weeks was up, and the clinic called to confirm my pregnancy. I couldn't believe it. I was pregnant. But I had also been down this path many times before. So, I just faced it in bite-size pieces for my own sanity's sake. The seven-week scan to see the heartbeat flickering … Ten-week scan and bloods for genetic testing. Twelve-week scan … I was so petrified every step of the way. Once we hit sixteen weeks, I had my first midwife appointment, and I remember having to do the mental health questionnaire with the midwife to measure and screen women for symptoms of emotional distress during pregnancy and the postnatal period.

Like hell I was going to look like a crazy person so I 100% fudged my way through the questions to ensure I was a vision of good health. But in reality, pregnancy was something I had wanted for so long, I felt shame and guilt that it wasn't as glorious as I had envisioned. I was expecting glowing Mumma goddess vibes. Instead, I had constipation, haemorrhoids, diabetes requiring insulin and cankles, and I am not even kidding! But that aside, I must admit, I did learn to love my body. I mean, how could you not? It was literally growing a human. Suddenly, I felt like my bumps were in all the right places. There was a small window of absolute body bliss for me.

In December 2016, I welcomed into the world my beautiful chubby miracle baby girl via emergency C-section … because of course, nothing about my journey so far was easy, right? Separated for the first few hours of her existence, by the time I finally got to meet my miracle baby and hold her for the first time, I was so overwhelmed with relief and love. I was so lucky to have a nurse on hand with the camera to capture that exact moment.

Enter Cadence Myee Telfer.

After six years of multiple miscarriages and heartache, never getting that heartbeat, naming Cadence was a no-brainer. Her name means rhythmic sequence in a melody. Her heartbeat was music to our ears and her first cry was music to the soul. The perfect name for the perfect miracle.

I finally had that hope of having my own child come true. With strong Islander blood, I was certain I would have an olive-skinned, brown-eyed baby. The universe had other plans for me again. Cadence has the fairest skin and the bluest of eyes with a golden ring around her irises. She might look like Dad, but the attitude is all Mum.

Nothing could have prepared me for motherhood. As much as I was involved in my nephew's upbringing with the countless sleepovers and holidays I had the boys for, I still really had no idea what I was in for. I really was unprepared. The first day Cadence was in the world, she remained butt-naked wrapped in a hospital blanket because I was unsure how to put her clothes on with the giant belly button clamp attached to her. The first time she cried, I buzzed for the nurse to ask, 'What do I do?' The sweet nurse simply said, 'Just love her.' I picked up my daughter and did just that, and she settled in my arms. Don't get me wrong, some days it takes a whole lot of 'love', rocking, nursing, feeding, cuddling, swaddling and burping to settle my girl. Nonetheless, I appreciate the midwife's advice, now, four years into parenthood and realising that children needing love really is the basic ingredient in anything we provide them as parents.

For the next eight weeks, I was in this newborn baby haze. Overwhelmed with guilt for not loving every moment, feeling like a failure at juggling it all, feeling inadequate for having a C-section like it made me less of a mother somehow. Becoming a mother was beautiful, it was agony, it was life-changing, it was hard. I couldn't tell my arse from my head, sleeping in three-to-four-hour blocks was a luxury, a shower was an extra, I rocked a mum bun and should have owned shares in dry shampoo. Breast milk was liquid gold, and I was quickly learning that mum guilt is next level.

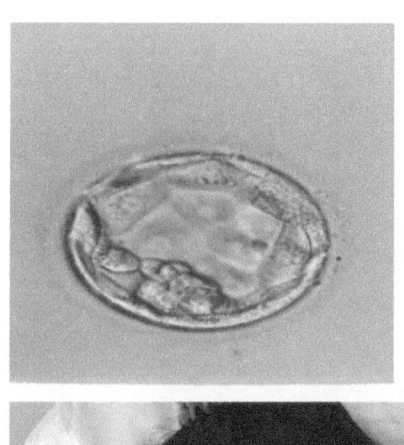
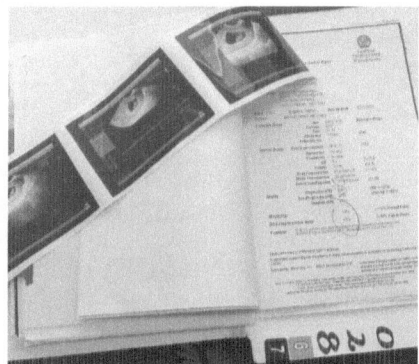
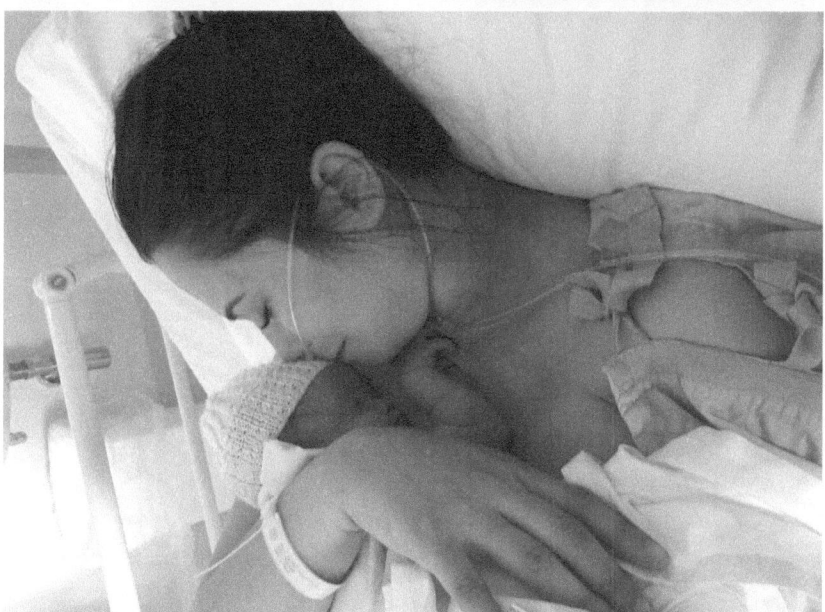

2016: Our IVF journey, our perfect blastocyst that became the perfect miracle baby: Cadence Myee.

BALANCE
HAVING IT ALL

Balance. [bal-*uh*ns]

noun

a state of equilibrium or equipoise; equal distribution of weight, amount, etc.

something used to produce equilibrium, counterpoise.

verb (used with object), **bal·anced, bal·anc·ing.**

to bring to or hold in equilibrium, poise.

to arrange, adjust or proportion the parts of symmetrically.

verb (used without object), **bal·anced, bal·anc·ing.**

to have an equality or equivalence in weight, parts, etc.; be in equilibrium

> *'Some days you eat salads and go to the gym, some days you eat cupcakes and refuse to put on pants. It's called balance.'*
> – Unknown

LESSON 25: SLIDING DOOR MOMENTS ARE A REAL THING.

Do you ever have those moments in your life that are like sliding door moments? They are the seemingly inconsequential everyday moments you are faced with that literally make or break the most important relationships and/or direction within your life. It's like being at a fork in the road and having to choose which one-way street to travel down, knowing you can never undo your decision or go back the other way ... and both paths lead you in very different directions in life ...

My first sliding door that impacted my existence was most likely the traumas of my past. While it does not define me, and I certainly do not consider myself a victim, it did, however, shape the caution that I would go on to apply to all relationships with males, along with my poor self-worth. My second sliding door would be cancer. It changed the course of life and my purpose in it to live in the present and without regret. This was obviously a huge sliding door moment! My third sliding door was Guy. I feel like when I was younger, if a relationship started to get serious and I knew 'the talk' would inevitably come, I would literally play out the relationship in my head from start to finish. I know right … How can I possibly know and/or control another person's feelings or reactions and responses? But there I was, being a control freak trying to minimise long-term and inevitable heartbreak for myself. If I couldn't see it becoming serious, I didn't proceed. Obviously, my first door most likely contributed to this crazy narrative, but now it's safe to say, for the first time in my life, it was with Guy that I couldn't and still cannot see any other path forward that does not include him. As such, I truly do not know what my life could have been had I not encountered Guy that first night at the sports club. This sliding door moment would be one of my biggest in life.

Lisa
The fourth sliding door moment was my career. After leaving the brain injury unit I was working in, I moved back into the community sector. I loved this space, the variety and the freedom. However, my employer at the time was more about the bottom line that brought the dollars in the door for her, than being client focused. The employees were often overworked, boundaries never respected, not listened to or valued and always taken advantage of. While I loved this sector, I had to move on. I decided to join a nursing agency. Not just any nursing agency, as there are many around, but there has only ever been one agency within Canberra that has stood the test of time and had the reputation to prove it. I joined that agency in July of 2013. I still had the variety of work, but longer shifts, which meant more flexibility while I finished my studies. Within the year, my boss became unwell, and her

daughter Lisa took leave from her public service life and stepped in for a while. Little did I know this human would become one of my dearest besties, like soul-sister level! I was still happy floating about, enjoying my workspace. Contemplating when I was going to put my big-girl pants on and go and get a job in case management and service coordination upon the completion of my additional studies.

Thankfully I contemplated this for a period. Long enough for Lisa to see something within me that I couldn't see myself. On 12 February 2015, Lisa invited me out to a little restaurant in the city for a work meeting. Now, I am rather intuitive with situations like this, so I had a feeling Lisa was going to propose a new role for me within her agency, as I had recently approached her about developing some templates for the workplace to assist in worker efficiency, as I was a super nerd and had these 'cheat sheets' I had created for myself when on shift. Turns out I was on the right track but had no idea to what extent.

Firstly, I was so nervous I ordered the exact same meal and drink as Lisa. I totally overthought it. *If I order something cheap, will she think I'm poor (I am poor. Totally broke-arse poor from doing IVF!), and I don't want to order something too expensive (because again ... I am totally broke!)* So, I played it safe. Then Lisa literally ate a baby bird's serving size, meanwhile, I was starving but felt like a gluttonous piglet. So I pushed my plate away; 'Oh, I'm so full too.' It was literally like I was so nervous I couldn't thread together a single independent thought for myself.

Then I also had this poker face I have always been good at ... aka resting bitch face ... just like Elsa, *Conceal, don't feel, don't let them know,* right?! So, while Lisa began offering me the opportunity of a lifetime and my mind was literally doing somersaults with excitement, my brain was telling me to play it cool, resulting in my face being completely emotionless. I wasn't giving anything away. Lisa had just asked me if Guy and I would be interested in going halves with her and her husband in starting up a new company that would provide services within the community sector. Now, it was literally just an idea to do something together, with no set time frames or definitive directions decided on, but I was already speechless at the mere thought Lisa thought I could be worthy to take such a chance on.

I remember questioning why my husband? While his public service role was people related, it wasn't his direct industry. Lisa explained to me that it would be such a huge commitment, it would work best if we were both onboard so our priorities would align. Sounded reasonable, but I didn't really grasp the benefit she was offering of both Guy and me a stake in a start-up company until later down the track. My head was swimming. I was so overwhelmed. *What? How? Why? Why me?* I went home that night to tell Guy all about it. I just kept saying, 'But why me?' I literally thought Lisa could do this with anyone else. She had an entire team to pick from … why me? What did I have to offer? What could I bring to the table? I was so extremely excited; however, this negative self-talk and flurry of questions would be something I asked myself every day for the next five years.

Obviously, there was a lot more meetings to nut out direction, scope, roles and so on. I was petrified Guy and I would have to buy into the company start-up costs, because I'm not sure if I mentioned this, but we were broke as fuck. Thankfully, all it cost to initially start-up was my soul. No, not really – I just had to put my heart and soul, time and energy into creating a company I could be really proud of. When cost started to be involved for things like uniforms and insurances, we were able to have Lisa and her husband loan our little start-up company the overhead costs.

I named my firstborn baby 'National Community Care' (NCC). I designed the logo with the IT help of my dad, created the branding and the functions we would require in the purpose-built system, I wrote all the community-specific policies, researched the shit out of the National Disability Insurance Scheme (NDIS), which was this brand-new scheme rolling out across the country, and chose uniforms and business cards, letterheads and more. I loved every single step of the process.

I remember going to the business accountant with Lisa and Guy to discuss NCC and how we would structure it. I vividly remember the accountants saying, 'The majority of start-ups don't make profit within a year and are lucky to make it past two years.' I felt like it was a disclaimer … 'warning – you might fail this'. *Like fuck I will,* I thought to myself. Challenge excepted. I worked for Lisa's company while setting up structures for NCC to ensure I still had income for myself. Once NCC was operational, I was the face of the company. I was taking the calls and emails. I was the carer out on the floor within our community delivering services, and Lisa was my mentor, accountant and payroll extraordinaire. She was like my bumpers on a tenpin bowling game keeping me on the right track. It was amazing. THIS WAS MY JAM.

LESSON 26: DON'T OVERTHINK THINGS.

Don't overthink things, said the overthinker …

Within our first full year of trading, our little start-up had paid back the loan money to Lisa, and still managed to turn a small profit. (Take that, accountant! No, I don't mean that, I totally adore our accountant.) Now, this certainly is not why I do what I do. I remember being gobsmacked about the concept of profit at the end of financial year. To date, I dread end of financial year and doing tax returns. I truly love this industry, and I love that I can say I enjoy and love my job and it benefits those we care for. Profit is merely a by-product of what we do. However, for a first-timer, I was chuffed with our efforts. It told me I was obviously doing something right.

Each year that passed by, my negative Nancy narrative was always in the forefront, making me feel like I was unworthy of my position and had to prove myself and my loyalty. Still not making sense of why Lisa tapped me on the shoulder for this adventure and this overwhelming sense of an unfulfillable debt I felt I owed her for the rest of my life. I put this pressure on myself to do bigger and better each year. Do not get me wrong, there's no scenario where I would do something I am passionate about half-arsed. I love what I do, and I know I am damn good at it, but with this feeling of debt I had, it was this added layer of pressure I put upon myself not to let Lisa down.

When we first started, every quarter, I would ask Lisa, 'Are we okay, are we on track?' I was so petrified of getting a tap on my shoulder telling me it was no longer viable. Despite Lisa always reassuring me and communicating with me, it was something that only took time for me to have confidence in myself to know I got this, and I am damn good at this.

From 2015 to 2019, it was Lisa and me. We did it all. We were reception, call intake, recruitment, HR, accounts team, scheduling and rosters, events coordinator, client onboarding and the on-call phones twenty-four seven. Lisa managed her nursing agency day-to-day operations, and I managed NCC day-to-day operations. We often got calls from brokerage teams asking to be put through to our accounts team ... 'Yes, that's us. How can I help?' Or a request to speak to the recruitment manager ... 'Yes, Natashia speaking.' Obviously, we were doing something right. The perception was that we were a large company with teams upon teams of management personnel. In reality ... it was just Lisa and me.

We absolutely love what we do, but do not be fooled, it is damn hard work, determination, grit and heart that keeps us going. There are no such thing as sick days. There is no long service leave or annual leave. If we stop, business stops. Now, I know business gurus are screaming, '*THAT IS NOT SUSTAINABLE!*' ... but we are seven years in now and still kicking. We thrive on the 'giveback'. Why? Because it is my heart and soul, and we are not above any of the tasks required to keep the cogs turning. No-one else will have as much heart in my business as I will. Our team has naturally grown. We have never had to drum up business or seek out and advertise for clients beyond our standard yellow pages advert. We have allowed organic growth to build the successful and reliable reputation we have today, and the key players within our management team are people we have head hunted personally as we felt they share our same values and ethics. This gut feeling/bullshit radar has always kept our house in order.

The upside to doing it all meant we had literally built the company in a way that suited our lifestyle. Essentially, we could operate our company daily operations from our mobile phones on the couch in our PJs if we wanted and no-one would know the difference. This same flexibility allowed me to undergo a few rounds of IVF and conceive my miracle baby in 2016 and a second in 2019. Again, no such thing as maternity leave, so as I was being wheeled in for my C-section, I was grasping the iPad as the nurse was telling me I had to put it down, just trying to finalise payroll to ensure my team wages were not held up just because I was delivering my first human child! (Counting NCC as my firstborn.)

While I navigated my way through that eight-week baby haze, Lisa took the NCC phone for the first four weeks, and I maintained rosters, emails, billing and payroll prep. Most of my email responses were sent at three in the morning while breastfeeding, but we made it work because that is what it took. After four weeks was up, Lisa gave me the phone back and it was business as usual. I struggled initially with this, but I was not accepting failure, so I pushed on. Guy had eight weeks off from public service life to really do this side by side with me, and beyond that, upon returning to his full-time job, he would often race home on his lunchbreak because Cadence was screaming and I had a client call scheduled, or because I simply needed a sanity check-in because it was fucking hard! In hindsight, I was totally suffering from postnatal depression but refused to allow myself to entertain the idea. This would eventually bite me in the arse later.

As the years tacked on, our team has gone from just me providing face-to-face services, to a team of over eighty employees and a reputation I can humbly say I am extremely proud of. You are only ever as good as your team. Our team are the beating heart of my business, so we ensure they are looked after and know we are standing shoulder to shoulder on level ground with them. After many previous roles with terrible management who loved to enforce hierarchy, I felt I had an unwritten handbook of what not to do; but effectively, it all boiled down to a couple of factors … being a decent and kind human and putting people over dollars. This approach sounds like common sense to me, so it was no surprise that it was successful. We had created ourselves a niche service making us the best at what we do, and over the years, we have been recognised for these efforts from a wide scope including the

Governor General Peter Cosgrove and Lady Cosgrove, Dementia Australia and a few local and national government agencies.

Lisa taking a chance on me has been the biggest sliding door of my life. To have someone see something in you that you don't even see yourself is pretty amazing. She brought me to life. She gave me a platform to create 'something' truly amazing. Initially, Lisa had no idea what it would be when she asked me to partner with her. I shaped it into what we have today with Lisa's unwavering support. Lisa provided the financial start-up for me to literally create my family and support them. I used to allow this gesture to hang over my head for many years, feeling I owed my life to Lisa somehow, even though this was totally thanks to Nancy, as all loaned money was returned, and each full trading year provided profit. Eventually, I would acknowledge and accept it's been my damn hard work and dedication that has given us what we have now. This is something Lisa would regularly remind me of, but wasn't something I accepted until I found *me*. Yes, without Lisa, I most likely would not have National Community Care as I know it today … but I do know I would have something similar with the same goal to make a social community impact. Maybe as an employee, maybe I would have eventually started on my own. I was always driven to do something within the industry and my studies were getting me there. Lisa has been an amazing mentor and bestie.

What Lisa gave me goes beyond any of the financial gain, and I know now that that aspect goes both ways. I don't even think Lisa realises what she gave me.

She gave me a platform to grow.

A heat lamp to feel safe.

A safety net to catch me.

She gave me her bum on the line with mine.

She gave me space to find myself.

And confidence to find my worth.

That is utterly priceless and totally irreplaceable.

Lisa is a big dreamer, a visionary, and most importantly, a go-getter! She is a total boss, calls it how it is, total bad-arse, the most amazing party planner, a thoughtful gift-giver, the biggest cheerleader you can imagine and has a heart of gold.

Lisa is the big sister I never had and has some pretty amazing hand-me-down clothes too!

Every person needs a Lisa.

Lisa is my home girl. My business partner. My work wife. My bestie. My soul sister. My person.

2019 Lisa and Me

LESSON 27: WORK-LIFE BALANCE IS BULLSH*T.

Do you ever feel like Dory swimming in the big blue? 'Just keep swimming, just keep swimming.' ... I often get myself in a funk and begin to question my abilities of being an adequate mother, wife, sister, daughter, employer, business owner, friend ... My head feels so overwhelmed with fog; my priorities get hazed some days. I feel like this period allowed negative Nancy to really take a front seat in what I felt was my epic failings in every department in life while I was striving to 'do it all'. Sucky wife, shit mum, terrible boss, distant sister, not present friend as I attempted to navigate my way through this new chapter as a mother and business owner.

This eternal struggle, to date, has never gone away. People say and promote 'work-life balance', but I call bullshit. Like Oprah Winfrey said: 'You can have it all. You just can't have it all at once.' Everyone believes if you want to climb the corporate ladder, then that requires sacrifice. But does it? Really? It doesn't require sacrifice; we just require equality ...

Yes, I feel I 'have it all', but what does that even mean? There is so much more to that label and its concept that it is never fully unpacked. Firstly, this concept only applies collectively if every human on the face of the planet wanted the same things. On an independent level, my claim to 'having it all' also has a disclaimer along with it ...

I have it all – but at a large cost and a constant juggling act to actively maintain all aspects within my life, oh, and I often drop the juggling balls.

Doesn't quite have the same snappy ring to it, now does it?! I am a self-confessed life-juggler and perpetual ball-dropper, but I guess the key to my success in maintaining balance is picking that darn ball up and continuing forward with the juggle.

So, here are my facts. Things I know today to be true ... without a doubt – thanks, Nancy!

I have an amazing husband that worships the ground I stand on, and I love him unconditionally.

I'm a loving mother.

Protective sister.

Supportive daughter.

Empathetic friend.

Honest employer.

Fierce advocate.

BUT ... I can hand on heart say, I can never be all those things actively at once. If any superhuman can tell me all facets of their life are a success at the same time, with equal time and energy shared, I truly take my hat off to you and ask you to tell me your source of witchcraft!

Work-life balance, for me, is maintaining and prioritising all those facets of my life at various times. For example, having sick kids often trumps all other facets of my life. A work meeting may trump a coffee catch-up with a girlfriend, or an emergency call-out to support a staff member trumps family dinner. They are all equally important facets in my life, but balance means sometimes only having the capacity to pour into those cups as required. I equate this to a veggie gardener. You have planted your seeds all at one time, or staggered. However, they each require different things to grow, and require your attention at different stages during that growth right through to harvest, right? So, of course, comparing your love life to your children, your career to your social life, doesn't work. Just like comparing potatoes, carrots and onions.

Balancing each of these facets is important to me and is ranked in my personal top five priorities to living my best life. If something is not fulfilling you in life or is having a negative impact on you, then why sit there and put up with it? Only *you* can change your personal circumstances, and even if your circumstances are affected by a larger external factor you cannot control, you can still decide how *you* will react to these adversities. Are you going to throw a pity party? Play the blame game? Hate the world? Or …

Put on your big-girl pants and roll with the punches? Enjoy what is good within your life. Life is so vast, there is so much to be grateful for when you really break it down and bring it back to your priorities and core values. Whenever something feels off for me, within my life, I reflect on mine. What are my top five priorities? Not as in my priority to-do list for the day, but rather the priorities of life I uphold. Are they in check with my core values and are they on track or require an adjustment of sorts? Your priorities can be an array of things that are important to you as an individual. For me, my five are:

Family: Spending quality and meaningful time with loved ones that put in an equal amount of effort to make me a priority.

Work: Not in a workaholic way; I know it's weird, but it fills my cup up!

Relationships/social interactions: Celebrating the good stuff and maintaining healthy relationships with friends. This facet also helps me feel like something other than 'just Mum'.

Health: Looking after myself. Self-care, healthy eating, gym. This is my 'just me' priority. Something I have for myself and no-one else. It really is the ultimate self-care for me.

Balance: This is key for me. Without this, I cannot do any of the above successfully.

Your priorities could include travel, finances, exercise, political freedoms, education, etc.

PROJECT KIND

You'll notice these priorities are not numbered, as they are not a hierarchy but rather a Venn diagram. Each priority has cross-sections with others. If one element of my five is out, then all become off balance for me. However, this may not be the case for all individuals.

To clarify, these are not goals, but rather priorities I need within my life. In my opinion, goals are the bigger picture, that wider lens, the tangible milestones that I'm trying to achieve. Priorities are the things that I need to say *yes* or *no* to in order to reach my goals and ensure my personal fulfilment. They keep it all aligned. They are like your non-negotiables of life. Nothing comes before them, otherwise serious adjustments need to be made to set things back on track to ensure I am operating at my optimum level. Of course, my priorities will look different to yours depending on what's going on in your life. It could include a multitude of priorities such as home, hobbies, sports, education, pets, friendships, relationships, family, self-care, spirituality, religion, finances, personal growth, professional growth or volunteering, just to name a few.

The reason I set these priorities and review them regularly is that I do find they help to reduce indecision about where to dedicate my time, structure my days in meaningful ways and allow me to stay on track. Priorities can obviously shift, and they *should* shift over time. But I've learned that, to make progress and not get burnt-out, it's important for me to focus on a few things at a time until they no longer serve me.

My main goal most days is to have mental clarity. When I let shiny-object syndrome take over – which can happen quiet easily, I might add – I try to prioritise all things, but I get stuck in my head and find it hard to concentrate and make decisions, which leads to procrastinating. Some days, I let shiny-object syndrome take over, because the five minutes I might spend on the shiny object beats the four hours I would spend thinking about it while ineffectively trying to stick to my priorities. But it is about using your judgement in knowing your strengths and weaknesses, and for me, knowing which battles to stick out and which to wave a white flag at always helps. I don't want to be overridden with anxiety wondering whether I'm making the right choices in my life or not. Life is far too short to live like that. I want to feel confident in my decisions. That's why I think priorities are so important. I love a good Post-it Note, list, note in my phone … organised chaos is the state I live in.

LESSON 28: DECLINE UNSOLICITED ADVICE.

As kids, we question the advice given to us by our parents. By our teens, we are defying that advice. We receive unsolicited advice within our careers, personal lives and pretty much every milestone within life. From dating, to starting a business, buying into a business, buying a home, choosing not to buy a home – all bring unsolicited advice from a flurry of people who think they know best. Of course, they know best for their personal circumstances … but that doesn't make their advice or experiences automatically what is best for you and your personal circumstances.

Life is not one size fits all. To be honest, it would be damn boring if it were! To date, I feel I manage unsolicited advice rather humbly. When I was diagnosed with cancer, every person had a great-aunt that had some crazy remedy for curing cancer despite having little knowledge about my personal circumstances. Having perspective around this allowed me to see that the person meant no harm. In fact, the advice-giver generally felt it was the only available option to provide me with comfort, with a small slither of hope and optimism for a grim situation I found myself in. When it comes to giving advice to people with medical conditions or illnesses, it's such a slippery slope. No person wants to be sick. Please remember that before you dish out your uneducated advice. No two human bodies are the same. Your witchdoctor herbal shake might work for you, but not for me. Thanks … but no thanks.

When starting my first business, the opportunity Lisa gave me was so kind that so many people couldn't believe that it wouldn't have some great cost to me in the long run. Despite working day in and day out until we had billable hours to derive an income, people seemed to look past this. For the most part, I stuck to my lane, knowing what I know and allowing nothing but the time, and eventually, evidence of my success prove them wrong. I didn't have time to waste trying to convince the naysayers otherwise. They had already made their assumptions and drawn their conclusions on a situation that had no impact on them. I'll admit, sometimes the advice given may be useful. It may conjure an interest to explore the advice further, but for the most part it was not relatable to my personal circumstances and was totally unsolicited.

Then comes the baby race. The unsolicited advice given here is next level. This is a race I thought I was disqualified from since the age of nineteen, but I still got advice about witchdoctors, surrogacy and overseas adoption. The three serious boyfriends I did have post-chemo life were all well-informed of my situation and destiny of being a barren spinster. I felt this huge insecurity about finding the life partner that wanted to accept me as I saw myself … defective. Why would any man want to settle with me? However, after meeting Mr Right Guy, for the first time ever, I allowed myself to admit I wanted a family.

Nancy loved to remind me that due to my deal with the devil,

I wasn't going to fall pregnant naturally, so for six long years, Guy and I didn't have what everyone else had. We didn't have a 'we bought our first house' moment or the 'we're having a baby' posts which seemed to be flooding my socials daily. Each baby shower I attended to celebrate my gorgeous friends still put a sting in my heart of what I thought I would never have. This was all a lovely reminder from the universe to keep me in check. Every cent we could save was spent on IVF. We didn't have private health cover, so everything was out of pocket. At $10,000-$15,000 a pop and eight years of IVF it's easy to see why we didn't own real estate or anything of monetary value. We were living pay cheque to pay cheque in the hopes of having a family.

It's not until you become pregnant, you realise it's like the entire human race has this secret pact not to disclose the particulars of these experiences to any female yet to conceive. We all know the human body is amazing and can withstand a lot, yet when it comes to pregnancy and childbirth, you think you know what to expect, but nothing can prepare you … life as you know it is over. I thought I knew this enough that I didn't have a typical baby shower, Guy and I threw an 'End of life as we know it Baby-Q', but even thinking we knew what to expect was still not enough. All the nephew sleepovers, all the baby books and baby classes in the world could not have prepared me for mum life.

Sadly, the unsolicited advice starts from the moment you're pregnant. No, wait. I take that back; it comes from the minute you are married. 'So, when are the kids coming along?' Yes, it's all good and well to say, 'Stuff what others say, it doesn't matter' – when you're a raging hormonal baby-seeking woman undergoing IVF, or a pregnant woman, or a sleep-deprived Mumma, it does matter! It's like a red flag to a bull.[8]

There's the obvious topics everyone loves to give you their opinion on – pregnancy foods to avoid, are you taking prenatal vitamins, NIPT/harmony testing, finding out the sex of your child, how long is your maternity leave ***cough** – proud small business owner ... what maternity leave?!* I was diagnosed with gestational diabetes, and every second person had some diet tip for me. Obviously, none of them cared to stop and listen to me or educate themselves on insulin-dependent GD, as they would have learnt it, in fact, had nothing to do with my diet and was beyond my control.

My tiny humans entered this world via unexpected caesarean section. I didn't have a birth plan. I didn't understand how I could plan for something with so many variables. I was not going to hang my hopes on the 'ideal' birth to have it go out the window then feel stressed and not in control for the rest of the experience. So, my only birth plan was: *'There is no plan. Just have a happy healthy baby.'* Did you know that this is the only surgery where five layers of tissue are opened? And us mums are expected to be on our feet within six hours, all while experiencing intense uterus contractions, the overwhelming release of oxytocin and all that Mumma love! Despite going through all of that, and now being responsible for a small human, I still was overwhelmed with guilt that I somehow was less of a mother because my baby was surgically birthed. Little did I know, this was just the beginning.

When that amazing tiny human is suddenly in your world it's all about breastmilk, formula or mixed, child care versus family day care, the immunisation debate, to swaddle or not to swaddle, pram brand envy, do you follow baby-led weaning, co-sleeping, too many naps, not enough naps, too many layers of clothing, not enough, circumcising boys, piercing ears, public schools, private schools ... it literally never ends. And heaven forbid if you have to go back to work to support your family – the world turns old-school and expects the mother to stay home forever like we are back in the 1950s! Then it's a world of day care parents, birthday party one-upping, preschool parents and schoolyard parents. They each offer amazing support if you find the right ones, otherwise sometimes they can also bring stress, guilt and a whole lot of mum shaming. I am so grateful my experience to date in the mum circle of friends has been supportive. However, it is not always the other parents you are shamed by. It becomes even more frustrating when it comes from people who have no children at all but they 'read somewhere', or their aunt's daughter's partner's sister said so.

So, here is what I learnt quickly … I was chickenshit before mum life. I would have never wanted to upset anyone by saying 'shove your advice', then when this tiny human arrives, that amazing Mumma-bear instinct kicked in, and I just knew what my kid needs and that Mumma-bear roar just continues to grow inside. Because if I (and Dad) can't do what is best for our child, no-one else will! Yes, it's as scary as hell, and yes, I have no idea what I am doing, but at the end of the day, when I do need advice, you can bet your arse I'm not going to ask the know-it-all's … I'm going to ask my mum … or mothers' group or Google! My mothers' group became our baby besties and my mum squad, my go-to gang! Supportive, no judgement and awake at three o'clock in the morning when we are too! No topic is too much, from birth stories, to recovery, dirty nappies, family tales and more. Honest opinions and heartfelt support because we are all going through the same shitty sleep regression leaps, all craving Mars bar slices and iced coffees with ice cream and chocolate sprinkles, all love a good mountain hike carrying our babies in baby carriers and all share a common dislike of the unsolicited baby advice.

PROJECT KIND

In November 2020, ABC Kids aired a popular animated television series aimed at pre-schoolers but captured the hearts of the entire family, and I am even going to go as far as saying parents love *Bluey* more than the kids. This particular episode I'm referring to is called 'Baby Race'. It perfectly depicts the early stages of motherhood. In this episode from season two, Bluey's mum Chilli is reminiscing about Bluey's baby days. While Bluey learnt to roll over first, her baby friend Judo was the first to crawl, which ultimately led to a baby race (in Chilli's mind, at least) to see who would walk first. While my experience with mothers' group was mostly a positive one, a place where I made some lifelong mum friends having shared one of the biggest chapters in our lives together, there was also a more negative component. That being competitiveness.

Competitiveness (always internalised) created by our own inadequacy as first-time mums – inadequacies that weren't necessarily real. Nonetheless, this competitiveness instigates the unspoken baby race. Like all mums, we tend to think our little love is just incredibly special, so much so, when they reach milestones it's as if it is on account of our amazing parenting skills. Surely, right? That first tooth popped because I am an amazing parent! Totally legitimate. My amazing parenting skills willed that tooth to cut.

Looking back at this now, it seems so absurd to be caught up in this cycle of self-criticism brought to you by Nancy for doing absolutely nothing wrong and behaving like a competitive MTV dance mum about developmental milestones. But with Nancy butting into every other aspect of my life, why would that mean 'mum life' would be immune to Nancy's negative powers? That first year of motherhood is like a little bubble where mums are equally adjusting to and learning this wide new world we find ourselves trying to navigate. None of us have a frigging clue what we are doing.

The best part about the baby race … within twelve months, you no longer have a baby. No-one bloody remembers whose baby walked first and last, whose baby was organic fed and who was first to eat chicken nuggets off the floor because I promise you one thing: eventually every child will eat nuggets off the floor! Mark my words. It's just that you are so caught up in all things baby you literally find yourself wishing your baby's first year away striving for each milestone! Before you know it, you have a sassy back-chatting kindergartener telling you off … oh wait, maybe that's just me?!

So, what is the best way to deal with the unsolicited advice and opinions of others? If you sound semi-interested, you run the risk of opening Pandora's box of shitty advice. But if you shut the person down too readily or what may be acknowledged as aggressively, you can damage your relationship with them, and while this can often be the option you want to choose, there is a way to respond that empowers you and won't give up your personal power. You may never intend to take on the person's advice but some of these responses cover all bases:

'I'll think about that.'

'Good idea. I'll do some further research to see if that's right for me.'

'That's an interesting opinion, but I prefer to do it this way.'

'I'm not looking for any advice right now.'

'That's not actually in line with my values.'

'I'm not going to do that.'

'No.'

The unsolicited advice is always going to come! It's like it's programmed into humans to vomit out the useless advice and opinions they hold. You can go blue in the face arguing with the advice-givers or you can learn from the experience. What is it that

PROJECT KIND

I learnt? Ignore the advice, stick to your lane and don't be one of those people! Don't dish the unsolicited advice – says me with an entire book on life lessons. Remember the overwhelming feelings you get when you are bombarded with the advice and opinions of others. Don't make others feel like that. In doing this, society is one person closer to a kinder future without the unsolicited advice.

GROWTH
WHATEVER IT TAKES

Self-Growth. [grohth]

noun

development as an individual.
the act or process, or a manner of growing; development; gradual increase.
size or stage of development.

'It is not the strongest of the species that survive, nor the most intelligent, but the one most responsive to change.'
– Charles Darwin

LESSON 29: IT'S OKAY TO BE BATSH*T CRAZY.

Over one million people in Australia experience depression each year. On average, one in six women and one in eight men will experience depression in their lifetime.[9] If you haven't experienced it within your lifetime, I guarantee you know someone who has. Depression and anxiety impact each of us. Despite these high statistics, we are still tainted by the concept that mental health is a taboo topic. So, all too often, it's not openly spoken about. I am the perfect example of this. Working in the health care sector promoting and advocating for my team to look after their mental health, meanwhile, when mine was out the window, I struggled to tell my family in fear of being seen as less of a person. Thanks again, Nancy …

By 2019, we decided to try for another IVF baby. We had miscarried again in 2018, and as strange as it sounds, I was not prepared at all for my 2019 pregnancy. We weren't sure where we would be living, the business had a huge project I was heading which was going to be significantly life-changing. Fitting a baby in almost seemed reckless, but there we were, doing it anyway, thinking the possibility of falling pregnant was less than a fertile couple having sex and conceiving, right?

Despite work life being hectic, pregnancy was more enjoyable this time around because I knew what to expect and went through all the motions feeling a lot more prepared. The likeness of this pregnancy being my last meant I was savouring every moment of the experience. I truly loved being pregnant. By no means was I the lucky kind with glowing skin, glossy hair and the only weight gained was the baby bump. I was fat all over, got diabetes, constipation, acne, body hair, iron infusions and so much more ... It certainly wasn't glamourous, but for the first time in my life, I felt comfortable in my skin. Like all the bumps and lumps were exactly where they were meant to be, and I loved the process of growing a beautiful human.

At ten weeks, I was sent for early diabetes testing. By eleven weeks, it was confirmed ... gestational diabetes again. On top of that, I required so much insulin I had to dial up the insulin pen twice to be able to get the required dosage, and my body was still not responsive to it. (And FYI, to those judgey mcjudgers out there, it was my fasting BGLs that pushed me into the GD bracket. My donut-eating diet was fine and my post-food BGLs were within a safe range.)

This time around, I told myself I would be responsible, and I would speak up during the mental health screening with the midwives. I was ready to answer honestly because I didn't want to have the same internal battle as I did last time. Somehow, I ended up falling through the gaps on this one again. My first appointment, there were no anxiety and depression (K10) checklists left so I couldn't fill one out, the next handful of times after that, it wasn't a priority within my appointment and/or assumed I had completed it in my initial intake appointment.

At thirty weeks, I had one of those 3D scans. Looking at my baby's features, I was so sure I had a little brown baby coming. Finally, some Islander blood would be coming through …

In June of 2019, we welcomed the most perfect sweet little soul.

Nate Michael Telfer.

A pale-skinned, green-eyed tornado. I might have found out the gender during pregnancy, ruining what many believe to be the only true surprise in life, but I can guarantee you I would never have expected in a million years, I, an olive-skinned Islander descendant, would have fair-skinned and blue/green-eyed babies! That surprise was plenty big and still blows me away every day I look at their beautiful faces.

My heart was absolutely bursting. Seriously. After having one baby, I truly thought it couldn't get any better and I couldn't possibly have any more room in my heart to share my love with another child. I called bullshit. I swore my girl was going to be my number-one child. Then, there in the operating room, it was most likely a chemically induced sensation, but as soon as my sweet boy was cut from my uterus, I immediately felt a warm wave start in my chest and radiate over my body. If I hadn't known any better, I would have sworn my heart literally expanded in my chest making room for my newest little love. He was perfect. Suddenly, I realised he was an even cuter baby than my daughter was!

After my beautiful, sweet boy arrived, we returned home, back to reality to find our mojo as a family of four. We soon came to realise the baby blues were only meant to last three to five days, and then the eight-week baby haze was bigger than eight weeks. My negative Nancy was up in my face and Natashia had left the building. Meanwhile, irrational negative Nancy had me hulled up in my bedroom with my baby, and I wouldn't leave my room or let anyone take him.

Irrational. Moody. Angry. Sad. Unpredictable. Unstable. Abrupt. Uncontrollable. Out of my damn mind! I knew all the things to do for myself, in theory, so I refused to get help because for some stupid reason I thought there was nothing they could tell me that I didn't already know. As the days passed, I felt like I was drowning in responsibility and failing at every aspect of my life. In fact, showering and brushing my hair were barely on my to-do list. I was feeling constantly tired, physically 'detached' from my surroundings, and in a state of constant generalised worry. I developed obsessive compulsive thoughts and/or behaviours with tasks I felt I was solely responsible for, declining any form of help from my loved ones. Everything was so serious, I didn't find the light, bright or fun side of anything. I wasn't eating, I wasn't sleeping, even when I wasn't up with my baby! I couldn't concentrate, and in general, I was just an awful human to be around. I felt like an empty shell of the human I once was. Like a cicada, my body had left my shell, leaving behind the perfect empty carcass that was my existence. I missed the girl I used to be.

My breaking point was seeing my two-and-a-half-year-old daughter speaking to Guy so disrespectfully, and all I heard come out of her mouth was the attitude and words of myself. It was like a good hard look in the mirror. Was I that horrible? How the fuck has my two-and-a-half-year-old daughter picked up on my poor behaviour before my grown-arse realised it? I am fucked. What has my poor husband had to endure? That was it for me. I felt such shame and guilt as a mother, a wife and as a decent human. We just spent tens of thousands of dollars to have a family, and here I am, resenting my responsibilities within it and feeling disgusted in myself for feeling this way. It was like a double punch to the face. Late that night, in a blubbering mess, ugly crying like Kim Kardashian, I got online and emailed a local postnatal depression support group and booked an appointment with my GP.

Sitting in the doctor's office, I completed the anxiety and depression checklist (K10), on which I scored highly. My GP suggested a mental health plan and thought, given my history of cancer, IVF, miscarriage and lack of maternity leave, that medication should be something I consider in my plan, along with professional help, talking with a psychologist specialising in postnatal depression (PND). The doctor asked me to go away and think about it for a couple of days and come back, check in and unpack my decision with her. I didn't want to do either of those things, but it was literally the definition of insanity thinking that I could just continue doing what I was doing and expect a different outcome. While I was hopeful this would happen, it was clearly an unrealistic expectation. To be blunt, I was in a dark place. I wanted the world to swallow me up. Yes, I loved my family, that was never a question, but I struggled to find *me*. I needed to implement something to change the path I was on, and it needed to be a big something. More importantly, accepting that only I could help myself out of this rut that I found myself stuck in. That miracle I was waiting for was not coming.

With a lot of Doctor Google, negative Nancy and discussions with Guy, it seemed what I had to do was as clear as day. So, I went back to my GP, got my referral for a PND specialist psychologist AND a script for sertraline, which is commonly known as the brand Zoloft. Deciding to take this was my second biggest internal battle. Second to seeking help in the first place. Despite working in the health care sector, being a huge advocate for mental health and even knowing all the amazing resources out there, here I was, putting all those stigmas upon myself thanks to Nancy! So, I did what works best for me … making it a logical decision. I had a big work project in the works. I'm talking a multimillion-dollar project to literally change the lives of those we would be looking after. This was literally a career and personal achievement I had to be on my game for 110%. At this point in time, work felt like it was the only thing in my life I confidently knew I was good at. So, logically, I knew my world did not have time for my wheels to fall off right now! If I continued to unravel, I was on a trajectory to a straitjacket. I had to get my shit together, and I needed whatever it was going to take to get me there and keep me on track.

I knew the antidepressants would take a good two to four weeks to be fully effective, however, I felt that time frame would pass much quicker than the wait I had until my first psychologist appointment, let alone the several appointments I would most likely require to unpack my thoughts and behaviours and identify and implement what would be suggested to me in my cognitive behavioural therapy (CBT). I knew I needed it all otherwise I seriously felt like I was on track to a one-way ticket to our local adult mental health unit. Given I had worked at the facility prior, this was a hard, non-negotiable NO for me.

The psychologist was a lot more beneficial than I gave credit for initially. Not only in identifying and unpacking that I am a massive perfectionist, but also that I am a giver. I knew that … but the psychologist assisted me in identifying that I give too much at times, and it can become detrimental to myself thus leading into my inability to look after my own needs. As the weeks passed by, we unpacked my history of abuse and cancer, and my inability to deal with those which all added to the situation I found myself in. I did find the psychologist sessions helpful in actively unpacking things as they occurred. Too often we put emotional stuff in the 'too-hard' or 'too-busy' basket and proceed forward. She assisted me in equipping myself with some tools and tactics to change my language and behaviours and show myself some kindness.

In one of the earlier sessions, my psychologist asked me if my family knew of my current situation. I went to answer with a bunch of words … but ultimately it boiled down to a simple no. No, I had hidden this away from the world. Other than Guy, Lisa was the only other human that saw me in my pit of disappear, and even then, that was only because one day was so bad, I couldn't get out of bed or stop crying and Guy called Lisa to come over and get my arse out of bed because he was at a loss with what he could do for me. I was mortified but grateful at the same time.

When I was diagnosed with cancer, I never had to tell anybody. Mum and Nat were with me when I received the news, and they did the rest. So, my psychologist tasked me with going to my family and telling them I was struggling and was on antidepressants. This seemed reasonable enough … until I had to do it. I ended up wimping out and sending it in a bulk message in our family group chats. I didn't want to feel their pity or disappointment. To my surprise, all the females in the family came back to me telling me they were either on antidepressants and/or were at some stage previously. Ironically, I felt sad that they couldn't have shared that with me prior, and yes, the irony is not lost on me. It appeared Nancy had one-upped me yet again.

Thankfully, my medication also assisted in fast-tracking me

back to a healthy reality. By no means do antidepressants change you in any way. You are still YOU – yes, strangely, people do believe they can magically change someone! I found my antidepressants took away the fog that was in my head. At the height of my PND, it was like I literally had become so indecisive I could barely make mundane everyday decisions. My meds removed that fog, allowing me to have clarity to make decisions. It also helped in controlling my reactions as I was finding most things I was responding to were over-the-top and emotional responses. The meds allowed enough clarity for me to respond logically. It's like my filter of appropriateness had been reinserted between my brain and mouth.

Fast-forward two years to now, I look back prior to having both my kids, and I can honestly say I was a very emotional responder in general. This led me to believe I most likely had some level of depression I was dipping in and out of since my cancer diagnosis. While we can never definitively say that, my psychologist believes it is likely. Two years on, I am still on my meds – I truly wouldn't have thought I would be, but you know what … I've accepted that is perfectly okay and probably for the best for everyone in my life! Right now, I have no desire to alter, decrease or stop my current plan … and no, I do not need your unsolicited advice on the matter *wink*.

To my mum friends, I see you. Politely disregarding that unsolicited advice, I feel you when you make the third dinner option that still no-one ate, I know your frustration when you feel you aren't going to make it to bedtime or that no-one listens to good-old mum. I know what it is to lose your shit multiple times a day because parenting is fucking hard. I hear you whispering under your breath, 'Are you fuckin' kidding me?' for the millionth time today. I see you trying to keep the mum guilt at bay. We have all been there. I see you. You are not alone.

PROJECT KIND

To those who struggle to breathe through the chaos of the daily grind. I see you. Those who can't muster up the energy to get dressed, the thought of leaving home so terrifying. I see you. You are not alone.

Be kind to yourself. You deserve love too.

2022 Nate Michael and Cadence Myee

LESSON 30: DITCH THE IMPOSTOR SYNDROME.

Self-growth is more than just growing, it is equally about what you outgrow and leave behind. It is only in this space you can truly live your authentic self.

I hate that, at some time or another, us women in business label ourselves as impostors. Impostor syndrome, for those lucky enough to not know, is loosely defined as doubting your abilities, feeling like a phoney or fraud and finding it difficult to accept your personal accomplishments. An extension of Nancy's handiwork, the term 'impostor phenomenon' was a concept developed by psychologists Pauline Rose Clance and Suzanne Imes in 1978 when the two women conducted a study focusing on high-achieving women and has been a belief spurred on for the decades since. There have been some big-name women who have expressed their experiences with these feelings including the former First Lady Michelle Obama.

I am not discounting the way an individual may feel; I can say I, too, have felt undeserving of past accolades, including most recently being named Canberra Businesswoman of the Year, however, I do feel as a society, we label unsure feelings as impostor syndrome, but if we just stop and unpack my most recent experience where I felt I wasn't worthy and didn't compare with my fellow finalists, these feelings, when I really sit in the moment, were discomfort because I was exactly that. Outside of my comfort zone. Celebrating my successes, putting myself out there wasn't my 'thing'. Those feelings do not make me an impostor. The label makes me an impostor. Practising swapping a negative for a positive, I could say I do feel uncomfortable, however, I am deserving. This success was not overnight, and it certainly was not easy; it was a success I worked hard for and continue to work hard for.

I do love that the view of this phenomenon is shifting. It may be at a snail's pace, but change is never easy. It is finally being realised by some amazing powerhouse women that the title 'impostor syndrome' implies there is something wrong with us and directs society's view toward fixing women, when reality is we should be fixing the environment. *Harvard Business Review* wrote an article in 2021 championing for diversity and inclusion[10] with the same sentiment I am portraying here. Seriously, this original phenomenon was founded in the seventies. Women's movement was happening, more women were entering the workforce and it was becoming the norm within society, however, homemaker life was still an expectation to uphold, so no wonder the women of the seventies felt like impostors. They were trying to enter a 'man's world', while still doing their society-placed 'woman duties'. If you ask me, that doesn't make them impostors, that makes them friggin' superheroes!

Feelings of impostor syndrome can manifest differently for each of us.

At work, it can be attributing our successes to luck rather than actual abilities and work ethic. At home, as a parent, it could be feeling clueless and unprepared, which can impact decision-making. At school, students might avoid speaking up or asking questions when they need assistance. In relationships, it can be feeling unworthy of affection. These feelings of self-doubt have the power to stir up a lot more emotion than we give credit for. That self-doubt becomes paralysing. Feelings such as anxiety and stress creep in and thus begins a vicious cycle.

So how does one overcome such feelings? You need to start asking some hard questions of yourself. You need to move past the icky feelings and become comfortable with confronting some of those deeply ingrained beliefs you hold about yourself. This can be so confronting and difficult if it is not something you were ever aware of having. What core beliefs do you hold of yourself? Do you feel worthy of love exactly as you are today? What do you envision to be worthy of your successes?

So, what do you do with that? How can you channel it into something factual?

- Share your feelings out loud with others. Chances are, your beliefs are irrational, and discussing these out aloud allows you to unpack them and realise your thoughts and facts do not necessarily align. Sometimes, simply saying it out loud is enough to recognise this – if not, the person you choose to speak with will most definitely clarify the situation for you.
- One step at a time. Don't focus on doing things perfectly, but rather, do things reasonably well and reward yourself for acting. I love me a vision board with all my rewards on there for when I reach my stepping stones. If it isn't in bite-size achievements, I'm not going to stick to it.
- Question your thoughts. Are your thoughts rational? Does it make sense to believe that you are a fraud, given everything that you know? Are you comparing? Stop comparing. Every time you compare yourself to others in a social situation, you will find some fault with yourself that is never a true measure as no two people are the same. We all come with different variables.
- List your strengths. Write down your accomplishments, your strengths, your *why*. Compare that with your self-assessment, and I am almost certain they will not add up, thus supporting the notion that your thoughts are irrational. Seeing what you

have achieved on paper can be overwhelming, but the facts don't lie.
- Social media cleanse. Forget the lemon detox diet, try the socials cleanse. It's a fact that the overuse of social media can be related to feelings of inferiority. This comes back to always comparing … Shut it down for a little bit and get outdoors.
- Stop fighting your feelings. Don't fight the feelings of not belonging. Instead, try to lean into and accept them. It's only when you acknowledge them that you can start to unravel those core beliefs that are holding you back, and the beauty in that is that's where the growth begins. No matter how much you feel like you don't belong, don't let that stop you from pursuing your goals. Keep going and refuse to be stopped.
- My favourite – turn impostor syndrome around. A true 'impostor' would never exhibit such feelings!

To truly abolish this awful label, leaders must collectively create a culture for women that addresses the systemic bias. Only by doing so can we reduce the experiences that culminate in this label of impostor syndrome. I'm not silly though, I know for the most part not all leaders are great leaders, however, you do not have to be the leader of your workplace or community to cultivate change. You can still champion to assist others in channelling healthy self-doubt into positive motivation simply by fostering a supportive culture. It starts with a simple step in the right direction to create systemic change. Be that change!

LESSON 31: LEVEL UP.

Levelling up is one of the most exhilarating feelings in the world. It's a process of consciously improving yourself in all aspects of life, and this is a lifelong process. It's like selecting a gaming character, each character in the game has a variety of skills which identifies if this is the character's strength or weakness. Unfortunately, humans don't come with a player profile overview and it's generally an internal review of self that identifies your strengths and weaknesses or areas you wish to improve. Levelling up can be levelling up any one of your strengths or weaknesses.

The small things you do daily impact your life the most. These are the things you do behind the scenes that no-one applauds you for. This is one common thread through every single motivational speaker you will ever google. Whether it's about getting your business off the ground, making that leap from a side-hustle to a full-time gig, upskilling your education, your social media content and marketing or simply wanting to be a good human … It is the basic things that create the solid foundations to later build upon. Consistency and showing up, having self-belief and pushing through the doubt is what gets you closer to the life you envision. This can change your life. Sometimes, it is about respecting yourself enough to know you deserve more and there is room for growth. Then, being brave enough to start. The real level up happens when you stop settling, stop people-pleasing and stop compromising your boundaries, and when you recognise your values and act accordingly.

Personal development is equally as important as formal education and professional development, and is my personal favourite. The day any one person can tell me they know all they need to know, I can show you someone who will never level up another day in their life.

Growth is always.

A continuous path of learning, absorbing, developing,

expanding, evolving, increasing. So, how do you know when you need to level up an area in your life? Most often it is a desire to be better at something. An example could be learning a second language. By the end of the year, you could be fluent in two languages. That right there is a level up!

My favourite kinds of level ups I not only love to experience but love to see others grow through are the mindset level ups. The benefits of these types of level ups are truly immeasurable. A mindset level up can be overcoming your inner critic, recognising the barrier you hold on yourself, realising your worth, accepting you do deserve that award and realising you have always been more than enough. They suddenly open your mind to the possibility of more. It is here, the level up becomes a *glow-up!* I refer to mindset level ups as glow-ups because when these truly occur, you radiate. It is undeniable. You start seeing yourself differently and so will others.

If your journey to self-reflection and self-development is a relatively new one, or perhaps a journey you've travelled for many years but is in need of a review, then implementing a good old-fashioned stocktake of your life is the perfect place to start. An example of this, for me, is I have consistently levelled up my career achievements and business achievements every single year. I feel my personal development and mindset has improved over the past couple of years. My physical fitness, however, has much work to be done. To really take stock of my personal attributes and reflect on what I have achieved and what I can improve, I implement my stocktake of the areas in my life that I feel are important. I then apply a number between one and ten to what I feel that attribute sits at. Remember, everyone's attributes will vary, and this links in with what we each consider to be core values and those non-negotiable areas in life. It could range from connections with people, career, family, education, fitness, learning another language, dancing, hobbies, sports. For me, the areas I actively take stock of are:

Business achievements	8 – I'm not done yet!
Career achievements	10 – pretty proud so far
Mindset	7 – I've come a long way
Professional development	5 – want to improve
Family time	7 – need to improve
Friends time	1 – want to improve
ME time	0 – non-existent
Fitness	3 – need to improve
Health	5 – need to improve

I would love for my family time to be rated at a ten, and friends and me time to be much improved. It comes back to that juggling act called balance. This list tells me, if I want to improve these areas, I need to make some life adjustments to cater to those needs to allow a level up. Most often this comes back to time. Nobody ever has enough time to do all the things we seem to be so busy doing. The best way I have found to combat this is to create myself a twenty-four-hour schedule. Every human has twenty-four hours in their day. Sometimes, seeing those hours on paper and how exactly you are spending them highlights areas for improvement.

For me, I am a mum, a wife, a sister, a daughter, a daughter-in-law, a sister-in-law, a friend – I try to maintain all of those relationships, while also running a multimillion-dollar twenty-four seven community nursing company, managing seventy-plus employees, clients, plus four other businesses, three of which I am director of, ensuring the kids are happy and healthy, attending their social events like birthdays, play dates, swimming lessons, gymnastics and cousin play dates. Getting myself to the hairdresser, my lash queen and fitting in a healthy diet and exercise. So here is how I make it fit …

I don't.

Here is a brief overview of my daily tasks that can either support or block my abilities to work on the attributes I wish to level up.

	Mon	Tue	Wed	Thu	Fri	Sat	Sun
6-7am	family	family	family	family	family	family	family
7-8am	family	family	family	family	family	family	family
8-9am	exercise	exercise	exercise	work	work	family	family
9-12pm	work	work	work	work	work	family	family
12-4pm	work	work	work	work	work	family	family
4-5pm	work	work	work	exercise	exercise	exercise	exercise
5-6pm	family	family	family	family	family	family	family
7-8pm	family	family	family	family	family	work	work
8-9pm	husband	work	work	husband	family	husband	family
9-10pm	husband	work	work	husband	husband	husband	husband
10-11pm	sleep	sleep	sleep	sleep	sleep	sleep	sleep
11-12am	sleep	sleep	sleep	sleep	sleep	sleep	sleep
12-6am	sleep	sleep	sleep	sleep	sleep	sleep	sleep

My twenty-four-hour period is full, and friends and me time doesn't even enter the week, and while exercise is allocated, it's always the first to get cut if I need to do anything else. Running a twenty-four seven business means technically we could receive a call at any time with a disaster we need to action immediately. But the flipside to that is, I can coordinate said emergency from anywhere in the world from my mobile phone. Balance! So, although I may have work tasks to be done during the standard business hours, sometimes I can get them done from the chair at the hairdressers or the treadmill at the gym or a sandy beach in Fiji. Is my week full? Yes, but if I review the schedule and begin to shade out what duties and tasks can be considered negotiable, suddenly, if I want to make something a higher priority, I have space to make that happen. After all, it is only myself that is responsible for my time and how I spend it. With all my new-found pink-zone possibilities, I can concentrate on getting myself to the gym more, I can schedule that catch-up coffee with the friend I've continually cancelled on, and I can fit it in without feeling I've had to sacrifice something.

Another habit I swear by is locking in your appointments. Book your hairdresser appointments for the year … get a lash subscription … a regular PT gym session on the same days, same times each week. The benefits of this habit are plentiful.

1. You have your shit locked down! One less thing you need to worry about coordinating between school pick-ups, board meetings and rostering.
2. You know exactly when you are not available when scheduling your twenty-four-hour roster (for example, my two allocated orange boxes on Tuesdays and Thursdays are standing weekly PT sessions).

	Mon	Tue	Wed	Thu	Fri	Sat	Sun
6-7am	family	family	family	family	family	family	family
7-8am	family	family	family	family	family	family	family
8-9am	exercise	exercise	exercise	work	family	family	family
9-12pm	work	work	work	work	work	family	family
12-4pm	work	work	work	work	work	family	family
4-5pm	work	work	work	exercise	exercise	exercise	exercise
5-6pm	family	family	family	family	family	family	family
7-8pm	family	family	family	family	family	work	work
8-9pm	husband	work	work	husband	family	husband	work
9-10pm	husband	work	work	husband	husband	husband	husband
10-11pm	sleep	sleep	sleep	sleep	sleep	sleep	sleep
11-12am	sleep	sleep	sleep	sleep	sleep	sleep	sleep
12-6am	sleep	sleep	sleep	sleep	sleep	sleep	sleep

3. You are supporting small local businesses in doing so.
4. You are committed to your self-care because of the convenience of the rolling booking.

For me, managing this is a level up in my eyes. Areas I always look to level up include meaningful connections with loved ones, fitness and mindset. So, when I can coordinate and schedule time to do that, I feel like a grown-arse woman succeeding at adulting. Your level up will be hard for some people to watch. Do it anyway. The more you commit to and love your decisions, the less you will need others to validate them.

Realising you deserve more and wanting better for yourself is the ultimate upgrade on all levels. Go on, let yourself glow!

LESSON 32: KINDNESS ABOVE ALL ELSE.
I truly believe kindness is the most beautiful gift in the world. It is a language that has no boundaries and an effect so far-reaching it can change lives. Kindness is a very powerful tool and so, sadly, it is often undervalued. It literally costs nothing, but the benefits can be immeasurable. The thing I love most about kindness is you truly can't fake it. Well, you can, but the entire world around you will know it because kindness is one of the most authentic, selfless things a person can give.

I have spent my life and career showing kindness to my friends and family, staff and those we care for. We could and should all be kinder. Kinder to ourselves, to others, to the planet. I'm not claiming to be a saint of kindness or anything of the sort, but there is so much we can do to show kindness. We operate in such a fast-paced environment that we often don't stop to appreciate others. Showing kindness to others is the perfect starting point in self-growth and a by-product of that is the potential to provide you with some positivity in return.

Kindness is not to be mistaken for common courtesy. Common courtesy is not a favour or a nice gesture, but rather, an expectation not to behave like an arse. However, common courtesy is determined in the eye of the beholder; a generalisation of this would include your basic manners and exchanging pleasantries with others. Kindness is that little extra and often expressed 'just because'. Kindness is shown to others for no other reason than to be kind.

In our world, of a few things I am certain. Respect should be given. Trust should be earnt. Kindness should be free. Often, kindness is based on respect. Now, I know a lot of people strongly believe respect is earnt. Food for thought ... perhaps this is the reason we live in such an unkind world — if kindness is only shown to those that people choose to exclusively show respect.

As a teenager, I was told all too often by adults that I had to earn their respect. A common statement across high school. But I disagree. I believe every person, regardless of how that person chooses to live their life, deserves the human decency of respect. According to the *Oxford English Dictionary*, 'respect' in the noun sense of the word means 'a feeling of deep admiration for someone or something elicited by their abilities, qualities or achievements'. Now, I believe this is the core definition most people hold. However, the *Oxford English Dictionary* verb definition for respect is 'to have due regard for someone's feelings, wishes or rights'. Now, this is where my view has grown from. Why shouldn't every person, whether you know them or not, be afforded the right to be treated respectfully?

Shouldn't every human be afforded your respect, and this should only change if that person does something that adversely affects you directly physically, emotionally or ethically? Perhaps the world would be a lot kinder if we were all a lot more respectful. Kindness, just like respect, is a no self-serving purpose, just genuine thoughtfulness. Small-scale kindness I have been able to give within my means has ranged from passing on my paid metre parking ticket to a stranger digging in their wallet for coins at the pay station to taking in 'baseball imports' – a term meaning an international baseball player that has come to our local baseball club to contribute within the club. A part of that process is that a family usually billet the player for the season the player is visiting.

Guy and I were in our first year together, had just moved out into our first tiny two-bedroom unit and had a spare room to offer. Enter Johnny. He was from Pennsylvania and had come to Canberra to play baseball with the Bandits. He moved in with us rent-free, bill-free, grocery-free. We took him to open a bank account and essentially settle within Australian life. In return, we asked Johnny to be responsible for preparing dinner just one night a week. Guy and I were not rich, in fact, we were saving for IVF; however, we saw the opportunity we could provide to for Johnny simply by showing kindness. We celebrated an American-themed Halloween and Thanksgiving to honour his traditions and he joined in with my immediate family for Christmas celebrations. In fact, we even housed his American girlfriend who came to celebrate Christmas with us as well.

The baseball club arranged a little second-hand car for him, and we got Johnny a job doing landscaping with my brother-in-law throughout the season. I remember, after Johnny received his first payslip for one week, he came running out of his room in a state of panic certain that the bank had made a mistake with his account as the balance amount had too many numbers. That first weeks' worth of pay was more than Johnny had seen in his bank account

PROJECT KIND

within his entire life! He came from a first-world country, but a country paying minimum wage and based on tips. This opportunity provided Johnny with the ability to change his future. By the time baseball season was over, Johnny was beyond thrilled at the amount of money he was able to make and save, believing it had set him up for life – and all it cost me was giving up a spare room in our unit that was vacant anyway!

A great example of large-scale kindness includes the #ClapForCarers campaign, which saw people across the whole of the UK come together to show their appreciation for health care workers during 2019-2020 of the COVID-19 pandemic. This simple act of kindness let all of those working on the front line know that they were appreciated and hopefully built up their spirits and boosted positive morale in what was such a trying and tiresome time.

Another beautiful cause on our Australian shores is the '1000 Hearts' project. With the simple intent to spread some love and compassion. The founder, Sarah, created this cause hand-stitching one thousand pocket hearts for people who nominated themselves as distributors to give away in random acts of kindness. What was created to be a one-off small act of kindness became a global community where kindness and connection are valued, and hearts are healed. Sarah's simple and kind idea has touched the lives of many far and wide including those impacted by the Orlando nightclub shooting, the bombing in Manchester and the Grenfell Tower inferno in London, just to name a few.

I personally admire Sarah's single goal to create a kinder world. I loved this concept so much when I came across it, I had to implement this project for our National Community Care team of carers and nurses to spread the kindness across our Canberra health care system, gifting the handmade felt hearts to residents and patients in need of some kindness. Kindness doesn't have to cost anything though, and it can be shown in several ways including:

Sharing your positive thoughts. When you appreciate the effort someone has made, or simply think they look nice, tell them. Regardless of who they are. A friend, an employee, even a stranger. By expressing how you feel, you may also see your relationship grow in a positive way. I guarantee it will cost you nothing and you will have made the person's day.

Listening more. Really listen. Actively listen. One thing we can all do more of is listen. Listen without judgement, and sometimes even without response, and enable others to trust you to simply listen. Try pausing before you speak and choose words with positive intention when you might be asked to provide input.

Appreciating the good feels. There are many things that we are wired to feel good about. This includes the endorphins we receive from showing kindness to others. This includes boosting serotonin and dopamine, which are neurotransmitters in the brain that give you feelings of satisfaction and wellbeing when you show kindness to others.

Setting a good example. Life gives us many chances to do good and be kind, so when you take those opportunities, you show others why it's a more beneficial choice. That in itself can be very rewarding. A perfect example of this, in my house, is a poor children's toy giveaway. Before any event where our kids may be gifted presents, we ask them to find ten things we can regift to the less fortunate. We then let the kids come with us to see the process through and experience the gesture.

Volunteering yourself. Donating your experience, time or money to good causes is one of the kindest acts you can do.

PROJECT KIND

Whether you are supporting local charities, volunteering as a committee member in an organisation, supporting friends or family, the simple acts of helping someone move house, running an errand for someone or babysitting for a friend can all be incredibly kind.

Lending or gifting. Another way to be kind to others is to share your belongings or buy a gift that the person will appreciate. Lending a book can spread knowledge and sharing your clothes can reduce the demand for new items. A gift of something useful will be welcomed. Both our children's clothes have gone on the be decent hand-me-downs to cousins Lani, Jayce and baby Lewis.

Daily kindness. One easy way to act kinder is to take stock of other people, wherever you are. Give up your seat on public transport to someone in need, give a smile to a passer-by. Say hi to a walker you pass every day. These small acts may not be rewarded but may diffuse any negative thoughts or situations that arise from not acting in a kind way.

Reconnecting. Call, email or text a friend you haven't spoken to in a while. Ask how they are, let them know you are thinking of them. Sometimes a simple text 'thinking of you' reaches further than you think.

Random acts. This type of kindness is reserved for perfect strangers. Writing a letter or sending a care package to an elderly or vulnerable person in your local hospice. Putting a Christmas card in the mailbox of the house that puts on spectacular Christmas displays for your enjoyment. Paying for somebody's parking ticket or someone else's petrol at the station. It is about paying it forward.

Self-kindness. This kindness is the most important. Being kind to yourself. Cutting yourself some slack. Looking after *you!* Self-kindness is the first stage of obtaining the skill of authentic kindness.

LESSON 33: BE UNAPOLOGETICALLY AUTHENTIC.

Stop apologising for being YOU. Understanding how to be your authentic self is essential in the process of creating yourself a meaningful life with meaningful and genuine relationships. Seems simple enough, but in the fast-paced social-media-mad world we live in today, finding authenticity amongst people can sometimes be difficult. Many people struggle with expressing their emotions openly and honestly, and instead, we spend our time downplaying our victories and apologising for who we are, shrinking ourselves to make others feel comfortable and filtering the shit out of our flaws.

Authenticity is about speaking and living freely and honestly in a healthy way that allows you to make decisions that align with your core. This allows you to be vulnerable and open but in a strengthening sense, along with setting boundaries to protect that vulnerability. It allows you begin to build a life that brings you meaning and joy. In doing so, you inspire those around you to do the same. In psychologist Brené Brown's 2010 Ted Talk, *The Power of Vulnerability*[11], she explains how authenticity is an essential part of developing meaningful relationships. When people show up with their vulnerabilities, it allows them to truly connect with and feel close to others. You don't need to be who you *think* people want you to be. If somebody wants you to be something you are not, the problem does not lie within you, my dear …

Ironically, fear of rejection often prevents people from expressing their authentic selves. So instead, we put our armour on, the walls go up, the mask goes on, we apply filters to our words and social media, we guard ourselves and fear takes over. This self-preservation mode activates, and we change our behaviour and filter our responses to fit in. When you are not authentic, it shows. People around you become disengaged with what you have to say because you have essentially lost your credibility. Your relationships appear forced, and in business, you begin to sound salesy.

Authentic business: When it comes to business, it is always the authentically operated businesses that find success long before those that don't operate this way. The irony is not lost on me. I think most of us that have built businesses started off as that home-based small business creating the illusion we are grander in scale than reality. There is nothing wrong with this approach, but it does need to be done authentically. It still needs to be your voice. Your mission. Your reasoning and your *why* in creating that illusion, or as I like to call it – a manifestation to the reality that will be.

When you run your business in a way that is not authentic, it becomes forced, rigid and out of touch, and your target audience can smell this a mile away. Yes, we genuinely need to make that sale and get cashflow happening, but if this is the sole focus on why you are doing what you are doing, and you are not having any success, I would strongly suggest a review of your business mission and values to realign yourself with your business goals.

When you operate authentically, your target audience (being your consumers) see you as a human, not just a computer-operated machine that has no room for error. This means when an error may pop up, there is a lot more understanding from the consumer. To operate authentically in business is to share your story. To share your *why*. Why do you do what you do? How do you do what you do? Why does what you do cost what it costs? When your consumer understands these factors, they can make informed choices which are more likely going to turn into meaningful connections resulting in profitable sales, simply by being you! Don't get me wrong, there is always a need for that professional boundary, but when you suddenly go from what looks like an automated online store to a human-run business, feelings are evoked from your audience and the game changes.

Personal Authenticity: When it comes to personal authenticity, often we get lost along our journey and a good reflection is needed to take stock of what is important to each of us. For me, motherhood hit the reset button and allowed me to revisit what my authentic self looks like. In 2019, diagnosed with postnatal depression, I felt I had lost myself. I wasn't authentically me within my own home, let alone any social or professional setting. I felt as if my PND had beaten me into submission. In the pits of my identity crisis, I was unsure who I was. Feeling like my only identity was dairy milk cow to a newborn, a shitty mum and a non-existent wife to my husband. Some days, all I wanted was for the earth to open and swallow me whole. This was a whole lot of fear talking. Through my cognitive behavioural therapy, I had to rewire my habits to find myself again. I felt I had lost my way. Again …

Through my PND treatment sessions, I was able to step up and take responsibility for my actions, and more importantly, my inactions during this period of my life. This is where my reset could occur, and I could actively start being true to myself, and in this point of my life, it was rediscovering what that life looked like for me now that I was a mum of two while running several businesses. Yes, this example is quite a large one to unpack, but it could be something as simple as wondering why you are still in the job you have been doing for fifteen years. It is only natural over that time, you have grown, evolved, seen many others come and go, and perhaps that job requires the level up you are searching for.

Cultivating authenticity: One of the biggest core values Guy and I actively practice instilling within our children has been based around the idea of raising our kids to be authentic. By doing this, it keeps us accountable as Mum and Dad to also operate authentically. Let's face it, all children are born into our world without fear or worry. These are emotions the child learns. So, we wanted to do our part to ensure we could give them their best possible start within our means to do so. It wasn't going to cost thousands of dollars on private school education or extracurricular activities. It is free and simple. We implemented three simple, but core, non-negotiable house rules.

Be kind. Be brave. Be true.

Be kind to others and yourself. Be brave and always try something at least once. Be true to yourself and honest to others. In hopes we have equipped our babies with strong values and moral compasses to walk their own paths later in life, as authenticity happens when you talk the talk and walk the walk and to do all of that unapologetically. Our favourite Dr Suess quote in our house is, 'Today you are You, that is truer than true. There is no one alive who is Youer than You.'[12]

This rule is something we implement for ourselves too. It ensures accountability in confirming our words, actions and behaviours consistently match our individual core identity. It brings awareness and raises internal questions about who you are and what you choose to stand for. Not just today, but every day. In doing this, we have more humans living their lives authentically, and this becomes the norm, making it easier for oncoming generations to do the same.

***

Authenticity is not to be mistaken for pushing your opinions on others as the only opinions that matter. Sometimes it is associated with the 'authentic' person not giving a shit beyond their own opinion, but this is not the case. Within the workplace, authenticity doesn't compromise your professionalism in the real sense. If you are playing the game to get ahead then yes, of course, you can expect to alienate yourself, creating an atmosphere of competitiveness rather than collaboration. However, the idea of being authentic within your workspace is when you are equally encouraging in opening a dialogue, actively listening to and valuing the ideas of all employees in a respectful manner. Just because you are the boss, it doesn't make you right, it doesn't make you above any other person on your team. The day you begin operating like this, is the day you lose your team. They don't need to be bossed; they need to be led. Be a leader. Without each members' input and role within your team, you would have no team to effectively lead.

Another aspect of living authentically is self-acceptance. How many successes have you had that you have downplayed in fear of misconception by others? Neil Pasricha is a *New York Times* million-copy bestselling author of *The Book of Awesome* series and *The Happiness Equation,* thought leader for the next generation, and one of the most popular TED speakers in the world. In his book, *You Are Awesome*, Pasricha describes authenticity as 'following your heart, and you putting yourself in places and situations and in conversations that you love and that you enjoy. You meet people that you like talking to. You go places you've dreamt about. And you end up following your heart and feeling very fulfilled.'[13] So, naturally, it would make sense that authenticity supports one to live in their truest and rawest form … unapologetically.

Everything shifts when you stop living for others and their approval and start giving yourself the permission you deserve to be exactly who you are. Embracing everything that makes you proud to be you will allow you to advocate for yourself. I've spent a career advocating for others, and now I finally do it for myself and assert my worth. I've learnt to step into my power and become the most authentic version of me.

COURAGE
IT WAS ALWAYS WITHIN

Courage. [kur-ij, kuhr-]

noun

the quality of mind or spirit that enables a person to face difficulty, danger, pain, etc., without fear, bravery.

Obsolete. the heart as the source of emotion.

'A comfort zone is a beautiful and safe place, but nothing ever grows there.'
— Natashia Telfer

LESSON 34: SHINE BRIGHT.

Mayflies are freshwater insects that literally start as an egg, turn into a naiad, emerge from the water, fully mature into adults, mate and lay at least four hundred to ten thousand eggs before dying. This is all within a twenty-four-hour lifespan. Twenty-four hours! Do you think mayflies are worried about mundane topics? Do you think Mayfly Martha is worried Mayfly Melissa has brighter wings than her? Do you think Mayfly Maggie is worried her house on the water reed is a mess? No way, they live fast and free. They have twenty-four hours to live their best lives and do not waste a single moment of it.

Another natural marvel is fireflies. They are incredible winged bioluminescent creatures. This literally means they create their own light. They don't steal it from anyone else, they don't dim their own lights or the light of others. They aren't profiting off selling their light. They simply live by the beautiful phrase 'you do you'. One of the kindest things you can do for yourself is allowing yourself to shine authentically.

This comes back to a concept that we must be modest over egotistical. There is a common idea amongst us that you are either humble and modest OR an egomaniac. So, when we pick what lane we wish to be perceived in when carving out our identities and places in the world, many of us pick the humble and modest lane. However, why do we stereotypically assume there are only those two options? I sat in the humble and modest lane for most of my life to date. Until I finally realised there is a lane in-between humble and egomaniac. It is in this middle lane where authenticity, courage, kindness and confidence reside.

So, why the middle lane? Because we are all capable of achieving some pretty damn amazing things. The humble lane are the quiet achievers. These amazing achievements often go uncelebrated and unrecognised. In the egomaniac lane, the achievements are shoved in everyone's faces to the point no-one enjoys hearing it while we humbly worry you might blow away with the number of tickets you have on yourself – but then there is the middle lane. This is where it is at. You can comfortably acknowledge your achievements. Celebrate them without feeling shamed or undeserving. The middle lane allows you that space to say, 'Damn straight I did that! Go me!'

This middle lane is only something I discovered and crossed over to in 2020, and it has without a doubt been the biggest game-changer of my life. In the height of COVID-19, I utilised this time to truly take inventory of my life, and it literally smacked me in the face. I have done some amazing things in my life … and I let each of those things pass by, not allowing myself a moment to recognise my achievements or celebrate my wins. So, as the following year approached, I vowed to make it the year of ME.

I proceeded with caution, but I proceeded! That was the key to all facets of my self-growth. It started with identifying my feelings when others around me shine. What do you feel? Is it jealousy that they are in a place you are not? Is it a proud feeling because you know what it takes to get that? Perhaps it's a sting of defeat as you project this inward in a negative sense, but you don't know why because you hadn't really sat with the feeling until now? Regardless, the feels you get in these situations, acknowledging your ability or inability to shine a light on what areas you may need to progress, is progress within itself. For me, I am always proud of my family and friends' achievements. I feel so proud to know them, to play a small part in their life, even if it has nothing to do with the accolade received. Their wins and successes provide me with all the warm fuzzy feels of excitement for my loved ones.

Unfortunately, the reality is, people often get threatened when other people shine their light on the world. This troubles me, even more so when businesswomen do it to other businesswomen. Our role as leaders is to empower, not try to bring them down. As women in business, we face enough barriers, each other shouldn't be one of them, but unfortunately, we can't control the actions of others. We can, however, certainly do our part when it comes to doing things for ourselves and ensuring we don't allow others to dim our light. These five key points have been winners for me each time I feel my light may be bothering someone else:

1. **Kindness. Always.** It is always easiest to snap back when someone attacks you. But at what cost? What does that bring? All it confirms is that you are allowing yourself to engage in a situation that has no good outcome. You are suddenly refocusing your time and energy on all the wrong areas in your life and that the person has successfully disrupted your glow. By

showing kindness, you are displaying a strength of leadership and character on a much higher level.

2. **Ask the questions.** Exploring how or why the criticism is being directed at you can unpack a lot. Firstly, it is important to know not all criticism is bad, and we can grow from constructive criticism when we show humility and ask the questions to allow us to understand. Sometimes, when asking the questions, it may also become apparent that the criticism is about the idea or method of work, or more personal, being about the individual.

3. **Disengage.** Let's face it, sometimes we just do not have the physical time or mental capacity to spend on those who consistently attempt to dim our light. Sometimes, those repeat offenders do not deserve your time and energy if they continue to be an energy drainer. Remember your time and mental health are the most precious currency we can hold, so disengaging in this kind of behaviour is always acceptable.

4. **Do good.** The best way to be empowered is to empower others. Nobody becomes a successful leader by beating their team into submission. There is no ratio of success allowed within one space. We can equally shine and equally support each other. It is also worth noting, no single person I have ever had the pleasure of knowing has created their success completely single-handed. I may have been honoured as Canberra Businesswomen of the Year 2021, but I have an entire team of kick-arse individuals who all contribute to the success of the business and in bringing my vision to life every single day. This award is equally contributed to by their amazing efforts.

5. **Compassion.** Always remember not every person has the knowledge and experiences you have had. Our past experiences are aways contributing factors to our behaviours and

future responses. Remembering this when we intercept that light-dimming person allows us to remain compassionate and see past the surface. Most often, the discomfort in this situation is the discomfort of the person throwing shade on your glow.

***

Lisa has always been one of my biggest cheerleaders and is always there supporting and shining a torch on me at any opportunity that presents. Most recently, Lisa secretly nominated me on Australian Nine Network's *Today* show with a segment called 'Random Acts of Kindness'. The purpose of the segment was to recognise selfless humans within our Australian community, and in return, the *Today* show awarded the nominee with their own random act of kindness. Oh, of course, I knew nothing about what was going on. Lisa and Guy had concocted a plan telling me I had to be dressed like I was going out for a work lunch … but ready to go at seven in the morning. Not knowing what was going on was killing me! I'm surprised Guy didn't break under the pressure because I was relentless in my countless interrogation questions. Lisa was late in picking me up. However, this was nothing out of the ordinary.

A little after 7am, I received a phone call. I was a little perplexed. It was Karl Stefanovic on the phone asking me how my morning was going. Thankfully, Ally Langdon stepped in and began to explain why they were calling me. I was directed to go to my front door, and I opened it to find Lisa, my sister Jayde, a camera man and a sound tech on my front doorstep. As the events would unfold, it turned out Lisa had nominated me for my efforts in the establishment of Alex's House and more recently, having repurposed two hundred of my subscription boxes into sunshine boxes I had posted out across the nation to those needing a little sunshine, as most of the nation was in COVID-19 lockdown at the time.

Both acts I was now being recognised for, and had photos splashed across national television. I had done this for the good of the recipients with no intent of getting a reward of my own. As such, when Lisa was standing on my doorstep telling the nation how amazing she thinks I am, she literally made me cry on national television, and Nine Network believed my selfless acts of kindness deserved the grand prize of $15,000. This was such a random experience I couldn't help but feel like that impostor again. I felt like I was just doing my job. It didn't deserve any airtime, let alone monetary value!

It took me a few days to sit with this experience, let it soak in and reflect. In doing this I was able to separate myself from the act. I came to realise and accept that the gesture that was rewarded was deserving. I can see why I was recognised for simply showing kindness to others.

2021 was the year I decided to start consciously backing myself and allowing myself to shine. In doing this, my world as I knew it completely shifted. My husband was finally able to resign from his permanent position within the public service industry because we were solid in our community company. I was nominated for a flurry of awards and even put myself forward for a couple. Writing my application for this was invigorating, noting my achievements in black and white. This reflective process was a win to me and a great way to take stock of my wins. To go on to be listed as a finalist, let alone a winner, was simply beyond.

I won awards! I put myself out there and I won awards. AusMumpreneur recognised me in their award placing me bronze in 'Business Excellence', bronze in 'Health and Wellbeing' and gold in 'B2B Business Services'. Next was Canberra Women in Business Awards. I was a finalist in the 'Social Impact Award' and won the prestigious title of 'Canberra Businesswoman of the Year'. The ripple effect this had was beyond nailing an acceptance speech or two. It shut down every shred of doubt I ever held onto. I could do this. I am good at this. Maybe I do know what I am doing, after all!

This realisation brought me connections beyond my wildest dreams and friendships I have come to cherish. It provided a platform for additional exposure for both my business brands and my personal brand through radio interviews and podcasts. So many podcast guest appearances. My businesses received more online traffic, and my community team continued to expand and provided us with a platform to reach our cause even further in our bid to make systemic change. On a personal level, I was provided the opportunity to be an International Women's Day guest speaker and panel member, committee member for organisations that align with my core values, magazine cover girl for a local mag, and a joint book collaboration with other amazing kick-arse AusMumpreneurs which would become our book titled *Courage & Confidence*[14] and of course signing with Women Changing the World Press to have the creative freedom to pull this book together.

So, my wise words of wisdom on this topic: Stop letting your potential go to waste because you don't feel ready enough or because you feel others will be uncomfortable. Allowing yourself to shine is a game-changer and suddenly your level-up game is strong, and next thing you know, you want everyone around you to shine and begin championing for their light to shine bright too. The world needs your light, so allow yourself to shine.

2021 Canberra Weekly Magazine Cover: Businesswomen of the Year

LESSON 35: NOTHING GROWS IN A COMFORT ZONE.

In all the laps around the sun I have completed, I have been faced with many experiences beyond my comfort zone. Doing things that are just beyond your comfort zone is when growth can begin. In my case, often my experiences were thrust upon me beyond my control and consent, however, there have also been times in which I have made an informed decision to allow myself to grow. To invoke growth, you need to seize opportunities and create your opportunities. This usually entails doing things that are uncomfortable and unfamiliar to you. It is taking a leap of faith to achieve your goals. You can't rely on others to push you outside of your comfort zone. At the end of the day, it is up to you to decide and act on what kind of life you want to live, who you want to be and the legacy you want to leave behind. When that zone becomes familiar and no longer uncomfortable, it's time to extend again.

***

When I started my first business, National Community Care, I did not have the faintest idea about how to run a business, much less how to be an 'employer'. Just like parenthood, there is no manual you are given, you simply figure it out as you go. Did I know what I was doing when I started? No way. Have I made errors? Hell yes, I have. Over seven years of operation, National Community Care has grown from myself solely delivering client services and writing policies, to Lisa and me expanding to an office of eight and a community team of seventy-plus. Within the health care industry, there is no room for complacency. I am very familiar with identifying my zone and acknowledge that a lot of the 'work stuff' sits outside of my comfort zone. I've learnt to accept this because it is only here I know I will never become complacent with what really matters, and because of this, my company has had the growth it has. From the introduction of new governance requirements, I have led the company into expansion, accepting the challenges we are faced with, taking risks, and furthermore, I have utilised this platform to encourage the same change in others across my team of staff and clients. I have gone on to support each of them in championing for extending their zones.

Today, I have been guest speaker at several events within the industry, in women in business groups and a handful of award acceptance speeches. When I first started National Community Care, public speaking was the most terrifying thing I could possibly think of. There was an ACT Government Healthier Work conference Lisa and I were invited to speak at. Lisa knew this was light-years beyond my comfort zone. She wrote the speech and identified which parts I would say. We got up there on the stage and Lisa began. It came to my part, and I absolutely froze still. Without opening my mouth, I made a two-syllable noise *'nah-ah'* indicating to Lisa I wasn't going to speak. Thankfully, Lisa and I are soul sisters, and she totally got my lingo and inability to speak. Lisa glided through with ease, not a single person in the crowd knew otherwise. After all was said (or not said) and done, I reflected on this experience. My choice to not speak was because I knew it was beyond my zone, but I didn't want it to be anymore. I also knew I was the only person who could change that by making a different choice the next time. I didn't know exactly how I would do that, but I knew it would be by doing more than I did on this particular day, and that in itself was the beginning of my public speaking growth and the rumblings of a little courage and confidence bubbling under the surface.

Now, there is always something beyond every person's comfort zone, regardless of how confident or accomplished someone may appear. It is about identifying your perceived risks versus the possible rewards. For example, overcoming my fear of spiders has no reward for me that improves my daily living, so I am more than happy to leave spiders outside of my comfort zone. When it comes to things that *can* improve my daily living, then I want to do just that! Improve. Just because it is uncomfortable, doesn't mean it shouldn't be done.

How do you step out into the unknown?

Identify.

To do just that, you must become aware of what lies within and beyond your comfort zone. This allows you to clarify what it is exactly that you wish to achieve. Start with identifying the parameters of your zone. You need to become familiar with where your comfort lies in order to know where you need to explore. Ask yourself these questions: *When was I last uncomfortable? How did that present? What was it that made me uncomfortable?* This identifies your tell-tale signs of when you may be uncomfortable. This is where you want to be!

Shift.

Next it is about changing your patterns of thought. Extending your comfort zone includes growth in mindset. If you have a fixed mindset, not open to change, you will need to develop your growth mindset. Much like the old saying 'you can't teach an old dog new tricks'. Only, you can, on the provision the dog is willing to learn. Just like when dealing with your inner critic, it is about shifting the intensity of your language. For example, if a comfort zone included 'I can't ask for that pay rise', but instead of 'I can't', it is about changing the narrative to 'I can't ask for that pay rise *YET*'. This allows you to consider the idea of stepping beyond your comfort to create the change that needs to occur and implementing actions between now and asking for said pay raise to make it happen.

Reframe.
So, you have the 'I can't' and 'yet' language on the radar. Next up is reframing the idea of what a comfort zone is. Naturally, the assumption is a place of comfortability, safety, protection, familiarity. To those who have shifted and reframed their comfort zones, this place becomes associated with the idea of being stationary, stagnant, still, motionless, lifeless, static, dull. When this reframing occurs, you realise this zone is not where you want to be at all. It's a place of nothing living as nothing grows in the zone of comfort.

Acknowledge.
If familiar is where you like to live, often revisiting and acknowledging some of your achievements is a great reminder of the possibilities you have. Accomplishments are often made because you stepped beyond your comfort zone. Acknowledging your past achievements is a perfect example of times you have expanded your comfort zone and survived! This tells you: you can do it. It is possible and you are the proof of that. It is also about acknowledging that both fear and courage are equally required to grow, for without fear, we become reckless, and without courage, we stay still.

Proceed.
Whether it is a crawl, one small step or a giant leap into the unknown, it is still the beginning of something new. Regardless of the outcome, you have immediately expanded your comfort zone. Well done!

Learn.

Learn from the experience regardless of the outcome. There is always a lesson in the experience for you to take away and grow from. What worked well? What could you have done better? What do you think stopped you from succeeding? How can you overcome that barrier next time? What is the silver lining of this experience?

LESSON 36: YOU ALREADY HAVE EVERYTHING YOU NEED.

As Glinda the good witch of Oz once said, 'You've always had the power, my dear, you just had to learn it for yourself.' Most of society equate courage with fearlessness. The assumption is courage enables a person to face difficulty, danger or pain without fear but that's a faulty interpretation. In fact, courage is acting despite the fear within. Courage is the willingness to respond despite any feels you may have. The Cowardly Lion, in the 1939 movie *The Wizard of Oz*, was told this sentiment by the wonderful Wizard of Oz: 'All you need is confidence in yourself. There is no living thing that is not afraid when it faces danger. The true courage is in facing danger when you are afraid, and that kind of courage you have plenty.'[15]

I am always fascinated and amazed with how many people believe they are not courageous or brave. The only thing that makes those statements true is the belief held by those telling me this. Courage does not have to be a huge feat like running into a burning building to save a pet, it doesn't have to be climbing Mount Everest or swimming with sharks or donating your kidney or starting a charity that stops world hunger. Don't get me wrong, all those things are ridiculously courageous, however, courage is present in all of us. If you really think about it, it is in the choices we make daily. We each use courage every single day, multiple times a day, in various levels.

I found my courage started flourishing the day I realised no-one was coming to save me. Fighting cancer was something I could only do for myself. I had one hell of a support team surrounding me, but when it came to it, it was all on me. Today, courage in my house looks a little different. However, it's courage nonetheless. Courage is getting up first and running to the heater to turn it on in the morning when it's a chilly -5°c in the Canberra winter. In our house, it is my kids knowing it is okay to tell the truth no matter what that may be; it is trying anything new and trying again when we make a mistake or get it wrong.

Courage, for me personally, was acknowledging not something I was, but rather something I was *not*. In mid-2019, I was not okay. I was struggling with postnatal depression but also making the choice to seek professional help.

Courage for me is still confidently saying, two years on, I choose to stay on my medications, and I'm okay with that and no opinion of any other person on the matter will change my mind.

Courage to my kids is squashing the bug in the bathroom.

Courage to me is squashing said bug in the bathroom without showing fear to my children.

Courage is childbirth, regardless of the method.

Courage is sitting an exam even though you think you are unprepared and doomed to fail.

Courage is deciding to quit smoking … every time you try.

Courage is booking that dreaded appointment you have been putting off.

Courage is speaking up for what you believe in.

Courage is knowing your limit.

Courage is asking for help.

Courage is questioning something if it doesn't seem right.

Courage is changing or breaking the rules if it feels right.

Courage is simply making a choice to continue one foot in front of the other.

Courage is within us all.

Acknowledging this can literally shift your mindset and open a world of possibility, simply because suddenly you realise you are, and always have been, courageous. Everything you could possibly require to be courageous already lies within you. When this is recognised, you have begun extending upon that. It is never too late to start living a courageous life. In fact, courage is simply another trait that can be developed with intentional effort and practised by recognising your fears and then willingly choosing to act despite them.

The key is to look at your fears as an opportunity to build your courage muscles, just as you would your physical muscles at a gym. This allows you to push through your discomfort and live the kind of life you have always wanted. If courage is always within, when we realise this, suddenly we can tap into and grow the confidence we often do not believe we possess.

Confidence is simply the attitude and feelings you hold toward yourself in your skills and abilities. The word 'confidence' originates from a Latin word *'fidere'* which literally means 'to trust', so to have confidence is to have trust in oneself. It is not about feeling superior to others, but rather, a quiet inner acknowledgement that you are capable. This leads to one feeling secure within their place in the world and ready to face whatever all the tomorrows may bring with a positive frame of mind.

LESSON 37: BREAK THE RULES IF IT FEELS RIGHT.

As a business owner I would never want my employees to break rules, so this seems a little odd, right? But I guess this topic is something I'm so acutely conscious about, I've written our workplace rule book in a way that supports any member of our team to ensure the best interests of a vulnerable person are above all else. I have been in the position, in several instances, where my personal actions have had immense impact on improving the quality of a client's life simply because I broke the rules to get the right result. Now, I am certainly not condoning breaking laws or inflicting harm upon any person. However, sometimes rules do need to be questioned. Just because an agency or government body set the rules, does not mean they have all the information to make the informed decision. I feel, as a service provider within my industry, I have a duty of care to speak up for those most vulnerable and ensure they are represented.

Nina

We were contacted by the hospital to assist Nina receive in-home supports as a part of her discharge requirements. For a lot of our most vulnerable citizens, this is not an uncommon request. Nina was a lovely, sweet lady who married her second husband quite late in life. Upon her development of early-onset dementia, naturally, her loving husband was granted guardianship of her to act in her best interests. Our carers would assist Nina twice a day, every day of the week.

Once Nina was settled and comfortable with her regular carers, reports started to roll in of uneasy feelings. A consensus that the home didn't feel right. As these concerns were not tangible, we followed our process of documenting and following up. Then came sightings of unexplained bruising, which Nina's husband always had the perfect explanation for. Only, Nina's husband told three of our regular carers three different versions of events. The carers each

PROJECT KIND

asked Nina what had happened, and while the response was never clear, it was suggested she was frightened of her husband. This became a mandatory reportable incident. As health care providers, we hold a duty of care to report the concern to the local police station. So, this is exactly what we did.

Sadly, the response from the police was that without a victim reporting the incident, there was no crime. Despite explaining our duty of care to report this, and that Nina was not medically capable to access resources to report an incident herself, there was nothing that could be done at that stage. Unfortunately, because Nina was under the age of sixty-five, she did not fall under the standards of the Aged Care Quality and Safeguards Commission. And because Nina was wealthy, her husband was funding her care with Nina's own money. This meant she wasn't a NDIS participant either. This meant there was no overarching commission looking out for Nina's best interests. No strict framework laying out the path in the event such awful things would occur. Nina found herself in the cracks of our system.

The following days and weeks continued with concerns raised, incident reports issued and police updated. While I knew my employees and my company were doing everything within our duty of care, this still was not enough to protect Nina. I had followed the rules and all the general guidelines of mandatory reporting within my industry. The breaking point for me was when Nina asked one of our carers, 'Take me with you, please. Don't leave me with him. He gives me those tablets to make me sleep.' This was now not only suspected physical abuse, but it was also domestic violence, physiological abuse and chemical restraint.

I knew I had done everything within my responsibilities as a service provider. But I still felt, as a human being, I had a long way to go to help this poor woman.

Enough was enough. I emailed every leader I possibly could in hopes somebody within their space could do something about Nina's situation. I emailed the ACT Civil and Administrative Tribunal to hopefully have her husband's guardianship reviewed and revoked. I emailed the ACT Public Trustee and Guardian in hopes they would see Nina needed their position to oversee her guardianship. I emailed the ACT police commissioner and domestic violence task force to act, and I emailed the Human Rights Commission to help Nina maintain her basic human rights.

Still ... nothing.

Now, I'm sure my emails were probably in an automated inbox that had to go through all the processes, but time was not on this woman's side. At this stage, poor Nina was becoming unwell and was admitted back to the hospital she had initially come from. I knew this was my chance. We contacted the social worker at the hospital and notified her that Nina had been readmitted to hospital, and that we suspected abuse from her husband/guardian. The social worker heard us. I knew she would as I had worked alongside this amazing soul in previous projects. The social worker took my information to the hospital board, and in the best interests of Nina's welfare, they extended her hospital stay. It was during this period I sent a follow-up email to all previously contacted parties.

This time I got a response.

The response was from the ACT human rights commissioner herself.

FINALLY. She heard me and was taking this very seriously.

Once the human rights commissioner was involved, suddenly, responses from all parties were onboard in support of Nina. An emergency review of guardianship was scheduled, and Nina would remain in the care of ACT Health until such time a determination was made.

The husband was not happy with us as the service provider and tried to seize our services to his wife thinking it would stop the wheels that had been set in motion, or perhaps that we would choose the billable hours over Nina's basic human rights?! He was sorely mistaken. I'm not farming sugarcane or cattle. I'm providing care to the most vulnerable people of my community. No dollar value can be placed on any person's basic human rights. My morals cannot be bought.

Nina's husband went on to involve his solicitor and tried to discredit and minimise the qualifications of our employees who had reported the concerns in attempts to make the accusations go away. This was just despicable. Not only does our company have Aged Care Quality and Safety Commission framework, but we also operate within the NDIS Quality and Safeguards Commission framework, because we operate under the Nurses Award, this provides an additional layer of operational requirements we choose to implement to ensure our team are qualified, trained and supported with only the best of practices.

In the end, it was safe to say Nina's husband's accusations were quickly discredited. The ACT Tribunal found not one breach in the husband's duty of care, but a staggering fifty-two counts of concern. As Nina had no living relatives, the Public Trustee and Guardian stepped in and took guardianship of Nina. This meant Nina would not be returning to her home or abuser. It did mean, however, she would be admitted to a twenty-four-hour home care facility. This was something Nina truly did not want. However, the facts were simple. There were only two awful options that Nina had in front of her: a) stay at home and in the cycle of abuse, or b) in a nursing home.

At least one of those options ensured Nina's safety.

The human rights commissioner went on to recognise and commend our company for going 'above and beyond' our duty of care. While that was beautiful recognition to have received, I'm equally saddened our actions are considered 'above and beyond' when they should be considered merely the bare minimum of what any service provider should be doing. This is simply a practice that needs to change, and the way our team managed this incident will be the way we will always continue to handle such situations.

Alex's House
Mid-2019, I gave birth to my son. The day I was discharged from hospital, we drove up the road to check on a worksite project that had been going for seven long years, and I had been a part of only in the last four of those years. When we arrived, I was so excited to see the house that once existed on the block had been demolished to make way for a specialised disability home. This was such a huge milestone in what felt like a very long four years. I made Guy snap a photo of Nate and me to mark the momentous occasion. The game was changing because we didn't give up.

Four years prior, our company was contacted by an advocate of four disability participants that were residing within a hospital. These beautiful souls had collectively resided at the hospital for eighteen years combined. Due to their complex clinical care needs, this meant the participants could not physically leave their hospital room, or at best, the ward. This meant they had gone without direct sunshine on their faces, grass between their toes and the smell of a storm rolling in our Canberra skies. This also included no Christmases, birthdays or any other milestone celebrated beyond their hospital rooms.

Why? To put it bluntly, because their care needs were too extreme for our government to provide them with the level of funding to adequately support them and a lack of suitable accommodation options to ensure their safety. I vividly recall attending our first meeting with ACT Health and the families to discuss the mammoth task we had in front of us.

I was so certain we would get the participants out of hospital; I just had no idea what it would take. I will never forget promising one of the participants' mothers in December of 2017 that it would be her daughter's last Christmas in hospital. I was so hopeful. Unfortunately, that would not be true and was something that drove me further to make sure they would get out of hospital.

For three more years, we attended meetings, and ACT Health partnered with us in taking this fight to the doorstep of the National Disability Insurance Agency (NDIA) to help educate them in understanding what needed to happen to adequately support these participants in achieving their identified goals. These participants were the forgotten ones, placed in the 'too-hard' basket. The square pegs not fitting in the round holes. Most of these participants required tracheostomy airway management, as such, didn't fit the standard check boxes of the funding applications. They didn't just need a carer a couple of hours a day; they each required twenty-four seven complex clinical care delivered by a registered nurse and a team of carers.

This took several years of creating policies to support their care needs, reports to support their funding requests and training to ensure we were staffed adequately, all while not knowing the process would take as long as it did. There were countless emails, regular meetings and not a single hour was billable. That's right. For four years, my company did not charge a single billable hour. I know most business-focused people would have initiated the parachute button after the first thirty to sixty days. But here I was, fighting the fight because it was the right thing to do. Just because these participants have significant care needs, why should that limit their basic human rights to live in a home of their own, much less live a life of their own choosing?

The advocate of these participants had taken the lead in making just that happen. He single-handedly engaged ACT Health, government leaders, local media outlets, NDIA, National Community Care and Disability Housing Solutions to make this basic human right become a reality for the four participants. Disability Housing Solutions are a Queensland-based specialist disability accommodation provider that came to Canberra and built the house that would eventually become known as 'Alex's House'.

As expected, the build faced many bumps in the road including the marked land for the property being objected to by the neighbours on the street, theft on the property, rain delays, builder delays, supplier delays and then COVID-19 restrictions. Finally, at the end of 2019, NDIA had reviewed the funding they would provide and moved to list registered nursing tracheostomy care under the National Disability Insurance Scheme. Finally, the biggest win of all! Unfortunately, that win was dampened when one of the four participants sadly passed away in hospital awaiting this second chance at life. In honour of this amazing lady, we named the property 'Alex's House'.

Now we had a beautiful custom-built house for the participants and funding looked like it was underway to be approved but the house was still empty. In the end, my company, National Community Care, decided we hadn't come this far to let these deserving individuals live in an empty lifeless home. They were already living in a clinical hospital room. NCC purchased every possible item you could think of. White goods, kitchen goods, furniture and home décor. By March of 2020, COVID-19 was spreading in Canberra, and the hospital ward the participants lived on was being converted into the COVID-19 ward. This meant the participants were at the greatest risk. Suddenly, there was a discharge date put on the table, and NCC had to make it work. This is exactly what my four years of work had been prepping me for. Bulk recruitment for nurses and carers was in full swing with ACT Health assisting us in ensuring adequate tracheostomy training and competencies were underway. It was during this time we identified that our Territory does not have a practice standard for tracheostomy care within a community setting. With absolutely no framework other than some broad NDIS guidelines, we identified a huge gap. One we would go on to close at a later point in time.

On 27 March 2020, Alex's House was finally ready, and the participants were successfully discharged from hospital to a place they could finally call home.

This will, without a doubt, be one of my top five achievements in life until the day I die.

I'm going to put it out there and say I am so damn proud I levelled myself up from a meek little people-pleaser to a rule-breaking game-changer. The rules to the game these participants faced automatically put them at a disadvantage. In fact, it didn't even include them in the game. This needed to change, and no-one seemed to be coming on a white horse to save them, so we did.

Sometimes in life, rules and expectations need to be reviewed, altered and broken. Ask yourself, *Who made those rules?* Are they rules you've placed on yourself? Or in my case, we were faced with inadequate rules that simply were not inclusive of the participants we were looking to support. If the action is with purpose, then choosing to break the rule that limits you is sometimes a necessary action.

2019: Left the hospital and went past the cleared land for the new disability house.

SELF-CARE
YOU DO YOU

Self-care. [self-kair]

noun

the act of attending to one's physical or mental health, generally without medical or other professional consultation (often used attributively): It's been a rough week, so this weekend is all about self-care through exercise.

the products or practices used to comfort or soothe oneself (often used attributively).

> *'Be enough for yourself first. The rest of the world can wait.'*
> – Unknown

LESSON 38: PAUSE, THE WORLD WON'T END.

'Let's begin by taking a smallish nap or two.' Winnie the Pooh was a wise old bear. Rest. Always so much easier said than done though, right?

What Winnie didn't know was that, as a businesswoman, we are made to feel rest is for the weak. In a man's world, rest means disadvantage. As a mother, rest is never an option, and we have this amazing ability to run on nothing but caffeine and fuzzy feels sometimes. A smallish nap or two would be great, but sometimes is just not a possibility.

But we often forget, if given just a moment, it is not until you stop, rest, reset and start again that you realise just how much more amazing you can be when you are recharged and working at full capacity. Seriously! It's like having an iPhone and not installing the updates. You can still operate your phone but eventually it becomes sluggish and problematic, either forcing you to update or put our device to rest. Have you noticed that? Apparently when the latest

OS is created, it is cleverly written for the newest device, ultimately meaning it can't help but run more slowly on our old hardware. So, like iPhones, sometimes we need to ensure we maintain the updates. In our case, as humans, this means self-care.

Sometimes it's not a pause we physically need from our own lives, but rather, a pause from an external factor can be just as important. A social media pause: no news coverage for a week. No newspapers or news apps. Sometimes it's external factors like pandemics or mass deaths, crime and war through our screens that drains our mental capacity. It sounds silly but it can be fatiguing to watch such death and destruction every evening on the 6pm news. I'm grateful for the likes of Netflix and live streaming TV platforms that mean our household can watch anything with no adverts or news clips of any of the devastation going on in the world. It could also be a pause from that friend that just sucks the life out of you with all their 'woe is me' problems. It is okay to put your mental health first by choosing to remove external factors to allow yourself half a chance to pause other areas of your life.

Working in the health care sector, mental health and self-care is not new in my world. This concept has always been in the forefront of our team, our office and our daily communications. This is something my company has been acutely aware of due to the high volume of health care worker fatigue that exists, and this was prior to the 2019 pandemic. To combat this and ensure it was a priority for each of our team members, midway through 2015 we decided that we needed to do something significant to make sure our amazing team were looked after. We looked around at putting in place things like an employee assistance program and speaking with local organisations such as gyms and equipment shops to offer discounted memberships, but we didn't seem to get the engagement or commitment from our team. Back in 2015, we were a small organisation, as such, we needed something bigger to be part of to support us in supporting our team. That's when we came across the ACT Government Healthier Work initiative and decided it was time to put a proper action plan in place for our team – a holistic one.

The plan is set each year for the following twelve months, with each season focusing on a particular area such as physical wellbeing, emotional wellbeing, healthy eating, sun smart, eco-friendly and heart health, to name a few. In each season, we engage with the team, providing strategies we implement for both our people and the workplace. We have now reached Platinum+ status and been recognised for our continuing efforts to workplace health by ACT Health and even Beyond Blue and former CEO Geoff Kennett. This program shifted the culture within our workspace, making these strategies become part of the daily fabric that is our team. The results of this have been astounding. Our staff are engaged and care about each other, it's not just a job, but a team who look after each other, even though they may not work together every day or even at the same place. In our business statistics, Lisa found: 'Our sick call intake has decreased significantly; employee availability has increased. Workers' compensation claims have decreased from two claims every three months, to one in the last four years. Our team refer other good workers they want to join our team, and one of the most important measures – the clients we look after acknowledge the level of support we provide our team with.'

When it comes to my own personal self-care, I always default to my 'if I stop, my wheels will fall off' statement, and yes, usually if I do stop, I inevitably get run-down, but this isn't because I stopped, this is because of the high level of stress I place upon myself to have everything in order. This means when I finally do stop, so do my stress levels, including stress hormones which mobilise your immune system against illness. Ironically, the only way to avoid this is to ensure regular rest and keep your stress in check. At the end of the day, the work will still be there tomorrow. If it isn't, there will just be more work after that. Now, before you think to yourself, *Wait a minute, you own and operate a community company that provides services twenty-four seven, what would you know about resting?* let me tell you that it is because of this exact reason I have learnt to know that rest looks different to every person. For some, it is being uncontactable and device free. For others, rest is working from home today. Some consider a morning at a day spa or a jog around the lake the rest they feel they need for their body and mind.

In 2010, when I was studying various courses working as a carer across nursing homes, the acquired brain injury unit and community sector, each shift I completed had a beginning, a middle and an end. You knew, when your shift was finished, you had completed all the required tasks for the person you were caring for. When I began my business, I struggled for a long time to know when to call it and end my working day. I would be up until two or three in the morning still trying to complete a task, finish writing a policy or roster one more day on the schedule. This was a part of the reconditioning I had to face otherwise I was on a fast-track trajectory to burnout as my current pace was not sustainable.

My husband had himself a decade-long career serving within Centrelink processes, emergency management, and risk and project management. A lifetime prior to joining me in our business. Public service life meant he paid for parking every day and was required to work in his office building from 9am to 5pm and not a minute longer. If a project needed doing, tough luck if it was past five, that's a higher-up position problem. Clocked off, meant clocked off. Annual leave and sick leave meant no-one in his workplace was going to contact him. This practice has always been seen by society as the benchmark for work-life balance.

Now, you already know my thoughts on work-life balance ... as an employer, sometimes there is no such thing. If I am sick, I can rest, but I might need to rest around an hour or so of urgent work that needs to be completed, or I am tag-teaming with Guy or Lisa. To me, that sounds pretty damn reasonable because I've created a lifestyle that works for me every other day of the year. For my husband, however, the employer lifestyle took a little adjusting to after being conditioned for a decade to be a nine-to-five worker bee.

When COVID-19 hit Australian shores, as a nation of conditioned worker bees, we had to collectively start thinking outside of the box and in line with our state and territory health orders. Suddenly, the idea of working from home was not only possible, but it was also supported, and in some cases, enforced. In so many ways COVID-19 brought on an evolutionary leap for society regarding flexible workplace arrangements, however, it was still so out of touch with the modern-day family, placing additional constraints for working families also trying to home-school their children when our schools were closed. As a result of this, additional stresses were introduced within our communities and mental health was thrust into the forefront of our minds, TVs and social media. FINALLY!

Self-care and mental wellbeing are now being rightfully recognised as commonly as physical wellbeing. There has always been a misconception that self-care is being self-indulgent or selfish by putting your needs above others (seriously ...). I feel like my parents' generation was a time where mental health was associated with mental institutions and straitjackets. Anything less than that just required you to get on with it. Today, thankfully, we know self-care to be taking care of yourself so that you can be healthy, you can be well, you can do your job, you can help and care for others, and you can do all the things you need and want to accomplish in a day.

Self-care looks different for every person. My mum would consider a self-care day tucked away in her craft room creating anything and everything. Guy would love a day without the work phone while playing eighteen holes of golf. For me, I couldn't think of anything worse than golf. Self-care as a mum is sometimes as simple as being able to wash my hair or pee uninterrupted for just two minutes. Beyond this, I love nothing more than vegging out at the end of the day when the kids are in bed, the dishes are done and the house is calm. It's now, I *need* to sit on the couch with a cup of tea. This is the perfect way for me to unwind at the end of the day before I go to bed. It doesn't matter how late my day might have ended, or how jam-packed it was, or how exhausted and tired I am feeling, I know my mental health needs me to sit on the couch for twenty minutes or so, put my feet up and watch something mindless on TV. This is the first time all day I am not actively thinking ten steps ahead. The benefit of this time is that when I go to bed, I do not have 101 things rolling around my head that I need to remember or do because I did all that while I was watching TV and tying up any loose ends from my day. This practice allows me to go to bed calm and drift off to sleep instantly …

energy

DRAINERS

- AVOIDING REST TO STAY PRODUCTIVE
- ONE-SIDED RELATIONSHIPS
- CLUTTER AND MESS
- EXCESSIVE PHONE USE
- GETTING STUCK IN COMPLAIN MODE
- PEOPLE PLEASING

RETAINERS

- BALANCE, WORK & REST
- SUPPORTIVE RELATIONSHIPS
- ORGANISING LIFE TO SUIT YOUR NEEDS
- DOING THINGS JUST FOR FUN
- APPRECIATING THE LITTLE THINGS
- SLEEP, WATER & SUNSHINE

LESSON 39: RECOGNISE YOUR OWN BURNOUT.

Listening to your body isn't about intuitively knowing which vitamin your diet may be lacking or what nutrient-filled smoothie you need to make yourself drink. But wouldn't it be amazing if we could actually do that?! It is simply about paying attention to the signs when your body is feeling something, and considering if it is a signal for something.

So often we feel aches, pains, stiffness or soreness and we just proceed with our daily tasks. Have you ever stopped to think about these signals your body is giving you? I am by no means a doctor of any kind, but I do know my signals are often symptoms of something requiring my attention. The minute my sleep is disturbed or ulcers appear in my mouth, I know I'm run-down from stress. These are my tell-tale signs, but of course, by the time they present, it generally means that I am already high on the stress scale and didn't even stop to realise. Sometimes it's not until the physical signals flare up that I review my situation and adjust accordingly, and I usually require some rest and self-care.

We grab the paracetamol when we have a headache, why not grab a moment of peace if we are overwhelmed and stressed? In 2019, the World Health Organization announced an updated definition of 'burnout' in the *International Classification of Diseases. (ICD-11)*. For those thinking, *What the hell is an ICD-11?* it is a medical textbook identifying every single possible disease, disorder, illness, injury and diagnosis under the sun. The *'11'* being the eleventh edition. In this text, it lists burnout as: 'A syndrome conceptualised as resulting from chronic workplace stress that has not been successfully managed. It is characterised by three dimensions: 1) feelings of energy depletion or exhaustion; 2) increased mental distance from one's job, or feelings of negativism or cynicism related to one's job; and 3) a sense of ineffectiveness and lack of accomplishment. Burn-out refers specifically to phenomena in the occupational context and should not be applied to describe experiences in other areas of life.'[16]

Across all the resources readily available on the web, they consistently mention a person feeling they might lack control of their situation. The person may have unclear job expectations or dysfunctional workplace dynamics. The person may feel a lack of social support and then my personal favourite … work-life imbalance. So, have you experienced burnout? I think it is safe to say most of us have experienced the definition of burnout at some point within our working careers.

Are you experiencing brain fog regardless how many hours of sleep you had?

Sexy time with your partner depleted?

You physically feel stressed and have physical tell-tale signs?

Are you running on empty?

Have your sleep habits changed?

Have you lost motivation?

Becoming negative and detached?

Okay, so you've realised you are starting to burnout, your body is screaming at you … now what? For me, I have always needed to come back to looking at the balance within my life. Often, my stress is due to a case of imbalanced priorities and core values. Without a correction, my tell-tale signs will continue to rage until I drop or do something to change my circumstances. So, how does one act upon what their body is telling them? There are a number of methods, and again, there is no one right answer for every person.

I personally find I need to deal with the stress-causing factor first. If I don't, none of my other coping strategies will be effective because I will ultimately still be thinking about said problem. So, for me, I found these tactics to be most useful:

1. Evaluate the situation and the options I must activate to navigate the problem.
2. Ask myself, is my stress caused by a factor I can control?
3. Is this something saying NO can alleviate?
4. Perspective. Allowing myself to being intensely aware of what I am sensing and feeling at every moment. It also includes extending that perspective beyond myself in looking at the situation from all parties' perspectives.
5. Can my stress be reduced by seeking support or designating parts of the workload to others to essentially share the problem? Like the corny but very true saying 'a problem shared is a problem halved'. Breaking the overwhelming problem down into bite-size pieces.
6. Sometimes it requires a change of scenery. Taking a moment to stop and take a step back, then going back and trying again with a clearer and calmer frame of mind is all it takes.
7. Try a relaxing self-care-based activity. Things like yoga, meditation, walking in nature or the shopping mall – my personal fave!
8. Move. Regular physical activity can help you better deal with stress. It can also take your mind off work or any other worries.
9. Adequate sleep. Sleep restores wellbeing and helps protect your health, but when you are stressed, this is often disrupted. Take the necessary steps to give yourself the best chance at a good night's sleep. For example, no screens past eight at night. Read a book before bed. Avoid caffeine. Set a relaxing end-of-day routine.

Your goal should be to be an asset in every sense of the word. An asset to your business, to your partner, to your family, to your friends, but above all, to yourself. To do any of this, it starts with listening to your body, saying no to things that don't serve your mind, body and soul, resting when you can and adjusting workload when the burnout indicators come on. At the end of the day, taking the rest you need for yourself will not lead to death, destruction or the downfall of your company. In fact, quite the opposite. Imagine if you were running your business and life at 100% battery ...

Through accepting that self-care is just as important as physical health, I've come to realise my ability to rest is just as important as my work. I refuse to believe that achieving my goals and dreams must come at the cost of burnout. That is not what my story is about.

LESSON 40: PUT YOUR OWN OXYGEN MASK ON FIRST.
Self-care is a critical facet of life, as is diet and exercise, good sleep and safety. Self-care assists us in building our resilience toward those stresses and adversities in life that you can't necessarily control or eliminate. When you've taken steps to care for your mind and body, you'll find you are better equipped to live your best life. Self-care isn't a luxury, but rather, a priority to ensure you are adequately equipped to handle the inevitable challenges life throws at us.

Think about that. On an airplane, we are always instructed to put on our own oxygen masks first, before helping a child or other adult to do the same. If you think that's a crazy idea, consider the fact that you will not be much help to anyone if you've passed out due to lack of oxygen because you tried to help everyone else first. Apply this to your everyday life.

Take care of yourself first, keep your cup full, then share with others. As the saying goes, 'you can't pour from an empty cup'. So how does one fill a cup? It is about meeting your needs. I consider this the nourishment of my body, mind and soul. It includes physically taking care of yourself, diet, sleep, rest and exercise. Emotional fulfilment like experiencing meaningful connections. Socialising could also be those connections, participating in hobbies just for you. For some, it can also be spiritual and religious needs. Regardless of what your needs might be, the idea is it will always be different for each individual, and overall, the goal is to fill your cup with things that make you feel well.

It's when your cup is full that you are at your optimum and can take on your world. But ... like all good things, a cup never stays full for long and they are easily drained by negativity, stress, rejection, loneliness, isolation, feelings of unworthiness, demands of others, failure and fatigue. Sometimes, there's no one thing that has emptied your cup, but rather, evaporation has naturally occurred, being in the daily grind of life and before you know it, you need a top-up. If you don't do things for yourself to ensure your cup is topped up, you will inevitably have nothing left to give or share with others.

This tends to be a tough concept for most women, as all too often we have been stereotyped to be the caregivers, putting others first. Heck, I made a career out of doing just that! We tend to think we don't deserve to take care of ourselves until everyone else is happy. But the reality is, everyone else is never happy. That list becomes never-ending and ultimately an impossible quest. To care for your health and wellbeing, it is important to find a balance that allows you to address whichever area of need requires some attention.

The idea of self-care to those who label it as selfish, often think self-care is a time-consuming task that takes away from your other priorities. It really is not. Self-care looks different for every person, and there are endless possibilities to assist you in filling your cup back up. Get in the habit of asking yourself, *What have I done for me today?*

Here is a list of just a few because I love a list and setting myself a good challenge:

- Truly savour your dessert or have two!
- Try a new exercise class.
- Actually use that gym membership.
- Listen to an inspirational podcast.
- Watch a movie.
- Go to the art gallery.
- Read for fun.
- Pay it forward at a paid parking machine.
- Call a loved one.
- Attend a workshop.
- Write a journal.
- Become an organ donor.
- Learn a new skill.
- Pick up a new hobby.
- Do something for someone because you can.
- Go for a coffee with a friend.
- Donate your preloved items to charities.
- Pinterest your next holiday or event outfit.
- Do a random act of kindness.
- Close your eyes and take ten deep breaths.
- Sign up for an online masterclass.
- Donate to a food bank.

- Hold hands with your partner.
- Volunteer somewhere.
- Go to a restaurant for a nice meal.
- Cuddle with your children.
- Write a note of encouragement for someone.
- Join a collective of like-minded people.
- Pay it forward at a drive-through window.
- Sleep in.
- Buy a homeless person a cooked meal.
- Google good news stories.
- Tell those you appreciate, exactly that.
- Get a spa treatment.
- Enjoy your favourite gourmet tea or coffee.
- Donate blood and plasma.
- Sing along to your radio while driving.
- Have a family movie night at home.
- FaceTime with a friend who lives far away.
- Go for a walk outdoors.
- Replace the donut with fruit.
- OR enjoy the donut!
- Drink a glass of water right after you wake up.
- Book those concert tickets.
- Take a yoga class.
- Have a moment of gratitude in the morning.
- Stretch for five minutes.
- Have a nap.
- Revisit your goals or vision board.
- Try a new smoothie.
- Go for a bike ride.
- Take a bubble bath.

PROJECT KIND

- YouTube funny cat videos.
- Play board games with your kids.
- Go for a scenic drive.
- Go on a hike.
- Donate to charity.
- Take your children for ice cream.
- Visit a farmers' market or a craft fair.
- Watch the sunset.
- Hug someone.
- Take your mum out for coffee.
- Book your next holiday in.
- Learn another language.
- Meditate for five minutes.
- Book a night away from home.
- Go to a sporting event.
- Eat chocolate for breakfast.
- Eat breakfast for dinner!
- Join a committee you are passionate about.
- Play with your pet.
- _____
- _____
- _____
- _____
- _____
- _____
- _____
- _____

Make self-care part of your daily routine. Make it as regular as brushing your teeth should be! (I say 'should be', because I know in my house, my kids have all the excuses in the world as to why they didn't brush their teeth!) During times of uncertainty and stress, it is crucial to review your daily habits and create rituals and routines for yourself that provide you with a grounding sense of peace and calmness. These activities are varied; for some, it is reading, journalling, walking in nature, going to the gym. For others, it is having tea, cooking or meditation. Sometimes you might even think you don't have an activity, but the next time you're doing something, you might realise, *Oh wait, this walk to pick the kids up from school is the perfect moment of self-care and self-reflection.*

Choosing to protect your energy isn't optional – it's essential. Part of this is taking care of yourself. It's nothing personal. Making that commitment to yourself sets boundaries to others that you will no longer be a doormat. You are no pushover. You know your worth and you are putting *you* first. After all, if we cannot put ourselves first, then how can we expect any other person to do so?

LESSON 41: WORK SMARTER, NOT HARDER.

Choosing to live my life without regrets has meant saying yes to opportunities that excite me. No to situations that take from me. It's been about taking on challenges that scare the pants off me but knowing when I'm beyond my depth and waving the white flag and calling in the cavalry. In essence, this is working smarter, not harder.

It sounds so cliché to say 'no regrets' or 'regret nothing'. I've found these statements more than often come from the younger generation just starting out in adult life with no actual true concept of purpose just yet. It's almost as if it is a throwaway line to foolishly say 'let's do everything regardless of how reckless it may be'. An association with the term YOLO. 'You only live once'. Or

FOMO. 'Fear of missing out'. At the age of nineteen, I knew all too well about that.

Then there are those on the other end of the spectrum who do face impending death that can clearly identify all their 'should haves, could haves, would haves'. Some of the people that I have spoken to in all my years within the industry wished for common things and regretted similar things in life. Much the same as those themes you find with a quick google of 'regrets'. Most commonly, I found many wished they had led a life true to themselves, rather than by the expectations of others, or that they regretted not valuing their loved ones more or not chasing their dreams whole-heartedly or having worked too hard, sacrificed too much.

For me, my cancer diagnosis was a huge awakening to finding a meaningful path. It was a life-altering moment that allowed me to learn from the shitty situation and make something from it. I would identify, at the age of nineteen, exactly what I didn't want to die regretting. I didn't want to regret a thing, but when I was faced with death, I was regretting not things I had done, but rather all the things I had not done. I wanted to have a meaningful purpose with something worth leaving behind.

This is a sentiment I actively live by. For me, I have had my fair share of impactful experiences which became huge motivators for me to start living as if any day could be my last. We never know how long we will live, so we must make conscious choices each day to live fully and make the most out of each experience we have. Don't get me wrong, I love nothing more than a wasted day of being a coach potato with a binge-watch on Netflix, but it's all a part of the grand scheme of that elusive balance in life.

After a business and two children, my balancing act looked a little different from the childless life I thought cancer had condemned me to. As such, I needed to do some serious readjusting to make it all work for me and my family. Regardless of your job or industry, there just are not always enough hours in the day to get everything done. As a result, I constantly feel like I am behind. So, what's the answer? More work hours? More hours in the day in general? I find myself saying that all too often.

Until this point in time, I was working long hours, and with a home office set up, it was quite easy to end up down the rabbits' hole until all hours of the morning. After the birth of my son and the overwhelming slap in the face from postnatal depression, I had to master how to work smarter, not harder. I needed to do this not only to survive my own mental torment but also to stay true to my core values in line with living authentically and without regret. Seeing my husband was an added bonus too.

Learning to work smarter, not harder, not only improved my productivity and performance, it also allowed me to tame a small fraction of that never-ending mum guilt. I needed to establish my own personal working boundaries. Being a business owner meant I was accountable to no-one. That meant no-one was coming to tell me I needed to leave early that day, no-one was telling me I'd had too much overtime or need to use up my leave days. There I was, promoting work-life balance for my employees, but sucking at it royally within my own life. To change my circumstances, I had to act and make some necessary changes to keep myself afloat. There are many out there such as email hour, calendar block-outs, productive meetings, bite-size work times, to name a few. But I needed to up my game and this is how I did it:

Cut the bullshit: Taking on any new project in my business always gets me excited and my mind is racing with a million different thoughts on where to start and what I need to do to get the job done on time. As a result, I start creating a to-do list that is massively bulky. (I do love myself a good to-do list.) The problem I always face is that most of the time they are so overwhelming I focus my time and energy on the wrong areas just because I want to tick off the 'quick' tasks to see progression on my to-do list. This ultimately leaves me no closer to completing the core of the project.

I combat this by taking my mammoth to-do list and breaking it down. Usually, it's in a variety of fancy highlighted colours and broken into a four-step matrix:

1. Urgent and important.
2. Urgent and not important.
3. Not urgent but important.
4. Not urgent and not important.

Identifying where my tasks sit break down to the following:

1. Urgent and important = I MUST COMPLETE ASAP.
2. Urgent and not important = I MUST DELEGATE ASAP.
3. Not urgent but important = MY SECOND PRIORTY.
4. Not urgent and not important = DELEGATED SECOND PRIORITY.

Delegate the shit out of stuff: I love to think I can do it all. In the beginning of my business, I could. I also did not have children or seventy employees needing support. To be honest, I still really suck at handing over work that I want to do. But that's the thing … identifying the work that needs to be done and the work I want to do. Sometimes, as business owners, we have to put the big-girl pants on and suck it up. At least until I can master human cloning, right!?!

I had to start delegating tasks and carving out additional roles from my one-stop-shop role. The consequences for me if I didn't was probably going to be a straitjacket in a padded cell or working myself into an early grave with a lot of regret!

Overcome shiny-object syndrome: This may not be for everyone, but it is a serious problem for me. A new project to me often means new stationery and planning books, new Excel timeline spreadsheets or a presentation I spent several hours on Canva making look beautiful rather than the actual content I am meant to be conveying … all the frills that distract me from the actual work that needs to be done. Don't get me wrong, I will get it all done, but I could have used my time so much more wisely. To keep this in check, I usually add a fifth column to my planning matrix:

5. The fun stuff = A REWARD ONLY WHEN THE REAL WORK IS DONE.

Automate the automatable: As a woman that loves clothes, I am 100% not going to do a Steve Jobs or Mark Zuckerberg and wear the same outfit every day to prevent fatigue as they claim it does. I'd rather take their word for it and automate other areas in my life. Any personal appointments I have like hair and lashes are standing rolling appointments. Kids' sport commitments are usually standing. I automated my employment application process and email responses. Meal prepping when I can and accepting that some months call for automating my diet and living on pre-packaged and delivered-to-my-door meals making it one less task I need to give thought to. The idea of this is to streamline the simple mundane tasks to allow you to concentrate on the important stuff. Now, can someone invent healthy school lunch options packed and delivered to your door already?

Open. Reply. Send: This rule is simple. If I open your email, I commit myself to respond. Because if I don't within twenty-four hours, it's lost. This used to mean that I read your email at two o'clock in the morning going to the loo, so would respond from my phone before going back to sleep. I had to adjust this further by only opening work emails during office hours. In the event the response was a weighty one that I suspect may not be received well, I will always save the draft and review in the morning before hitting send. This is still a practice I continually have to work on, to say I have a couple of unread emails in my inbox would be a gross understatement.

Work routine: As much as I like to think I am a carefree spontaneous person, I am equally a creature of habit. Creating a strict work routine, particularly in the mornings when energy levels are optimum, means I can be the most effective. This includes preparing for any meetings I may have, attending to those emails that came in overnight and having that first cup of work coffee for the day. I also implement packing up my workspace and creating the next day's task list with any urgent tasks that I will need to focus on first thing the next day, and the simplicity of in and outgoing trays assists in providing a focus point.

And then there is my favourite …

Team: Surround yourself with the right people.

CONNECTION

BUILDING AN EMPIRE

Connection. [k*uh*-**nek**-sh*uh*n]

noun

the act or state of connecting.
the state of being connected: the connection between cause and effect.
anything that connects; a connecting part; link; bond.
association; relationship.
a circle of friends or associates or a member of such a circle.
association with or development of something observed, imagined, discussed.

> *'Meaningful connection is formed when we share our truth.'*
> – Michelle Maros

LESSON 42: BUILD YOUR DREAM TEAM.

When we first started National Community Care, between Lisa and me, we did it all. We grew. But our growth was ultimately going to be limited as our scope and ability to take on anything further was limited. It became about finding the right people to have on our team.

It takes a lot to trust others with your business at times, but it comes back to aligning your employees with your company values and the brand you have built, and ensuring you have the right people on your team to continue and build upon that culture. For me, it was about paying attention to who I am with when I feel I'm operating at my optimum. This is always a good indicator of who I need in my life. Equally so, popping my head up when the chips fall to see who out of those individuals are still present. This can be applied both personally and professionally.

For NCC, given it is literally based around providing people with care in their homes, meant it wasn't too long until I could no longer be that person, plus answering the phone and emails. There were literally too many places for me to be at the same time. Recruiting for carers was going to be a natural process, but I didn't just want any carer working for me. Don't get me wrong, I do believe if any person wants to be a carer, that is a beautiful and selfless service to provide. However, in community there is an additional element of vulnerability as you are sending your employees to client homes one on one.

This meant I needed to ensure I had a team that could hit the ground running, that understood the level and quality of care our company provides and would become an asset to the team and the culture I was trying to build. Of course, the industry had base-level entry requirements, but I knew we could do better so we set our company base-level entry at a standard I know I would be happy to have my parents receive care from.

I had never been somebody's employer before and didn't really have a clue with what I was doing, but …

- ✓ I did know the service I wanted to provide.
- ✓ I did know what if felt like to receive amazing care.
- ✓ I did know what it felt like to receive poor care.
- ✓ I did know from my previous workspaces what approaches did and didn't work.
- ✓ I did know how it felt to be an employee in an extremely overworked and underpaid industry with flexibility promised but never given and always unappreciated and never heard.

So, I took what I did know and used this as my driving force to create a business and a dream team from the ground up. I had to build a team to carry the values and vision I had built and allow them to create and continue the culture and worth ethic. So, how did I know if I had the right person on my team?

Instinct. I know that sounds ridiculous, but I needed to ensure the candidate was going to possess common sense and a good attitude. Both skills aren't exactly something you find on a résumé, and if I did, I wouldn't believe it. I wasn't a fancy employer of people. I had never done this before. We had implemented our company employment entry-level requirements, so provided the candidate met those requirements, the rest of the decision was based on our face-to-face interview to gauge their common sense and attitudes. I wasn't taught how to ask all the selection criteria questions like you would find in the public sector. So, I created a handful of questions that told me more than any résumé ever could.

- *Tell me something about yourself that is not on your résumé?*

This gives me a small window into the life of the candidate. Are they volunteering every weekend at their local hospice? Perhaps raising five kids as a single parent? Avid softball player?

The answers to these often tell me what other skills they may possess such as time management, priorities, core values, ability to be a team player. So often candidates want to focus on the qualifications and merits, thinking this is what employers␣what to hear. Maybe that is true everywhere else, but I don't want to be like other employers. I'm running my own race over here. Besides, all that information should already have been captured in the candidate's résumé and application form. What I want is to get to know the human that wants to join my team.

- *What are your top three priorities in life?*

If a candidate thinks I want to hear 'work' in their top three priorities, they would be mistaken. What I am looking for here is honesty. Is your priority training to get to the next Olympics for table tennis? Awesome, how can we help you do that?! Is your priority finishing university and getting that dream grad placement? Fantastic, I know we can definitely help you achieve that! This rolls into my next question:

- *What is your professional long-term goal and how can we help you get there?*

We understand that, in most cases, our company is often a stepping stone for the candidate as they forge their own career path. We are always supportive of this and have had the honour of shaping some amazing nurses within our health care system, however, I do expect transparency from my team. By knowing the candidates' intentions, I can somewhat determine the time frames of their goals to weigh up the time and energy I would spend training and upskilling the candidate versus how long they intend to stick around. For example, a carer who has just finished studying at university, awaiting their postgraduate program to start in the next three months does not excite me. I would be spending those three months training and upskilling the candidate who would then be leaving us upon the completion before I've had a return on my investment. However, a second-year nursing student … this tells me they have at least two years before they would be looking to proceed forward so that is a good amount of time for me to invest in that candidate, making the arrangement equally valuable to both parties.

PROJECT KIND

- *Why my company? Had you heard of us prior to applying?*

This question is by no means a deal-breaker, I don't suspect every candidate has heard of our company, but I do find this question is a great way to gauge public perception for those candidates that have heard of us previously. We always find those who have been referred to us by our own employees make some of the best employees themselves as they are aware of what we do, how we operate and why we are different, and they still want to be a part of our team. This tells me they are here for the right reasons. This question will always highlight those candidates who have also done their homework and at the very least looked up your website to know what it is they are looking to join, and the super keen beans will know we are not just your average service provider.

I have implemented a similar approach when it comes to our security vetting processes regarding the candidate's reference checks. I didn't need to know 'how long was candidate K employed at your organisation?', or 'what would you say the candidate's strengths and weaknesses are?' I wanted to know the **real** stuff. Not the pre-emptive stuff.

- *Would you say the candidate is compassionate and empathetic?*

You just simply cannot do the job if you do not possess compassion and empathy. I need to know the candidate gives a damn about our cause and if your referee can't answer this question or doesn't have the experience working with you to know, then chances are the answer is already on the wall.

- *Does the candidate upline all matters accordingly?*

I need to know the candidate can follow directives and workplace policies and procedures when it comes to up lining and won't go rogue. Do the candidate's words and actions match?!

- *Does the candidate work well in a team and independently?*

Does the candidate play well with others? And is the candidate trustworthy enough to work independently? Often the reference will disclose any performance management issues they may have experienced in the past here. This is never a reason not to employee a candidate but can often reveal to me if the candidate's performance concern was successfully managed, which would make this a non-issue now and could even be considered a strength in turning those candidates' experiences into a silver lining and utilising the strengths and nurturing the weaknesses.

- *Would you personally employee the candidate to provide in-home care to your loved ones?*

If I asked this question first, the answer could very well end the reference check immediately, but I wouldn't seem very boss-like if I shut down the phone conference after one question … This question often catches the reference contact off guard. It invokes an emotional and honest response from the reference and tells me everything I need to know.

***

The above approach would lead me to go on to employ close to two hundred carers and nurses in the first five years of operation, and some of our most reliable employees have been with us for that entire period. With this kind of growth, my role was significantly increasing. In 2020, when Alex's House was set to open, Lisa and I knew we needed to seek the right person to join our team and oversee the clinical coordinator role. I needed someone who got our vision. Who would join us in our fight and become an invaluable asset to the company.

Cue Tahla. This girl was a fun, energetic, detail-orientated ball of light, along with all the right governance, risk framework and clinical qualifications, of course. Lisa and I knew, despite the four-year project of getting Alex's House prepared for operation, neither Lisa nor I had the appropriate clinical scope to oversee it upon its official opening. Did this mean we were going to stop the project? Heck no. It simply meant we had to find the right person for the role and expand our metaphorical business utility belt. We needed to ensure the person we took on shared our values and saw the bigger picture. Brave enough to ride the crazy journey with us, fighting for that systemic change to improve our industry all while we continued to just figure it out as we went.

Lisa and I have always managed to find and attract the right people. When this occurs, to date, all of our key management players have approached us wanting to work for our team in some capacity because they see us and our mission. Tahla had done just that. She was working within Lisa's agency, and we saw her worth. In the four years of preparing for Alex's House, we had a handful of candidates come and go, but in the end, Tahla seemed like the perfect fit for both our company and the participants that would be living in Alex's House. Having Tahla onboard got me back to concentrating on 'the next big thing', confidently knowing she had everything else under control. That next big thing was also inclusive of Lisa and me starting a business with Tahla.

Complete Clinical Consultancy and Training Solutions. CTS for short! We identified a ridiculous educational gap in our industry that left our clients vulnerable and service providers at risk. We were outsourcing tens of thousands of dollars a year on specialised clinical training for our complex nursing team to training companies based in Sydney. This was not conducive to the COVID-19 restrictions, travel bubbles and lockdowns we endured for a while. Tahla and I went back to school and studied training and assessment. Between the both of us, with our experience and qualifications, we have been able to create and deliver some pretty kick-arse training content. For the first time in a long time, we had learners (our employees) praising the training they had received because we managed to actually hit the mark. All of this was just an absolute confirmation that what we saw in Tahla was greatness.

This is exactly what building your dream team is about. Outsourcing the skills that are either beyond your scope or your interest to somebody else who thrives in that space and expanding the skills of those you want to see grow and flourish.

LESSON 43: FIND. APPRECIATE. WORSHIP YOUR TRIBE.
Firstly, I understand the word and use of the word 'tribe' may be offensive to some. I do see you and disrespecting your ideology of the term is not my intent.

According to the *Oxford English Dictionary* a 'tribe' is defined as 'a social division in a traditional society consisting of families or communities linked by social, economic, religious, or blood ties, with a common culture and dialect, typically having a recognised leader'. As a Rotuman Islander girl, I understand this term in its traditional sense of a society with inclusions of blood lines, religion, culture, dialect and recognised chief leaders, however, this doesn't necessarily promise togetherness.

I also see that, over time and evolution, the term can expand within its exact and unchanged definition.

As women of today, I also understand the term to capture the essence of families or communities coming together socially, economically, culturally and even through dialect to some degree. For example, a group of friends come together with commonalities, often sharing similar values and culture, and metaphorically speaking, the same dialect – being on the same page.

To me personally, a tribe is a group of people of your choosing that share commonalities in life. These are the people you choose. This may be a blood relative, but equally, it may not. I think it is so important to say out loud that, just because someone is your blood relative, does not automatically guarantee an alignment with your idea of core values, so why should you be expected to stand with relatives that question your being or core values, or worse yet, impose their core values on you? This is when mental health takes a turn as we are expected to fall in line when it comes to a blood relative. No person is worth the cost of your mental health. Let me say that again …

No person is worth the cost of your mental health!

My idea of a tribe is a positive association, it describes a bond shared and aligning your core values. As such, this can include blood lines, friendships and work colleagues that share any of the above. These people are the people who get you, who are on the same wavelength. The people who share the same brand of quirky, crazy or oddness that you do. The ones who understand why you do what you do, or if they don't understand, they either ask or they just accept without judgement, and either way is fine. They understand your soul song, and love and respect you for simply being you and want nothing but good things for you, and you equally feel the same for them.

Unlike the days of being in the school playground and asking someone to be your friend, finding meaningful connections in your life as an adult isn't as easy. Then you add on the barriers of today's society including 'swiping right', no-shows, Zoom calls, social distancing and social media platforms, this makes the feat truly difficult. The ironic thing is you don't really set out to 'find a tribe'. Personally, I have been lucky enough to attract the right people into my life, and always at the right time. I think that's what it is about. Majority of the time it is only in hindsight I realise the necessity of the said person's arrival into my life in the cosmic serendipitist way that it usually occurs.

Naturally, we subconsciously gravitate towards people that feel familiar. We crave companionship and belonging, regardless of how independent we think we are. Friendship is part of the human experience and can be one of the most rewarding aspects of life. Meaningful connections can be forged from a variety of places including school, university, work, sports teams, social groups. Some of these are formed naturally, other times is about going out and aligning yourself with like-minded people to optimise your chances of making that connection. For example, if you were a recovering alcoholic, you probably wouldn't join a sports bar social group, but you may find a lifelong friend in AA as you both travel the path of sobriety together.

For me, I have found so many meaningful connections over the years through signing up to online groups that also hold face-to-face events and collaborations. Business Chicks, CBR Woman, She Mentor, Canberra Women in Business, AusMumpreneur. All collectives of like-minded women with similar goals and values as myself.

These are all formal collectives of people and it makes forming bonds so much easier when most of the BS is already filtered out.

I also sought out informal networks like 'Canberra December Babies of 2016'. This informal group was where I met my first 'mum friends', so that when I was up at three o'clock in the morning feeding a screaming baby, I had a mum tribe right there with me facing the same hurdles in life at that moment. Fast-forward five years and now we collectively hold butterflies in the pits of our stomachs as our December babies go off to kindergarten. This commonality has kept our bond strong and forever intertwined.

So, what constitutes a meaningful connection? How does one cultivate a meaningful connection?

Commonalities. Well, obviously. Identifying shared similarities is often the start of a relationship and these often eventuate into deeper conversations that shine a light on possible common core values you share.

Fun. The essence of friendship is the positive and fun stuff. It's this stuff that aids in the cultivations of a friendship worth pursuing.

Communication. Understanding each other's lingo is where it is at. A serious Sally and a sarcastic Susan might not match up well at first glance but it's about understanding how you communicate your needs to your friend and how your friend can effectively communicate theirs to you.

Listen. The most interesting people we meet are often those that ask questions and listen. I mean really listen. They encourage others to speak, and then they listen. Most of us wait to respond in autopilot setting without actually truly listening to the other person.

Genuine. Respecting another person is fundamental for

cultivating a lasting relationship. Have pure intentions for the other person. Don't pretend to like them. This does no person any favours. It is important to note there is a big difference in pretending to like someone and being a decent and respectable human being. Decency should be the default setting of every human but sadly is not. My experience has been that most have likable qualities, but not everyone is likable – but the key is I can still be decent and do no harm.

Confidentiality. We must not compromise by breaching confidentiality. We inherently do not trust people that gossip. It has associations with mistrust. You often see gossiping used as a strategy in attempts to grow a connection. 'Did you see what so and so did?' However, gossip triggers negative collaboration, which might seem like a genuine connection, but gossiping is almost always negative. Who wants to be around negative people? Answer: other negative people.

Show up. No matter what. This approach can be applied to vetting your current relationships. Who shows up for you? Who do you choose to show up for? When called to serve in friendship we must show up to demonstrate our commitment to the other person. Real friends show up in the good times and the bad. If you have people in your life that consistently are not showing up, recognise that they aren't friends – they are what I call surface friendships. Also known as acquaintances. Each of us have many of these. It's the true friends that always show up, a friendship is not meant to be one-sided and sometimes we need to know when to let go.

Boundaries. Know them. Often, we are all quick to give our two cents' worth on a friend's situation. Yet, we despise when we are given unsolicited advice. Only supply upon request! Instead, try empathy. Friends lean on friends, and this can only be done when you stop for a moment and see a situation from your friends' perspective. Boundaries also includes not keeping tabs or score. Too often, many of us are compelled to keep score in our friendships. Your intent should be to contribute in a meaningful way to friends without the expectation of anything in return. This is what builds meaningful and lasting friendships.

Variety. Meaningful connections are not a one size fits all. We have different relationships for different phases and causes within our lives. Often, these roles are stereotyped with traits of the person you cast in that role.

There's the brutally honest friend that never sugar-coats shit. You can always count on them to give you their honest, authentic opinion, and you love them for it. For me, my dear friend Jes holds this title. She's straight real.

The inspirational friend. This person never fails to empower you to be your very best self. They inspire you to push yourself out of your comfort zone and help you grow in life. If you didn't already guess it, Lisa is my soul sister right here.

The confidant friend that knows all your deepest darkest secrets. You could trust them with your life, have done some crazy things together and you're so grateful to have them. If I die, Keiralee knows where all the bodies are buried!

The caregiver friend that always wants to know you got home safe. They genuinely care about your feelings and are always there on your doorstep when you need, whether you know you need it or not. My sister-in-law. Family by marriage, friends by choice. Brooke is so selfless and always on our doorstep in a blink.

The comedian friend is the one you can always count on to make you laugh until your stomach hurts, they never fail to cheer you up and remind you to never take life too seriously. They often don't know they are the funny friend you need in your life. This is Tahla. She is my comedian friend that can always make me laugh, but she is so much more than that. Tahla has more to her than meets the eye.

Surrounding yourself with the right people can be game-changing.

Seek people that inspire you to be the best version of yourself but also accept you at your worst. The idea of finding the right people in your life is choosing those who accept you as you are. People that are good for your mental health and fill your cup. Seriously, even my hairdresser and lash queen share the same values and drive in business as myself and that is why I choose to be a repeat customer. Success in anything in life is about surrounding yourself with people who aren't intimidated when you shine. They don't expect you to dim your light for their comfort, but rather encourage you to shine brighter, and sometimes are even the ones shining the spotlight on you, believing in you every step of the way. Those who are blinded by your light don't share your vision. You are never too much. Perhaps it is merely the vision of others that is too small. This world needs people to stand tall in their truest and rawest form and do what they do because they can. 100% unapologetically. It is only when you do this, you just might find yourself unknowingly shining a light for somebody else trying to find their way … and that is friggin' spectacular.

LESSON 44: SETTING BOUNDARIES IS MANDATORY.

This is inclusive of both your workplace boundaries and your personal boundaries. Very different but equally important to maintain.

When it comes to workplace boundaries, you've got the obvious:

don't eat someone else's food in the staff fridge, rinse your cup out or pop it in the dishwasher – all types of courteous behaviours for general office etiquette. Sometimes, what we consider general office etiquette is still required to be documented in policy and procedure because undoubtably someone in the office will have different ideas on etiquette. Then there are some of the bigger calls that, as the boss, you must just suck it up and make. Despite building a dream team, despite all the support and appreciation you feel you are openly displaying to your employees, sometimes the message is still lost in translation, and we end up with a sticky situation no good employer likes to be in because it is like we are speaking different languages. I am not one for confrontation at the best of times, however, when it comes to my company and what I have built it to stand for and the reputation the team collectively work so hard to maintain, the minute anyone questions my company or my personal integrity on these matters, the gloves are off.

Within our workspace, we have always operated under an 'open door' policy and full transparency. This way of operation has served us successfully in our seven years of operation. Rather than waiting for performance reviews to raise minor performance issues X, Y, Z that happened six months ago, we will check-in via informal methods to correct the non-issue without turning it into 'an issue'. Nine times out of ten, formalising a concern in a quick email to say, *Hey Fi, yesterday it was brought to my attention you forgot to turn the internal lights off before locking up. Just a reminder to ensure this process is done each night of closing. Thanks heaps, Tarsh,* generally does the job. Fiona acknowledges her error and shoots back a quick response, *Hi Tarsh, so sorry, I totally spaced yesterday. It won't happen again. Fi.* And just like that, it's not an issue ever again. We operate our business as grown-arse adults, working with equal grown-arse adults. We all need to be accountable for our actions and inactions. As an employer, when I ask any of my team members, 'How are you?' I legitimately mean it! It's not just a pleasantry. If asking the question is opening Pandora's box, then I should have asked the question long ago. I will always ask my team how are they, are they okay? I want them to know that there is always a line of communication open should they need to raise any concerns with me. I'm not some big bad director sitting in an ivory tower with a management team the employees must go through. If any employee has a concern, they know they can contact me directly.

Equally so, our team know they can contact us at any time should they have any concerns that need a follow-up or immediate attention. It does not matter if we are at home with sick kids, away visiting family or even in a bridal party. We will still be there for our employees in need because that is our commitment, and we have taken this on as a duty of care to our collective team wellbeing. By doing this, it alleviates the need for a formal sit-down meeting behind closed doors, and totally nips it in the bud before we have a disaster on our hands, right?! Don't get me wrong, there are always some performance issues or serious complaints raised that require formal proceedings such as disciplinary meetings. So, seldomly when these matters do arise, it has never come as a surprise to the employee because either a) it's a serious breach of policy and you always know when you've crossed a line, or b) it's compounded performance issues that have continually been raised with the employee in informal chats and email exchange between the employee and management.

When we have to travel this path, our team know 100% we will be following with disciplinary action because that is exactly what our policy framework has been created for. No ifs or buts. These are boundaries that are just simply non-negotiable because the consequence in the business is far too great. Performance management and disciplinary meetings are never about appointing blame, but rather, about recognising strengths and weaknesses, room for improvement and taking on constructive criticism to better any future situations that may arise, or hopefully, don't arise. Can our policy framework be expanded in a particular area to remove any ambiguity that the employee may have perceived? Does the employee require a reinduction to our framework? Have we identified a training weakness we can support? Is there something as an employer I can be doing better to support the employee? The outcome of these formal meetings is always dependant on the attitude presented by the employee within the meeting. I need the employee to take responsibility for whatever part they may have contributed to the situation and be equally responsible for working with us to come up with a solution.

I know confrontation isn't my strong suit, but it doesn't mean I will not toe the line if you are in breach of company best practice. To assist me on this front, Lisa and I engaged an employment advisory company to assist us for all things employment related. Creating contracts, ensuring the award we operate under is the correct award, notifying us of any upcoming government or award changes that impact our operations, and best yet, they provide twenty-four seven on-call support for any enquiries. We use this service for all employment issues. Need to performance-manage an employee, we run that through the employment advisor. That is their space of strength, being all things legal, and we pay a pretty penny for the external company to ensure our company proceeds in the best interests of us and the employee as we navigate our way forward to an amicable solution. Best part is, in the event a situation turns south and heads to court, on the provision we have followed the directives given by our employment advisory, they will front any legal costs. Huge stress relief. Amazing, right!

Over our seven years of operation, our ability to pick amazing employees is usually on point. But every now and then you have that one that comes in, ticks all the boxes on paper and then creates chaos, disrespecting all professional workplace boundaries. Terminating employees is up there with being one of the toughest gigs in my position, along with audit and attending client funerals, but it's a job for a woman with her big-girl pants firmly in place. If I solely focused on the few unpleasant experiences I've had as an employer, it would be miserable, and I would have never had taken the leap. I would also be undermining the amazing kick-arse things our team has done, does do, and will continue to do for our clients and our local community.

A few years ago, we had reached an impasse with an employee with multiple issues raised prior in all the right channels, informal conversations, formal emails, and then a serious breach of privacy and confidentiality. We proceeded with the formalities, the employee attended the meeting and acknowledged her breach and took ownership of it. In the meeting, she understood, given the nature of said breech, there was no coming back from such an incident, as such, by the end of the meeting we were able to amicably determine an outcome. She had admitted to a serious breach and termination was the only path forward. She accepted this, was professional and courteous about the matter … until she wasn't.

Turns out, this employee had a change of heart on the way home and took matters into her own hands, returning to further breach a non-disclosure agreement that was in place during and after employment. The employee went on to slander our company on public social media forums, and even went as far as issuing a cease and desist to a client's formal advocate for simply doing his job in acting in the best interests of his client's basic human rights by reporting the breach of privacy and confidentiality. As awful as that situation was, ignoring my boundaries would have resulted in a far worse situation. When it comes to workplace boundaries, and in particular, client rights to privacy and confidentiality, it is simply black and white.

As for that formal advocate, he was that same formal advocate that we worked alongside with the establishment of the complex disability home, Alex's House. Furthermore, I am so proud to have this amazing human who left his advocacy agency and chose to work with National Community Care. *My team.* This amazing selfless human wanted to work on *my team.* That was a huge proud moment for me. This man rocks the dad vibes and has been a mentor of sorts to me throughout my years in the industry and in navigating the wide world of the NDIA. However, he is so humbly gracious I don't even believe he realises his own power. He is a disruptor, a fighter for justice, possesses the truest of north-facing moral compasses I have ever known and isn't afraid to make some noise to get the job done for those most vulnerable. He deserves a superhero cape.

Grieg … thank you for simply being you

***

When it comes to personal boundaries, that is often where some of the grey can lay.

The definition of boundaries literally means anything that marks a border, a limit, a metaphorical line in the sand. They are built out of a mix of conclusions, beliefs, opinions, attitudes and social learnings. These boundaries are not obvious like a fenced perimeter or a giant flashing neon sign reading 'do not enter' or your workplace boundaries in your black-and-white digital rule book. Personal boundaries are invisible bubbles that articulate your limit which are often based around your moral compass.

Some of our bubbles are impenetrable barriers, others can be malleable and adaptable, and some are barely tangible – but all are boundaries, nonetheless. Even though our boundaries can be challenging to navigate, they are essential to our health, wellbeing and even our safety. Our personal boundaries help define ourselves by outlining likes and dislikes and set the distances one is willing to accept. Setting and sustaining boundaries is a skill, and a skill that is applicable in personal and professional life.

Impenetrable: Solid walls that cannot be moved unless forced. For example: no means no.

Malleable: Boundary can be altered if situation calls for it. For example: I don't check my work emails on the weekend, however, I am expecting an important one I cannot miss.

Intangible: A very loose boundary. For example: this new year resolution I am going to the gym every single day … wait, it's February already? F*ck.

Healthy boundaries are necessary components for self-care. It is equally necessary that we make our boundaries clear to avoid a breach. Without respected boundaries, we can feel diminished, taken advantage of, taken for granted or intruded upon. Whether it's in work or in our personal relationships, poor boundaries may lead to relationship breakdowns, resentment, hurt, anger and burnout. Boundaries help us take care of ourselves by giving us permission to say NO to things, to not take everything on. Boundaries draw a clear line around what is okay for us and what is not. It is important to remember this looks different on every person.

In life, we already have many boundaries automatically in place for ourselves. Boundaries such as the law and socially acceptable behaviours. The law governs a lot of what is acceptable and what is not, which in turn, often shapes our views on these things. But I'm talking about boundaries you identify that you need to alter or implement to set a harder limit. When it comes to setting boundaries, you must remember that you are not responsible for the other person's reaction to said boundary. You are only responsible for communicating your boundary in a respectful manner.

Setting boundaries isn't always comfortable, even more so when you are naturally a people-pleaser. So, when you realise something needs to change and you need to implement a hard boundary, people may push back if you say no to something or try communicating your needs more clearly. People may try to test your limits, to see how serious you are about drawing the line. It may just mean that you need to be clear and consistent until people adjust to the new way of interacting because you do deserve to take a stand.

Your personal boundaries stem from knowing your worth. It's not about believing you are better than any other person or that your opinion is greater. Self-worth means you know you have value, you are deserving of respect and your boundaries should be equally respected as any other.

Boundaries allow us to preserve our energy and ensure we are not always pouring from our cup. It is about understanding that, just because you may be happy to lend a hand to your bestie who is moving house, doesn't mean you also have to do the heavy emotional lifting when someone texts about their latest drama.

This was a skill I had to learn when becoming a boss, as equally as I had to find, facilitate and build meaningful connections. I needed to create my business based around what is essentially my personal branding. I needed to articulate what that was exactly to ensure my employees knew the boundaries and framework to operate within, and the message and mission would be visible to our world of clients. My boundaries needed to have clarity, confidence and connection. So, I set out to do just that. Creating boundaries like a **boss** requires five key steps.

Be assertive: Stick to your guns and ensure you implement effective communication in expressing your boundaries. The famous 'how to use I' statement is used in psychology and by many life coaches across the globe. It is a statement that invokes you to be assertive but not confronting, making it a much more compassionate and effective way to communicate your needs.

'I feel _____ *when* _____
because _____

What I need is _____
_____,

Learn to say no: Long gone are the days where we were conditioned to say yes to every opportunity. A 'no' is just as good as a 'yes'! 'No' is a complete sentence. There are many instances where it is acceptable for you to never feel you need to provide anything more than a no in response without offering any excuse. When it comes to your personal boundaries, I fully support a, *'HELL NO!'*

Safeguard your space: Every person in the history of the planet deserves the right to a space to feel safe. When it comes to boundaries, this can extend to not just your physical space, but also your emotional space, your time and energy, and even possessions such as your tech devices, journals, diaries, calendars etc.

Know your hard limits: Just like in *Fifty Shades of Grey*, you need to know what your absolute non-negotiable hard limits are when it comes to your boundaries. Too often, we push our instincts aside because we convince ourselves we may be jumping the gun or tell ourselves we are being unreasonable because this seems the easier solution requiring less action from ourselves to reroute the situation. If it doesn't get any more comfortable, it is clear to say it is a red flag and a hard limit may be nearing.

Be authentic: You, just like any other person, have the right to your own thoughts, feelings and needs. You should also be able to express them freely.

Using this approach, I developed our company boundaries. Also known as our company handbook. Our fundamentals. The rule book. Our guidelines. Our true north. This book has exponentially grown over the years alongside the company, but it has always ensured our team knows the brand they represent and exactly what is expected of them, what it is that we provide and how exactly we choose to do that.

LESSON 45: HATERS GONNA HATE.

Have you ever noticed, when you step outside your comfort zone and experience a level-up, someone in the back is always throwing shade? Being a heckler, casting a cloud on your glory, raining on your parade? Downplaying your win! Firstly, once upon a time, with the help of Nancy, I used to do this to myself. Now I am no longer my own barrier, I have noticed that there will still always be that 'friend' or family member that can't just be happy for your moment of glory. Not just for me personally but also for a lot of people I hold dear.

Naturally, it is human nature to recall all the negativity you receive, and boy, do I have a long list … where do I start?

You're not a real Islander.
You're not a real Australian.
How come you didn't die from your cancer?
Oh, you only work in the community sector?
IVF isn't natural. Maybe it's just not meant to be.
Miscarriage, lucky it was only early in the pregnancy.
D&C? That's nothing, we've all been there.
Oh, you're mix feeding your baby?
Antidepressants don't really work; they are just a placebo. You just need to think positive.
Oh, you're going to send your baby to a germ-filled day care?
But you don't know the first thing about running a business?
So, what did you have to sacrifice?
But you didn't go to university?
Oh, so you're a podcaster now?
So, you were nominated for an award, and you actually proceeded with the application?
Wait, what? You have to pay for your application? So, you bought your award?
Since when did you write books?
Businesswoman of the Year 2021? Seriously?

I could go and discredit all these statements in a blink.

For example, miscarriage is a lost child regardless of the gestation period. The process and level of hormones released is the same and is equally as devastating.

OR, yes, my baby is mixed fed. Because fed is better than hungry and damn straight my sanity is important too.

OR, yes, damn straight I won Businesswoman of the Year. No, their standards aren't slipping, in fact, it was the largest number of applications for consideration in 2021. *Insert middle finger*

PROJECT KIND

But you know what ... at some point in your life, you just get tired of unhealthy connections, whether it be people or things or stupid negative uneducated and spiteful comments. As you grow, certain things become intolerable. That's perfectly okay. In fact, that is a level-up, girlfriend! It took me too many decades to accept the simple fact that no matter what I do, or do not do, someone is still going to displeased. So, I am not wasting another minute defending the way I choose to live my life.

Do good, they will talk. Do bad, they will talk. So, do you, and let them talk. I've always found that often it is the people who aren't happy within themselves that are mean to others. Let them misunderstand you. Let them gossip about you, their opinions aren't your problems, just as your opinions are not theirs. Don't allow it to have any bearing on your existence. It's about staying kind, committed and free within your own authenticity. It is only here, in this space, you can ensure you never doubt your worth and you stay true to yourself. Automatically rising you above.

Sometimes, it is accepting that people will not know your side of the story. This may very well mean that some people will draw conclusions on your behalf. Let them. If this is what they choose to do, rather than asking you directly to make an informed judgement about you, then screw them. You don't have to prove yourself to anyone. The real key is being disciplined about what you respond and react to. Not everyone or everything deserves your time, energy and attention. Stay in your light. As my mum has always told us, 'If you have nothing nice to say, then keep your mouth shut.'

One of the biggest barriers besides your mindset when levelling up your life can be the company you keep. Sometimes a by-product of levelling up includes outgrowing people, and there is nothing wrong with that. The people you may be outgrowing are generally the same people who will question and push the boundaries you set. So often, this process is tainted with labels and stereotypes that accuse you of becoming 'stuck up', or that you are suddenly above others when you attempt to part ways, or even hold on for dear life. However, this isn't the case at all, and I bet if you have ever been labelled these things, the people responsible were most likely the people you've outgrown.

Outgrowing your friends often means that you are both in different stages in life, and perhaps the activities and interests you once shared are no longer relevant within your lives. Every living thing in life evolves, so of course, that includes relationships. This can occur due to a few factors, including age – maybe it's no longer a priority to go nightclubbing, or perhaps your careers and families took you on different paths, you may have had personal or emotional growth that you feel the other has not, resulting in feeling like you are not seen, heard or understood now.

Ask yourself: Are you dreading catch-ups? Do you constantly take a raincheck or look for the easy exit plan? Would you be friends if you met today or do you hold onto the link of the past? Do you filter yourself around your friend? If the answer is yes to any of those questions, chances are, you aren't being your authentic self with your friend and are most likely dimming your light due to the fact that you may have evolved as a person. As people get older and move on with their lives, it's normal that life changes. Letting go of old friendships can make you feel guilty if the other person hasn't done anything wrong, but it's natural for your social circle to shift as time goes by.

In our years of schooling and early adult life, as a society, we tend to proceed with the belief that the duration of a relationship trumps all else. It is the pinnacle of identifying a solid friendship.

PROJECT KIND

The longer the relationship is, the more serious it is assumed. In some instances, this is true, however not all instances will this mean a bond is stronger based only upon time. Yet we find ourselves often feeling obliged to maintain said relationships that have, in truth, become more of an acquaintance than a friend. Sometimes, it's their relationships that require some re-evaluation.

Sometimes the signs are all but obvious we need to end the relationship. It can include:

- They betray your trust.
- They put you in danger or an unsafe environment.
- They pass on harsh judgement.
- They don't respect you.

But then sometimes it's a little more subtle but still a red flag just the same:

- Avoiding catch-up commitments.
- It feels as if they suck your life force.
- They aren't there for you when you need them.
- They have a knack of making you feel like a shitty friend.
- You enable each other's bad habits.
- You are expected to like and dislike the same people at all costs.
- You barely have anything to talk about.
- You hold each other back.
- You do all the emotional work.
- They don't value your time and efforts.
- They resent your growth.
- They belittle your achievements and tease you.
- Your communication styles just don't meet in the middle.

It is important to note you may feel like it is you being the shitty friend. Perhaps it is you. That is okay too. The idea is about identifying when the shift has occurred and freeing both parties of the relationship in order to effectively move forward.

Ignoring red flags because you want to see the good in people will cost you greatly later. I am always a seeker of good. So much so I often overlook somebody's faults to see their strengths. This isn't because I am a sucker or that I think the world is all rainbows and lollipops. It's because I'd rather avoid the uncomfortable friend break-up, but sometimes we need to let go of things that no longer serve us to make room for clearer minds and brighter futures.

How to break up with friends acquaintances:

Now let's just clarify something … if you are certain you are terminating a relationship here, the person you are ending said relationship with someone who is obviously no longer a 'friend' in the true meaning of the word. So, you are really breaking up with an acquaintance that used to be a friend …

Respect: Where physically possible (geographically) do it face to face. This is a sign of respect for the ex-friend because obviously once upon a time you both did have immense respect for each other. You shouldn't lower your standards just because you feel they may have. Be the bigger person. Maintain your integrity.

Clarity: When ending a relationship, you need to be clear but kind. To the point but thoughtful. Don't leave it ambiguous like there is hope they could possibly win you over, or worse, they end up steamrolling you into submission if you are not definite about your stance.

Empathy: Remember, the demise of a relationship is often because feelings are changed as a result of things that have or have not occurred within the relationship. Your ex-friend may not have seen the break-up coming. Express your sadness and allow for the ex-friend to react and show empathy.

Avoid: Don't let the conversation turn into a blaming or shaming episode of *Jerry Springer*. Don't engage in arguments or give in to protests.

Lastly, **Remember:** Some people will judge you for changing and others will celebrate you for growing. Choose your circle carefully. You deserve to have a support network that does just that … supports. One of my favourite quotes I see across a lot of social media is, 'Be so confident in knowing what you bring to the table that you're willing to eat alone until you find the right table.' – Unknown. Lisa and I are very proud of who we invite to sit with us.

SUCCESS
BEYOND MY WILDEST DREAMS

Success. [su*h*k-**ses**]

noun

the favourable or prosperous termination of attempts or endeavours; the accomplishment of one's goals.

the attainment of wealth, position, honours, or the like.

a performance or achievement that is marked by success, as by the attainment of honours.

a person or thing that has had success, as measured by attainment of goals, wealth.

Obsolete. outcome.

> *'You can't go back and change the beginning, but you can start where you are and change the ending.'*
> *– C S Lewis*

LESSON 46: THE RIGHT TIME TO START IS NOW.

Success. How do you know when you reach it? Is it an end goal? Is it something tangible? Is it a feeling? Is it unattainable? There is no single measure of success. Just like the notion of 'having it all', there is no single answer for how to be successful in life because success looks different for every person. Success to one person may be 100% career orientated, while to another it may be completely family orientated! Regardless of the vast possibilities of what success may look like for each of us, we can find reoccurring themes in the tactics, strategies and behaviours of those we, as a society, label as successful. In doing this, we can implement these into our own daily lives.

***

When?

The most common question I get asked in business, besides what got me on this path, is, 'How did you know when the time was right to start?'

Truth bomb moment – I didn't. There **never** really is a 'right' time. All the planets could be aligned, all the pieces to the puzzle in place, the weather on point, and you will still find a reason why now is not the right time. Nancy is spectacular at assisting you in this area.

People with half your talent are making serious waves while you're still waiting to feel ready. Honey, if the stars couldn't align for Romeo and Juliet, the chance of them aligning for you are just as unlikely. It comes down to how much we really want something, and what lengths and sacrifices we're willing to make during the process to achieve what it is we want to do. When we tell ourselves the timing isn't right, it usually boils down to fear. Fear of failing, fear of not knowing how to get it. Fear of what others may think of our great plan. Fear of it succeeding, then what!? When it comes down to deciding if you're ready to start something new, it's more about your own mindset than any other barrier. Be it a new gym class, a diet, a business venture, a side-hustle … the principle is the same.

Do you believe you are in the frame of mind right now to start and have success? If you can honestly answer with anything from a 'yeah' to a 'heck yes' then you are ready to take the jump. Much like skydiving. When I was nineteen, I had finished chemotherapy and the boys wanted to get me a present I would never forget. They didn't tell me what it was; even on my birthday as we were headed for the airport, I still could not have fathomed I would be skydiving. When it comes to skydiving, you can do all the training in the world – you can ensure your parachute is packed properly and your equipment is in good working order. You can complete all your safety checks and have highly qualified professionals with you, you can have the perfect weather for jumping. Your plane can arrive at the optimal jumping height of 14,000ft ready to go. The only thing between you and your freefall is your ability to let go and jump. To trust the process and know you have managed every possible variable leading up to this point.

It is scary as hell – both skydiving and starting a business. But isn't that where all greatness occurs? Just outside that comfort zone of ours? When it comes to operating a successful business (or a skydive) there is never room for complacency. Yes, just like skydiving, when you start a business, it can feel like you are freefalling to your death for what feels like an eternity. But then the parachute is ejected and your pace changes. Suddenly things calm down, you can catch your breath and find your mojo as you glide and navigate your way to the landing pad. There are many ways that can be done, just like the many business styles people may implement. You need to work out what is best for you and your business.

If you are like me, that answer was probably too ambiguous for you, and you were after something tangible. That black-and-white answer as to when should you start your next venture?

On the provision you have done the legwork, now. The time is now!

'What is legwork?' you say.

I'm talking about your research, your homework, your recon, your scouting mission to know that your business idea is a viable one. Great businesses aren't just created and successful in a day. In fact, it was my accountant that seared the comment into my brain: 'The majority of start-ups don't make profit within a year and are lucky to make it past two years.' Here are some of the areas I have always focused on when starting up:

Market research and forward planning.

Are you jumping into an industry that is already flooded with what it is you are wanting to sell? That's okay, BUT what makes your product or service the premium above the others? What sets you apart from the others? Is there a need for the product or service you want to provide? How will the world know what you have to offer? What are your competitors offering? What areas can you dominate? Are your charge rates competitive but reflective of your worth? Is this sustainable? Cost-effective long-term?

Suppliers and overheads.
What up-front costs do you require? Do you need software to operate? Do you need product from external suppliers? How many hours will this take from you before you forecast a wage or profit? Insurances to operate, website and branding. These all incur overhead costs. Does your service price cover this to ensure you are recouping costs? Your charge rates need to be reflective of the service you are providing. Don't undersell yourself.

Branding.
What is your logo? What colours are relatable to your product? Is your branding to the point? Is it clear? Did you know there is psychology of colour in your branding choices? Seriously! Across all the medical appointments and hospitals I have ever attended, every single logo was blue based. The idea of the psychology of colour indicates that certain colours evoke certain emotions. It's those same emotions that become a major factor for your client/consumers when they make purchasing decisions. For example, the colour red evokes emotions of strength, passion, excitement. It also evokes appetite! Have you noticed red is used extensively in marketing in the food industry, due to its ability to trigger appetite?

PROJECT KIND

Major brands including Lay's, KFC, McDonald's, Coca-Cola, Hungry Jack's, Pizza Hut, Red Rooster. Red also indicates energy and confidence, and as such, some of the world's most powerful brands make use of the colour red. Target, Netflix, Coca-Cola and YouTube are some strong, confident brands.

When it came to branding and creating my company, National Community Care, I wanted to be different but not outrageous. People don't want to take risks when it comes to their health and the care they receive. So, my brief became not only different and not outrageous, but also safe. Now I was getting somewhere. Green is said to represent freshness, growth, safety and relaxation. Green is the easiest colour for vision which meant, for my brand, it was inclusive to the clientele. I think it's worth noting that your branding also does not have to be realistic, do you think Steve Jobs thought an apple logo would represent his computer empire? Probably not, yet here we are, and the apple logo is iconic worldwide. However, this brand did take decades of consistently showing up to gain its renowned status.

Promoting.
How will the world know who you are, where you are, what you sell and why you sell it? Websites are easy enough to set up these days, and you can save a lot of overhead cost by maintaining it on user-friendly platforms such as Wix, Squarespace or Jimdo. But how does someone find your website or your social media pages? Other than inviting all your friends and family members, how do you generate meaningful connections in a virtual space that will generate your business? It is about knowing your brand. For example, National Community Care could advertise across social platforms, however, these platforms aren't usually resources one thinks to use

when seeking nursing services, so our marketing strategy is much different when seeking clients. However, social media is the perfect place for recruitment of employees.

My subscription box company, Project Kind, relies on email subscribers, social media followers and engagement with customers across these platforms. This is something most of us just fumble our way through when first starting off, however, there are amazing humans that focus on marketing solutions that you can choose to engage. This could be through a formal marketing company or a virtual assistant. There are editable marketing templates and social content calendars out there and amazing online workshops and groups you can join. Basically, there are marketing solutions for all business owners, of all business sizes and budgets.

If you have a solid idea and a strong foundation, then the only thing holding you back from starting today is you. Sometimes that can be hard to hear. The only way you can overcome a barrier starts with identifying said barrier. Perfect doesn't exist, the right time doesn't exist. Feeling 100% ready doesn't exist. Stop waiting for things that don't exist to start whatever it is you want to start. You need to create it for it to exist. Good things might come to those who wait, but I'd like to know how long they had to wait … Why wait when great things come to those who *do*. Be a do-er.

2005 Skydiving for my twentieth birthday post-cancer

LESSON 47: CELEBRATE THE GOOD.

It's no surprise to most of us that when we get a chance to sit on the couch and flick on the TV, the radio station or browse the online news platform, we are likely to come away believing that the world is rapidly descending into chaos and disaster. This is on account of the negative bias. Negative bias refers to the fact that it has become human nature to focus on the negative. As such, media outlets know their product and their consumer, and they portray their news in a way that will consistently emphasis exactly that, hooking the consumer in every time.

Have you ever noticed the news and media are filled with crimes, death and death tolls, destruction, protests, war and then there is literally one single good-news story which is generally the smallest and last bulletin? That good-news piece is almost published as if it is a novelty piece that pales in significance to the negative news. That is bloody depressing. This negative bias is exactly what fuels our negative Nancy and makes us hold on to the negativity we receive which always inevitably drowns out the positive. I hate that this is even a thing. We are already predisposed to negative bias. Then the media uses that to their advantage as a smart business marketing tactic, and ultimately, nurtures a perpetual cycle of negativity.

I choose to actively make celebrating the good stuff a core value both personally and professionally. Don't get me wrong, it took me a long time to externalise my wins, but now that I do, I feel so foolish for not having done so much sooner. I was prisoner to my own self-doubt. But why? It's not like I failed at the said situation. I succeeded, so why do we hold such modestly around these amazing milestones and achievements? Coming right back to impostor syndrome … No, no, no, no, no!!!

Regardless of the size or complexity of the good worth celebrating, choosing to actively live in this mindset suddenly brings colour and light back into your world. When you 'shine bright' and allow yourself to shine, I spoke about how opportunities can present and often good comes from those opportunities. Celebrate them unashamedly. In doing this you truly can accept your success. You didn't just stumble here by accident. You certainly didn't get here overnight. Don't allow the good to pass you by, otherwise, truly, what is the point? If you truly cannot celebrate your own successes and be proud of what amazing things you have achieved, then it just becomes so easy to get stuck on the hamster wheel and become disengaged with life.

After six years of awaiting to be officially placed into remission and declared cancer free, I threw myself the biggest party and called it my 'Life Party'. Literally celebrating the simple fact that I am alive because I beat cancer. Every year since then, on 19 January, the day I completed my treatment, I pause, reflect and celebrate my blessings. At thirty-six weeks pregnant with our first earthside miracle baby, I didn't want your standard baby shower with lame baby games. I wanted to celebrate with all our friends both female and male. So together, Guy and I threw an 'End of life as we know it Baby-Q'. Birthdays last all month long (for me, at least).

Today, in our family home, we wake up and always start the day by asking Google what the weather will be. We always somehow manage to find the silver lining to the forecast and celebrate it accordingly. Sunshine – awesome, the kids can scoot to school. Rain – gumboots and muddy puddles. Thunderstorms – cuddles on the couch after school. We celebrate swimming lesson skill milestones, kids wiping their own backsides equals high fives (after you have flushed and washed your hands!) and sleeping in their own beds for the entire night. (These are worth celebrating!) Tuesdays are known as ice cream Tuesdays because every kid in our house, old and young, should experience the joy of ice cream on a weekly basis and a school night makes it even more exciting! The celebrations in our house do not automatically constitute rewarding with gift-giving or prizes of any kind. A celebration can be verbal positive reinforcement. It could be getting to pick what we cook for dinner tonight, or getting to pick the Netflix movie, or let's face it, sometimes it is taking the four-year-old down to Kmart to pick a $5 toy.

Within my business, we do the same with the staff. Lisa and I have always celebrated our staff. Their wins are our wins whether it be births, deaths, birthdays, graduations, citizenship, marriages, even divorce. If it is important to our team, it is a celebration worth having. A workplace celebration can take many forms. Some occasions, where possible, we physically go to the location of the employee to surprise them with cake, flowers and gifts. Other times it could be during the team meeting or arranged in a private one on one. It's never a one-size-fits-all approach. We like to think about what the employee would appreciate. An avid crafter being gifted tickets to the folk art festival would be perfect, but one of our university nursing students would probably prefer a voucher or monetary bonus. That additional thought of personalising our approach confirms validation to our team that we honestly give a damn, and we value them whole-heartedly.

If these celebrations bring our employee a sense of joy, appreciation, belonging, happiness and/or light even for a moment, then it is always totally worth it. Celebrating the good has nothing but benefits:

- Releases feel-good chemicals into our brains.
- Helps reinforce positive behaviours and attitudes.
- Reduces stress.
- Promotes motivation.
- Cultivates optimism.
- It is an energy giver, a cup filler.

So, what are some creative ways to celebrate your own good moments? I'm glad you asked …

- Have a YOU day.
- Buy flowers.
- Buy that outrageous dress.
- Go for a massage.
- Drink champagne … because it's a day ending in Y.
- Eat dessert before dinner.
- Buy a cake. Why is cake only ever reserved for birthdays and weddings?
- Toast yourself for being amazing.
- Treat yourself to something you wouldn't buy on your average day.
- Own it and memorialise the celebration on a celebration pinboard or Instagram Highlight.
- Treat yourself to an adventure from your bucket list.
- Change something. A habit, a hairstyle or colour. Change your make-up palette.
- Date your own damn self. Treat yourself to a movie or art gallery on your own.
- Throw a party.
- Have a celebration dinner with your nearest and dearest.

- Buy the lipstick and rock the shit out of it.
- Buy and plant a tree.
- Get a pedicure.
- Buy a star.
- Go and try out that float tank.
- Join that reformer Pilates class.
- Try a Bikram yoga session.
- Upgrade your tech: phone, laptop, tablet, computer, earbuds.
- Upgrade your desirables: hair dryer, car, TV, Thermomix.
- Go out for dinner.
- Order yourself a grazing platter for dinner.
- Get your favourite takeaway for a night at home.
- Go on a day trip to the closest beach.
- Buy those earrings you want but totally do not need.
- Book that trip, that holiday, that concert that you have been wanting forever.
- Print and frame your success. Newspaper article? Book cover? Magazine cover? Certificate?
- Capture and frame a photo of the moment.
- Collect your successes in a digital file to keep and cherish forever.
- Print and bind said collection into a coffee table book.
- Do something silly like roly-poly down the grass hill with your kids.
- Get dressed up with a little extra!
- My favourite is dressing UP on Friday. While most workplaces have casual Friday, I'm more about celebrating the arrival of the weekend and wearing something snazzy!

LESSON 48: ALWAYS KEEP PERSPECTIVE.

Through a lot of the lessons I have learnt in life, one of the common factors across many of them has been to learn and strengthen my ability to keep an open mind to the perspective of all theories, options, thoughts or sides that may be involved. Seeing the bigger picture allows you to proceed knowing you are doing so with informed knowledge.

Why is seeing the bigger picture important? Like I highlighted in Lesson 11, the key to having the 'right' approach to perspective is acknowledging that your view is not the alpha perspective, and more importantly, that all perspectives matter. Having the ability to hold perspective keeps us grounded. Don't get me wrong, I believe both big-picture and detail-oriented thinking are crucial, and in fact, complement each other.

By thinking big, you're less likely to worry and panic over the finer details that ultimately won't matter in the long run, and a big-picture person is likely to see how a roadblock impacts the big picture and how that can turn into an opportunity. This is a great skill to possess if you're leading a team, but as most things in life are, it is never as simple as it seems. It is always the detail-orientated people that make the magic happen.

So, which am I? you ask yourself. One way to find out is by seeing what you tend to focus on naturally.

1. Do you set a project goal and just focus on getting to the result?
2. Do you give so many details in your project you easily end up down a rabbit hole?
3. Do you tend to keep a bird's-eye view on things, and feel frustrated when working on projects where you can't see how it connects to a broader plan?

For me, I am a number three, making me a blend of both big picture and detail orientated. I see the bigger picture, and the ins and outs of all the finer details and am easily frustrated when I can't see or understand a process of something. However, this approach can look different depending on the situation at hand.

Example one: in school, whenever I would have math homework, Mum would send me to Dad for help. My dad has always been a boy genius. He would explain whatever the solution was to me. Let's say, I had to work out the circumference of a circle. Pi is used to find area by multiplying the radius squared by pi. On top of this, I had a calculator with the pi value programmed in. But to my mind, it was stupid. It didn't make sense. Why is pi 3.14? Who said pi is 3.14? Why was it called pi? How did pi become pi? My dad would tell me, 'It's pi because it just is.' That method got me the right answer, yes, but it did not appease my curiosity. I would go on to research why pi was 3.14 and learn the history of it. For me, this meant I understood the whole process. To my dad, he pointed out I would still get the same answer regardless of my history lesson …

Example two: finding out I had cancer. Suddenly, none of the details matter. Who cares if Helen owes me $200? Who cares if I ate ten too many jam donuts? Who cares if I didn't get to the gym this week? Who cares if my sisters raided my wardrobe again? Who cares if Katlyn thinks I'm a bitch? NONE of those things will impact me today, tomorrow or when I am dead. Cancer … now that impacts every moment from here on out. #perspective

Practising and developing your perspective muscle is seriously life altering. Suddenly you are open to seeing the other person's view. You don't need to agree with them, but often, understanding how they got to that perspective is eye-opening and can provide room for negotiation on the provision the other person is willing to be equally as open-minded and consider how you reached your point of view. Unfortunately, the perspective muscle seems to be a rare commodity within the human race.

Flexing your perspective muscle is about acknowledging every emotion is valid. This doesn't mean the thought surrounding that emotion is fact, however, the way it is making one feel can be very real. We each have our own truths regarding our emotions, and it is never up to another person to make us feel worthy, validated or happy. Those feelings are all an inside job, yet so many relationships seek validation and happiness from one another. Food for thought, maybe this is why our divorce rate was recorded by the Australian Bureau of Statistics at one in every 2.3 marriages in 2020.[17]

Changing or broadening your perspective is an active decision only you can choose to make. To exercise this perspective muscle, we can consciously seek happiness for ourselves. By doing this, you will see things more positively and seek things of a positive nature. By doing this, you are shifting the default negative setting and allowing yourself to be a happier and more positive person with a broader perspective. When it comes to shifting that negative setting, this includes curbing your complaining about anything and everything. Nobody enjoys listening to a perpetual complainer. They are always labelled negative, sour or life-sucking, to name a few. Does it really matter if your Uber driver took a wrong turn? Does it really matter if the light was left on in the bathroom? Does it really matter who ate the last peppermint slice biscuit? Does it really matter if your child spilt juice on the kitchen floor? None of these accidents are life-threatening. Our responses to such instances should reflect accordingly.

I can hand-on-heart say a big portion of my success in life and in business has come down to my perspective and my ability to see past my own backyard. It is about empathy, kindness and courage. All traits I confidently know and absolutely own. Success does not happen by accident, but by habit. It comes from our ability to be intentional in our interactions, not only with others, but ourselves, and cultivating those meaningful connections. It is okay to have high expectations of yourself, but that is much different from beating yourself up or expecting the impossible. It is normal to let others' criticisms get to us, but do not let it stop you from doing something great. This is the essence of perspective. The greatest tool a leader should possess. It is in having this, you realise that any success you achieve hits differently because you have stopped giving a shit about what other people think and just do you.

LESSON 49: KNOW WHEN TO WALK AWAY.

Do good and good will come is a belief that spans many cultures across our globe. In a world of such chaos, surely if we are collectively agreeing on a matter there must be truth to it, right?! It's practically a science. Unfortunately, not always. Not every human is going to be as genuine as you hope, and not every human will have your best interests at heart. This is because, at the end of the day, our instinct is to survive above all else. To look after number one.

This does not mean as a kind and decent human you need to change the way you operate. If this book has highlighted anything throughout the chapters, it is about being authentic and true to your core values when you navigate life, wherever that path may take you. Maintaining your integrity while doing that is the highest honour, and knowing when you need to walk away is essential to your wellbeing.

PROJECT KIND

Now, my husband will be first in line to tell you I am no quitter. I am the most stubborn person he knows. That says a lot because I would have thought my kids took the cake on that front. I must admit I am stubborn. Strong-willed. Sometimes righteous. But – I also know I am very capable of recognising when it is time to walk away. Okay, okay, yes, I am a sucker for always giving others the benefit of the doubt to not be a shit human, up until the last possible second … I know when I was dating Richard, it took me a while to realise I was flogging a dead horse, but I got there. I walked away, and I have done this with many lost causes in my adult life.

There is such a social emphasis that being a quitter is a declaration of defeat, a sign of weakness. But I believe there is so much more to it than that. Sometimes it is doing exactly that – letting go and walking away is how you win. It is knowing that you refuse to accept anything less than your worth or standards and that you are strong enough to realise you do deserve better. We shouldn't have to sacrifice our happiness, our sanity or our light for the sake of any one thing or one person who would not do the same in return. In doing this, we are choosing our best interests. Our wellbeing. Our own mental health. That is not selfish. That is self-love, self-respect and strength.

It took me until my adult life to realise this, so when I did, it became a core value Guy and I chose to instil in our children. Like all loving parents, we endeavour to ensure our kids to have a strong sense of their self-worth. This is weaved through our family core values and house rules to be kind, be brave and be true. Sometimes, to walk away from something, it requires all three of those acts. Kindness to yourself to do such a thing. Bravery to act in your best interests when no-one else will. And truth to know that something may no longer serve you in a productive or healthy way.

Disclaimer: *Before I go on with my story that will reflect the concept of walking away, please note this story is in relation to my daughter. By no means do I claim to be a parenting extraordinaire. I wasn't given some magical handbook at birth, and I often tell the kids I will sell them to the monkey house. Just like all parents, I'm totally just winging it, surviving one day at a time, with absolutely no idea, just a hope to raise a half-decent human.*

When my daughter had just turned four, she didn't want to attend her swimming lessons anymore because the new swim class she would be going into had – in her four-year-old words – a 'boy teacher' and she didn't want a boy teacher. Now, my daughter is stubborn, so I knew I would be flogging a dead horse if I decided to battle her on this one. So, we told Cadence if this was her decision, then with that comes responsibility and consequence. That included my daughter being responsible for going down to the swim school and being kind, brave and true. Cadence had to speak to the receptionist to let her know she wished to swap classes … and to my utter surprise, my little girl was kind, brave and true. She did just that, and not only did she do it, but she did it confidently and proudly.

The lovely receptionist was able to accommodate Cadence's request, and this meant Cadence was content to stay in swimming lessons. She had a win; Mum had a win, and she would still be learning the important skill of swimming!

By supporting her choices and pointing out that our actions are not just faceless acts, I taught her a lesson that it is perfectly okay to walk away, however, we need to take responsibility when we do so. The consequence of not knowing how to swim meant no more beach trips to Ma and Pa's house or swimming at her cousin's house in their pool. These were not consequences Cadence wanted to face, so she made an informed decision to request a transfer of classes.

Yes, I could have toed the line, pulled rank and made her go to swimming with the male teacher. But would she have fought me about the matter the entire way? *You bet.* Would she have enjoyed going to class? *Absolutely not.* Would she have participated in the class? *I know for a fact she wouldn't have even gotten in the pool if she didn't want to.* Like I said, she rivals my stubbornness. Would this go on to possibly have her resist even harder the next time she had a male teacher? *With her stubborn streak, I could almost guarantee it.* Would hitting my head against a brick wall be more successful? *Damn straight.* Mumma knows best ... some of the time, at least.

Cadence navigated her way through acknowledging her self-worth and personal comfort zone and did something about it. I wish I was half as brave as she was at her age. The very next school term, Cadence also went on to have a male gymnastics coach who she confidently respected and enjoyed going to his classes. I whole-heartedly believe this was because I provided her a safe space to make that call on her own. I'm no mum expert by any means and I'm first to raise my hand in the shitty mum stakes riddled with the mum guilt, but I was pretty proud of my girl.

Another example I have is an experience of my dear friend Ruby. I've known Ruby for fifteen years now. Ruby is a life-loving, happy-go-lucky high-achieving go-getter. She's confident, bubbly, beautiful and follows her dreams wherever they may lead her. I admire Ruby's zest for life. Over the years, Ruby has had a handful of businesses all varying in size and success. One of her bigger ventures was opening a boutique hot dog franchise. Ruby became the best damn hot dog queen in town. Unfortunately, Ruby's situation was not conducive for the long term, and with no business plan in place, she was left out in the cold having to walk away from her business partners.

Recently, when talking to Ruby, she was seeking advice or any recommendations for business start-up courses, stating she had a lot of fear and old failures floating around her head that was ultimately holding her back. It caught me off guard. I had always admired Ruby's grit and determination to give things a go. She's always been an 'all-in' kind of girl. Then it hit me, Ruby's inner critic was in the building, and she was doubting her kick-arse abilities! 'Ruby, don't you see? It's not a failed business venture. You recognised your worth and made an informed decision to walk away. That, to me, is a very smart business decision!' I'm so proud of Ruby, and no matter what she chooses to do in life she always lands on her feet. Remember – you got this, Ruby Rhubarb!

So, what are the tell-tale signs that perhaps it's time to walk away? It could be a relationship, a job, a possession … regardless of what it is that you may need to walk away from, if it impacts, limits, stunts, stops or hinders your boundaries and standards, your happiness, your peace or your sense of reality and worth, then it's time to go. It really is that simple. These things should never be up for negotiation. That is self-worth 101.

Remember, you haven't done anything wrong. At times, we are faced with an impossible situation, and you do what you must do to restore the balance and self-respect within your life. Knowing when to walk away is a skill that will serve you well in all facets of life.

PROJECT KIND

LESSON 50: BE A SILVER LINING SEEKER.

'I am stronger because I had to be, I am smarter because of my mistakes, happier because of the sadness I've known, and now wiser because I learned.'
– Unknown

One simple but powerful way to enhance your quality of life is to find silver linings within the arduous situations we face. It might seem impossible at times when you find yourself in difficult situations, but I assure you, if you look, you will find a silver lining. Like all habits and behaviours, if this is not something you naturally gravitate toward, it may take you a little extra conscious work to seek the silver, but it is possible if you allow it. When we think about why we don't naturally look for the good in the shitty situations, we realise it is because sometimes we need to sit there in our pity and be miserable. Feel all the feelings. Go through the motions. That is normal. That is healthy. Then comes a point we need to start seeking solutions and find the silver in the situation. It's here we build our resilience and improve our view of the world around us, because let's face it, nobody wants to have gone through a shitty experience and not at the very least walked away with a lesson of some kind, right?!

For me, every single experience, trauma or life-changing event I have endured has provided me with a lifetime of lessons. Some of the experiences were utterly awful and I wouldn't wish them upon my worst enemy, but I have always found the silver lining. In some instances, it took me a little longer to seek, but they are always there waiting for you to find them. In seeking this, through all the good, the bad, the heartbreaking and the awful … I can truly say there is not a single piece of it I would ever dream of changing.

Over the last decade, there have been some amazing correlations between studies and the idea that optimism and silver lining seeking can have positive impacts in a variety of areas within our lives. Seems like a no-brainer, right? Because for just a moment we aren't just defaulting to our negative thoughts that is human nature. Some of these have included an association between optimism and high pain tolerance among cancer patients.[18] A study linking healthy aging[19] and even better occupational outcomes.[20] I thought these studies hit home for me particularly! My examples throughout this book are extreme. However, I love the simplicity in silver lining seeking that it really can occur in any given situation. So, if you are looking to consciously make a positive change, start with the everyday stuff. Doesn't get any realer than that.

For example, this morning we all slept in. As a result of this, I was in a flap, while Guy and I were trying to get the kids fed, dressed and lunches packed as well as getting ourselves ready for the working day. The breakfast dishes were piled up, uniforms weren't ironed yet and my hair was about eight days overdue for a decent hair washing. If I let it, that could have set the tone for the rest of my day. Annoyed, flustered and in a state of panic and rush. This is literally where I would often choose to reside only twelve months prior ... but today, instead, I went and hid in my walk-in wardrobe for a moment, stared at all my clothes (with absolutely nothing to wear, right!?!) and thought to myself, *Find the silver* ...

The silver was there in spades.

Firstly, I woke up in a safe and warm bed with a roof over my head, with food and running water available to me.

Given my second home in literally a Third World country (Fiji) where most clothes are washed in the backyard with the old-style washing boards and long bars of soap, my First World problems are not lost on me, and this perspective always allows me to see the silver when it comes to the 'haves' and 'have nots'.

I am blessed to have two healthy and happy children that I get to wake up to.

I have a loving and supporting husband that was right there with me juggling the morning chaos together as a team and a united front.

Running late meant we all had to pull together to get all the jobs done as a family unit.

It meant the kids had to assert a little more independence to be ready on time.

I would also get to enjoy a longer shower this evening when washing my hair without being in a rush.

And if all else fails, it could always be worse.

By doing this, I shifted the negative path I was heading down, was able to find the silver to shift my perspective and improve my morning. To start the shift in your mindset and start seeking the silver, it comes back to the small consistent actions we choose to do daily. Try these steps:

- Recall five things that make you feel like your life is enjoyable at this moment. It could be something like good health or a meaningful connection, having accomplished a task. The purpose of identifying these feel-goods is to shift gears and get your mind in a positive space. For me, I am easily shifted when I think about how grateful I am to have my IVF miracle babies. Melts my icy heart even on the coldest of days.
- Next step is to then think about a recent time when something didn't go your way, you faced a negative situation or you felt frustrated, irritated, mad or upset.

For example, I didn't leave my office in time to pick my daughter up and take her for ice cream.

- Use the example that comes to mind and put it into a sentence or two on paper, in your journal or even your notes section on your phone. This helps to set the scene of how the situation or experience unfolded.
- My sentence would look like this: On ice cream Tuesday I had over-committed myself to running two new employee inductions meaning I was going to finish later than usual which meant Guy had to collect Cadence and take her for ice cream.
- Next, go ahead and list three things that you could see as positives within the situation or experience. It is in this space the lessons are plentiful as you shift your mindset to begin looking at the scenario in a brighter light. My three positives:
  - Cadence still got her ice cream.
  - Both Guy and I have the ability to work around our family to do the mundane things like school pick-ups.
  - I love mundane activities. It reminds me I fought to be here to have mundane!

Throughout my journey, my favourite silver lining would have to be my kids truly believing anything is possible with a little hard work and whole lot of grit. That makes me so proud.

THE ULTIMATE: BE YOU.

So, what's my greatest lesson learnt thus far?

There are all the expected lessons one would imagine after facing death such as: *life is short, spend it wisely, YOLO (you only live once), do everything, regret nothing,* and these were all very much my mentality at the age of nineteen and into my early twenties. Thankfully, my brain fully developed by twenty-five and had the opportunity to face a lot more life experiences including few crazy exes, a husband, a career, IVF, loss and beautiful miracle babies, so I feel I have somewhat come full circle to really appreciate all the things in life. I mean **ALL** the things.

Experiencing and feeling the pain of a headache, the runny nose you instantly get when the crisp Canberra -5°c air hits your face in the morning, the sleepless nights, whether it be stress related or baby related, then instead of sleeping, choosing to lovingly watch your beautiful humans peacefully sleep. The panic and adrenaline of a fast-approaching deadline. The heartache of loss and the absolute overwhelming feelings of love when you see your loved ones succeed. Experiencing the absolute joy on the faces of the kids on Christmas mornings or wiping away their tears when their first pet inevitably dies. Navigating your own emotions as you mourn the loss of a loved one and seeing the process unravel for your children as you all fumble your way through the emotions together. The heart-skipping moment when your child asks you to kill the spider you are equally terrified of but like hell will you let the kids sniff out your fear.

Explaining to your kindergartener why countries invade other countries, then seconds later telling her eating boogers isn't good for you. Having your team achieve amazing things for those your company provide care for and seeing the quality of life improve for the clients is beyond priceless. The feel-goods of upskilling your team, empowering them to grow. Eating ice cream for breakfast or breakfast for dinner. Feeling and morbidly enjoying the feels of second-day soreness after a killer workout. Buying the dress you'll probably never wear but absolutely love and that makes you feel happy when you look at it as it hangs in your wardrobe with the tags still intact! Expanding horizons personally and professionally and making meaningful connections with like-minded humans. Feeling uncomfortable as you extend that comfort zone. Realising and knowing your value. The worth you bring to the table. Every. Damn. Day.

I have come to learn, one of the biggest lessons is experiencing and feeling all the feels. This is what being truly present and truly alive is about. Regardless of your journey, your career choices and family status. It's only when we face and overcome experiences such as trauma, loss, heartbreak, fear, pain, self-doubt and low self-worth that we truly experience the euphoria of all the goodness too. The love, joy, gratefulness, the confidence, the self-belief, the level-ups, the personal growth, the milestones of your loved ones and all the overwhelming moments you realise you have done some pretty kick-arse things and allow yourself that moment to celebrate and be damn proud of yourself …

Authentic kindness is not a destination you just one day reach and then you have forever, but rather, a way of choosing to live. A lifestyle to adapt … it's in these moments when you are feeling all those feels that you realise you've hit authentic kindness. It's easy to be kind to others. It's not so easy to be kind to yourself. It is about always remembering, so long as you are living, there are always lessons to be learnt and much kindness to be given. The moment you stop seeing the lessons and sharing the kindness is the moment you stop growing. It doesn't matter if you are looking to level-up your life personally or professionally … it all starts and ends with your mindset. Formal qualifications of others might be impressive. They might even be intimidating, but I promise, you are the only person qualified for the job when it comes to knowing yourself. You are never stuck. You always have choices and only you can change your circumstances because you are in control.

It's okay to make mistakes, but always learn from them. Remember, you are not your thoughts, and you are not responsible for the actions of others, nor their inactions. Life sucks sometimes, but nothing is permanent, you can rise from anything. It is the sucky times that allow us to strengthen our resilience and grow to better and brighter places in life. You do you, and if that is batshit crazy, that's okay too. Rid the negative. Break up with that shitty friend. Don't engage with the naysayers. Fuck what others think. They are gonna go ahead and think it anyway. Don't feed into that shit. Fight for your cause. Disrupt the shit out of things that need shaking up. Break the rules if it feels right. Stand for what you believe in but be mindful and respectful of the beliefs of others. #perspective

Remember, your purpose is not one fixed thing, and you can change your path at any stage of your life should you choose. You can divert and redirect it at any moment you please. Be the lead character in your own story. Be your own damn superhero. YOU. ARE. ENOUGH. You can think new thoughts. You can learn something new. You create new habits. All that matters is that you start. There are too many reasons not to start, be the reason you do. Embrace your individuality. You do you. Look after you. If you don't, you can't expect anyone else to give a damn.

Invest in yourself. Reinvent yourself a million times over. Level-up your company and find your glow. Discover what makes you, *you,* and do it unapologetically. Build a tribe that aligns with you and makes you want to be a better human, that supports your reinvention and your limitless level-ups and will celebrate the good with you. Always seek the silver linings in life. Be the light and shine a light for others. The most precious things in life are the people we love, the homes we create and the memories we make along the way. Ensure your tribe know you see them.

So, what is next for me?

You can find me somewhere in-between mum life, endeavouring to inspire others and spreading kindness around like confetti, working on myself, dodging negativity, fighting for the causes I am passionate about and slaying my goals both personally and professionally while always dropping a juggling ball or two as I'm trying to balance it all and hoping to raise my kids to be brave, kind and true humans all while practicing that allusive self-kindness.

REFERENCES

Chapter definitions: www.dictionary.com/

Lesson 1: You are not a label.

[1] *'Positive Leadership'*, K. Cameron 2018.

This research was initially founded in 2004 by Emily Heaphy and Marcial Losada Dled (2004) https://scholar.google.com.au/scholar?q=Emily+Heaphy+and+Marcial+Losada+DIed&hl=en&as_sdt=0&as_vis=1&oi=scholart who was later found to uphold incorrect data in some areas of their research. However, Kim Cameron's book, *Positive Leadership* (2018) (Random House US), also went on to support 5:1 ratio and was cited in the *Harvard Business Review* – https://hbr.org/2013/03/the-ideal-praise-to-criticism

Lesson 2: Your inner critic is a big jerk.

[2] 'Nancy's a B' – *Kindness and Courage* Episode 2, Natashia Telfer 2021.

Nancy's a B · Kindness and Courage (spotify.com)

Lesson 3: Don't stand in your own way.

[3] 'How to Stop Self-Sabotaging' *Psychology Today,* Ahona Guha DPsych, 2021.

How to Stop Self-Sabotaging | Psychology Today Australia

Lesson 7: Recognise and embrace your differences.
[4] Referenced: EQ Minds: https://www.eqminds.com/

Lesson 13: Limit Yourself Pity Parties.
[5] '5 Stages of Grief' Dr Elisabeth Kübler-Ross
https://www.ekrfoundation.org/5-stages-of-grief/5-stages-grief/

Lesson 21: Don't do drugs.
[6] 'Causes of death', Australian Bureau of Statistics 2020
https://www.abs.gov.au/statistics/health/causes-death/causes-death-australia/latest-release

Lesson 22: You deserve a happy ending.
[7] *The Political History of the Devil*, Daniel Defoe 1726.

Lesson 28: Decline unsolicited advice.
[8] Referenced to my juggling_mumma blog 2017
https://juggling-life.com/2017/08/11/unsolicited-baby-advice-baby-besties/

Lesson 29: It's okay to be bat-sh*t crazy.
[9] 'National Survey of Mental Health and Wellbeing', Australian Bureau of Statistics. 2008

Lesson 30: Ditch the impostor syndrome.
[10] 'Stop Telling Women They Have Imposter Syndrome', R Tulshyan, J Burey, *Harvard Business Review*, 2021.
https://hbr.org/2021/02/stop-telling-women-they-have-imposter-syndrome

Additional supporting information:
'The imposter phenomenon in high achieving women: Dynamics and therapeutic intervention'. PR Clance, SA Imes. Group Dyn. 1978

'The imposter phenomenon'. J Sakulku, J Alexander. *Journal of Behavioral Science*. 2011

'Feel like a fraud?' K Weir. American Psychological Association.

2013.

Lesson 33: Unapologetically Authentic

[11] *The power of vulnerability,* Brené Brown, TedTalk 2010

https://www.ted.com/talks/brene_brown_the_power_of_vulnerability

[12] *Happy Birthday to You,* Dr Suess, Random House 1959

[13] *You are Awesome*, Neil Pasricha, Gallery Books 2019

Lesson 34: Shine Bright

[14] *Courage and Confidence*, Katy Garner, Peace Mitchell, KMD Books 2022

Lesson 36: You already have everything you need.

[15] *The Wizard of Oz,* Metro-Goldwyn-Mayer 1939

Lesson 39: If you are tired, rest. The world won't end

[16] 'International Classification of Diseases', *ICD-11.* World Health Organisation 2021

https://icd.who.int/browse11/l-m/en#/http://id.who.int/icd/entity/129180281

Lesson 48: Always keep perspective

[17] Marriages and Divorces Australia, Australian Bureau of Statistics 2021

https://www.abs.gov.au/statistics/people/people-and-communities/marriages-and-divorces-australia/latest-release

Lesson 50: Be a silver lining seeker.

[18] 'Optimism and the Experience of Pain: Benefits of seeing the Glass as Half Full', B Goodin, H Bulls, Springer 2013

https://www.researchgate.net/publication/236071768_Optimism_and_the_Experience_of_Pain_Benefits_of_Seeing_the_Glass_as_Half_Full

[19] 'Optimism, Age, And Depressive Symptoms' *Journal of Personality and Social Psychology.* C Wrosch, J Jobin, M Scheier.

2016

https://spectrum.library.concordia.ca/id/eprint/980887/1/JP_2016_LOT.pdf

[20] 'Effects of State Optimism on Job-Related Outcomes' *Journal of Organizational Behavior.* D Kluemper, L Little, T DeGroot. 2009

https://www.researchgate.net/publication/227702268_State_or_Trait_Effects_of_State_Optimism_on_Job-Related_Outcomes

ACKNOWLEDGEMENTS

Firstly – **ME!** I just wrote a fucking book! You can bet your arse the cover of this book will be blown up poster size, framed and hung in my house with pride! I'm pretty damn proud of myself right now. My words, my experiences, my results from the actions and work of my doing. So proud.

Peace and Katy: You are both radiant beacons of light. Thank you for believing in me and this book. Every meeting reinvigorates my excitement for the 'project'. It has been an absolute privilege to publish this book under Women Changing the World Press.

Dr Baxter: After all this writing, I literally cannot find the right words to convey just how grateful I am to you. You saved my life. From cancer and from myself in my pits of PND. Your compassion, support and uncanny ability to always run over time is amazing and unwavering and I absolutely love that about you.

My Family: Mum, Dad, Eb and Jayde: For what it is worth ... thank you. You literally saved my life.

Guy: Thank you for the countless weekends of keeping the kids out of my little home office while I scrambled to get words on a page. You are my true north and my warmest light. Your presence always fills my soul. You are my partner in life in every essence of the word. Thank you for doing life with me equally every single step of the way. Together we raise our family. Together we run the businesses, together we take on the world.

Cadey and Nate: My littlest loves. You literally are my heart and soul. Without a doubt, my proudest achievement is the gift of being your mum. I am so proud of the kindness that shines in both of you. I promise nothing but weekends full of zoo trips, park plays, ice cream and movie afternoons because Mumma's book is done!

Lisa: Pretty sure I covered most of my Lisa love in your entire chapter and several others but in case you missed it ... thank you. Thank you for seeing something in me before I even saw it in myself. You are always one of my biggest supporters and I love that both our bums are in the boat! Thank you for choosing me to be your soul sister in this lifetime and the next.

Jes, Keiralee, Nat, Hayley, Katie, Tahla, Brooke, Rhonda and Claire: The amazingly supportive friends I never see but love that when we do, it's as if no time has passed. No judgement, just true meaningful connections. I appreciate your friendship. Truly.

The amazing NCC team: Do you know how amazing every single one of you are? The answer is beyond! Thank you for the heartfelt care you provide our community. You always have risen above, stood together and been truly inspiring. Thank you for choosing NCC and thank you for being you!

Ma: Together you and Pa literally embody the essence of true love. The real and rare legitimate kind. I hope to have a marriage with your son as happy and long lasting as yours. We love you. 'Soooooo much' and so many adventures to come.

Elijah, Iggy, Noah, Mahlia, Lani, Trey, Halle, Jett, Zaik,

Bindee and Jayce: Our favourite nieces and nephews. Watching you all grow into your kind selves is amazing. Stay true to yourselves always.

Alex: I've finished the book. I promise I will stop nervously pulling my lashes out now.

Emma: I feel you have your work cut out for you now, the greys have multiplied bringing this book to life. Thank you for always just being you.

The tribes: CWB, CBR Woman, AusMumpreneur, Business Chicks, No Ordinary Women, The Sistahood, PK Tribe. Thank you for true and meaningful connections in business and in life. So many of you – Sheena and committee, Olga, Gab, Katy, Peace, Karen, Emma, Bods and the BC crew, Fiona, Erika, Emma L, Bec C, Lindy, Jeanie, Sandy, Jenny, Bianca, Vanessa, Annette, Marika ... The unwavering support, encouragement and love from every single amazing woman I have had the privilege of meeting and connecting with is truly mind blowing. I see each of you, and I appreciate you all wholeheartedly.

www.ingramcontent.com/pod-product-compliance
Lightning Source LLC
Chambersburg PA
CBHW020912020526
44107CB00075B/1665